Global Television:
Co-Producing Culture

IN THE SERIES Emerging Media: History, Theory, Narrative
EDITED BY DANIEL BERNARDI

Joshua Hirsch, *Afterimage: Film, Trauma, and the Holocaust*

Global Television

Co-Producing Culture

Barbara J. Selznick

TEMPLE UNIVERSITY PRESS
Philadelphia

Temple University Press
1601 North Broad Street
Philadelphia PA 19122
www.temple.edu/tempress

Copyright © 2008 by Temple University
All rights reserved
Published 2008
Printed in the United States of America

∞ The paper used in this publication meets the requirements
of the American National Standard for Information Sciences—
Permanence of Paper for Printed Library Materials, ANSI Z39.48-1992

Library of Congress Cataloging-in-Publication Data

Selznick, Barbara J., 1970–
  Global television : co-producing culture / Barbara J. Selznick.
    p. cm.
  Includes bibliographical references and index.
  ISBN-13: 978-1-59213-503-5 (cloth : alk. paper)
  ISBN-13: 978-1-59213-504-2 (pbk. : alk. paper)
  ISBN-10: 1-59213-503-X (cloth : alk. paper)
  ISBN-10: 1-59213-504-8 (pbk. : alk. paper)   1. Television broadcasting–Social
aspects.   2. Television broadcasting–Influence.   3. Globalization–Social
aspects.   4. Americanization.   I. Title.
  HM1206.S45 2008
  302.23'45–dc22
                                                                    2007050272

2 4 6 8 9 7 5 3 1

For Sanford, Lily, and Ellis
I love you.

Contents

Acknowledgments

Over the course of researching this book I spent a great deal of time reading and learning. This project benefited from suggestions, ideas, and support from more than a few scholars, friends, and family members. There are many people who, along the way, influenced and enriched this project. I must particularly acknowledge a great intellectual debt to Amy Beer, who focused my interest in co-productions; her recognition of the importance of international co-productions influenced this book in its entirety. Other people who (with or without their knowledge) provided assistance and encouragement include my colleagues in the School of Media Arts at the University of Arizona as well as other generous scholars and good friends: Tim Anderson, Karla Berry, Caren Deming, Tamara Falicov, Karla Fuller, Barbara Goffman, Tim Havens, Mary Beth Haralovich, Nicole Koschmann, Jennifer Jenkins, Julie Lindstrom, Yuri Makino, Eileen Meehan, Jeffrey Miller, Michael Mulcahy, Debbie and Rich Neves, Homer Pettey, Pat Phalen, Patrick Roddy, Dot Roome, Judd Ruggill, Kevin Sandler, Julie Sandor, Beverly Seckinger, Lisanne Skyler, Beretta Smith-Shomade, Dan Streible, Al Tucci, Vicky Westover, Mimi White, and Justin Wyatt.

The staff at the School of Media Arts continually provides support and insight. Jill Bean, Toni Dorame, Sue Keeth, Sylvia Miles, Christina Swanson, and Pat Varney regularly make my life easier. My students have been inspirational. For almost ten years, students in our school watched episodes of *Highlander: The Series* in introductory, upper division, and graduate courses without (much) complaint and with a keen analytical eye. The students who passed through my courses contributed to this book in numerous ways. I also had the opportunity to work with some particularly wonderful graduate students who deserve special thanks: Alicia Barron, Kathryn Bergeron, Rachel Boyes, Chiara Ferrari, Debbie Jaramillo, Leslie Matthai, Lucas Micromatis, Deron Overpeck, and Sarah Salwin all provided significant research assistance.

Daniel Bernardi's insightful suggestions as well as his faith in my research were invaluable in helping me to focus and complete this project. I truly appreciate his support and friendship. Micah Kleit at Temple University Press was also enthusiastic and helpful throughout. My thanks to Micah and everyone else at Temple University Press for their assistance.

Support for this project was received from the School of Media Arts, the College of Fine Arts, and International Affairs at the University of Arizona. Portions of this manuscript appeared in "Europudding: International Co-Productions and Televisual Representation," *Spectator* (USC), 20 (Spring/Summer 2000): 53–62; "World Class Budgets and Big-Name Casts: The Miniseries and International Co-productions," *Contracting Out Hollywood: Runaway Productions and Foreign Locations*, edited by Greg Elmer and Mike Gasher, 157–176, Lanham, MD: Rowman and Littlefield, 2004; and "The Complete Story: Religion and Race in Global Non-Fiction Programming," *Global Media Journal*, 6 (Fall 2007), http:/lass.calumet.purdue.edu/cca/gmj/fa07/gmj-fa07-selznick.htm.

Finally, I must thank my family. Elyn and Mark Frieser, Kathryn Thomas and Steven Wilinsky, and Elliot, Adam, Rebekah, and Isaac Wilinsky are very patient with my tendency to disappear and overwhelmingly supportive when I resurface. As always, my parents Betty and Allen Wilinsky offer more encouragement and love than I could hope for. Their faith in me continues to give me strength. Sanford

Selznick provides me with so much more than a great last name. He motivates me, entertains me, and covers for me. His smile and kind heart can light up a room. My final thanks are for my children, Lily and Ellis, who reflect all the best qualities of their father. Their joyful passion for life, steadfast determination, and endless resources of love and laughter inspire me. For showing me each and every day what really matters in this world, I dedicate this book to Sanford, Lily, and Ellis.

Introduction

McTelevision in the Global Village

"To speak of the globalization of culture is to speak in the first instance of the globalization of capitalism, *and hence of a globalization of the commodity form which is expressed in a fully internationalized, interdependent and interlocking market."*

(FROW, 9)

"At best, [globalization] is no more than a catch-all category to refer to various trends towards more complex patterns of international circulation, not only of media products, but also of technologies, finance, people, and ideas."

(SINCLAIR, JACKA, AND CUNNINGHAM, 22)

Although by now this revelation is obvious and perhaps even clichéd, any scholarly examination of the international marketplace must acknowledge that the practices and meanings of "globalization" are complex and multi-faceted. Even the term globalization must be problematized, as we recognize that, in the marketplace, not all nations count equally; nor have national governments and borders ceased to matter. The world is not one big global village—in terms of economics or culture. In a discussion of culture especially, the concept of globalization gets tied to notions of nationalism, homogeneity, and commercialization. Culture— whether popular or mass culture—tells people something about themselves, helps to define identities, and explains the worlds in which they live. Culture teaches people what is right and what is wrong, what is inevitable and what will never be, what is worth thinking about, and what should be ignored. In an examination of global culture, observers invariably question what ideas and values get lost along the way and what rises up to take their place.

This book addresses John Frow's above assertion that the internationalization of culture is concretely tied to the economic structure in which it occurs and John Sinclair et al.'s suggestion that we break apart the concept of globalization to uncover the particular processes by which the international circulation of culture takes place. Focusing on a particular mode of production—the international co-production—I will consider this mode of production as a means by which transnational television is created as both an economic and a cultural commodity. This analysis will further highlight the ways that internationally co-produced television affects not only the cultural landscape of mass media but also larger cultural issues such as identity formation and commercialism.

Perhaps the most significant issue surrounding globalization is the threat that it poses to nationalism. Although some theorists, suggest that nationalism should be seen as an early concept in the move toward globalization, there is no denying that the spread of global capital, regulation, and culture threatens the dominance of nations as an organizational structure of society. One reaction to the breach of national strength is an increased focus on the local as a source of identity and knowledge. Both a tool of and a reaction to globalization, the strengthening of local ties offers a way of grounding identity and loyalty in a very fast paced and much criticized global world. At the same time, localization rarely offers a concrete threat to global capital in the way that a strong nationalistic movement might. Local preferences and loyalties can easily be mobilized by transnational corporations and incorporated into global practices.[1] Within this framework of globalization, culture is considered an important tool for spreading ideology and encouraging global capitalism. National culture, for example, according to Philip Schlesinger, is the "body of values, practices and identities deemed to make particular nations different from others" (372). In an attempt to erase nationalism as a source of identity, national culture, then, must be overtaken by some kind of global culture.

Mass media, particularly film and television, have served as one of the most efficient purveyors of such a culture (Featherstone, 57).

As the world economy privatized, media companies increasingly consolidated to create a handful of large, transnational, horizontally and vertically integrated media companies. Although mostly based in the United States, these transnational conglomerates are not designed to promote U.S. nationalism. As Richard Gershon explains, "As the world's economy becomes more fully privatized, the goal of nation states and the goal of [transnational media corporations] will increasingly find themselves on a collision course. For it is the purpose of nation states to strengthen the cause of political and economic sovereignty whereas the goal of the TNC is profitability" (35). Transnational media corporations are focused on creating profits, regardless of national allegiances.

The privatization and deregulation of the television industry in the 1980s and '90s, discussed below, paved the way for transnational television ownership. The programming of common television shows around the world and the production of programs that could be shown internationally became "commonsensical." The idea of national programming, while significant at a governmental level, began to lose its primacy for producers. While most national audiences certainly continue to prefer local programming with domestic stars and languages, producers learned that more money could be made with international programs, even with shows that were not the *most* popular, but just popular enough to get on the air in several national markets.

Furthermore, media producers and distributors found that they could not simply transmit "national" product overseas (Sparks, 115). Rather, they needed to produce programming with an international audience in mind. The expense and complexity of such productions led to several innovations in programming. For example, formatting became much more common, especially in the 1990s. Through formatting, producers sell the execution of an idea for a television program (such as *Wheel of Fortune*, *Who Wants to be a Millionaire*, *Pop Idol*) and the program is then re-produced for a different national audience. The commodity becomes the format, not the actual program. Formatting in the 1970s focused on finding successful programs that had been created for national markets and adapting them for different audiences. For example, U.S. producers formatted the successful British sitcoms *'Till Death Us Do Part/All in the Family*, *Man About the House/Three's Company*, and *Steptoe and Son/Sanford and Son*. In the 1980s and '90s, however, producers began to consider the potential of programs as international formats before even creating the original versions.

Like formatting, international co-production did not originate in the 1980s but did rise in popularity as a mode of production at this time as a reaction to the shifts in the international media marketplace. International joint ventures, an umbrella term for different kinds of co-productions, are the processes by which at least two companies in at least two different countries work together to create one media text. These kinds of productions come in many shapes and sizes. "Official" international co-productions are created through co-production treaties between the nations in which the companies are based. As of 1998, Paul Taylor counted the existence of 129 bilateral co-production treaties and six multilateral treaties (1998, 134). Such treaties help set the terms of the co-productions, including in them specific requirements surrounding factors such as the financial obligations of the co-producing partners, the nationality of creative and technical personnel, source materials, locations, language, and so forth.

Not surprisingly, the U.S. government has never entered into any co-production treaties; such treaties would establish limitations and rules that might hinder the "free flow of information." This, of course, does not mean that the United States does not take part in such productions. Technically, these productions are termed co-ventures—co-productions made without a treaty. Essentially, the difference is that instead of having terms of the co-producers' involvement spelled out by a treaty, these terms are negotiated by the co-producing partners themselves. While generally in international co-ventures there is some creative input on the part of all companies involved, this may not always be the case. In a pre-sale, for example, which some people do and some people do not consider a co-venture, a partner may simply agree to purchase the media text for distribution in advance. A pre-sale is very helpful for providing funding for a project, but also, by demonstrating at least one company's commitment to the film, producers are more easily able to obtain additional funding and distribution deals.

For the purposes of this research project, I have included both co-ventures and treaty co-productions as "international co-productions."[2] Wherever necessary (and possible) I will indicate whether a treaty existed between the non-U.S. co-producers. Additionally, when the partner takes co-producer credit, I am including pre-sales as a form of international co-production. My decision in doing this was founded on the "growing anecdotal evidence in the TV trade press that the customer often gets the programming made to order" (Paul Taylor, 145). In other words, it is highly likely that a distributor who agrees to a pre-sale arrangement will have some impact on the creative content of the unfinished product, if only indirectly. As we can see, international co-productions are a complicated business. Significantly their role in the process of globalization is similarly complex and allows us to pull apart the idea of globalization, as suggested by John Sinclair et al., and concretely connect cultural production to the flow of capital in the cultural economy.

To further set the terms of this research project, I should note that the focus in these pages is not on how companies outside the United States use international co-production to oppose Hollywood's hegemony (as will be discussed briefly below), but on how Hollywood itself embraces international co-production to achieve certain goals. This book examines the impact of globalization in the United States by exploring its role in creating and airing international television culture. This book takes seriously the idea that the process of globalization within the television industry has affected the United States. As primary gatekeepers within the media industries, what happens within U.S. media is significant. Furthermore we must recognize that although the major Hollywood production companies are associated with the United States, they may no longer actually be based in the United States. Rather, as previously discussed, these large transnational media corporations, in search of profits, concentrate on multiple markets. The push toward globalization within the media industries, I argue, has influenced the industrial structure and cultural contributions of U.S. television. To this end, through the lens of the international co-production, this book focuses on the complexities of media globalization by examining the impact of international media on U.S. media industries and culture.

Within the framework of globalization, international co-productions play a significant role. At various times, such productions are seen as both the carriers of Western capitalist media making inroads around the world and as the last bastion of hope for national media; sometimes as a mix of both of these. As Paul Taylor explains, international co-productions exist within the borders between the two main ways of conceiving of the visual mass media: as a cultural industry and as an entertainment industry. The "cultural" view, most popular in Europe, sees film and television as a reflection of "the identity and experiences of the originating country" (101). Those who consider film and television to be "entertainment," focus on media content as an economic output that's primary value is its ability to be bought and sold in the marketplace (Paul Taylor, 101). Although the entertainment industry perspective is certainly gaining in prominence, international co-productions can be motivated either by the desire to enhance a nation's culture or the interest in making money or both (Paul Taylor, 113, 124).

As will be discussed below, international co-productions, particularly those based on treaties, are at least framed in terms of their ability to enhance a national media industry (by allowing the country to identify itself with a larger budget production) and national culture. To qualify for certain subsidies and production incentives, international co-productions are required to satisfy certain "national" conditions. For example, a production may need to meet some or all of the following requirements: hire national (or now in the case of Europe, regional) creative personnel, include national themes, or set the film or program in a national location. As the history of international co-productions will illustrate, national interests were a fundamental incentive for the expansion of international co-productions everywhere except the United States. Even the term international co-production privileges national origin as a way of categorizing media texts (Elley, 20).

At the same time, however, international co-productions must appeal to transnational audiences and include themes, personnel, and locations from other co-producing partners' countries. In order to succeed as international products, these productions must limit their national particularities and reflect global issues and concerns. Paul Taylor explains, "International co-productions have the curious quality of having the look and feel of both foreign and domestic programming in each of the partner countries. The quality of being mostly familiar and a little different reflects the unique creative and co-financing arrangements that made their production possible" (152).

We can see then that understanding international co-productions means fleshing out their existence in between the existing categories in which film and television are currently placed. International co-productions are both artistically and economically motivated; they are foreign and domestic; in the case of treaty co-productions, they are both privately and publicly financed (through tax incentives and subsidies); they offer economic benefits to both the wealthiest and the more peripheral media industries; they act as tools for spreading dominant culture while offering opportunities for transculturation. International co-productions, therefore, are an extension of the idea that "'internationalization' and 'localization' need to be understood as co-extant tendencies operating within even the same markets" (O'Regan, 76). Now we can see that these tendencies do not just exist within single markets, they exist within single media texts; within individual, internationally co-produced films and television shows.

The proliferation of such productions, which seemed to provide something for everyone, makes sense, especially during the 1980s and '90s, when the increasingly transnational nature of the media marketplace was becoming apparent and necessary. Such productions could be justified both by those who wanted to herald their cultural benefits and those who wanted to focus on their economic rewards. Their existence within the overlap of growing trends within the media allowed international co-productions, for a time, to represent the best hope for many different factions of the media industries. Perhaps then, it is not surprising to see that so many accounts of co-productions include some version of the idea that "international partnerships and co-production ventures have emerged as one of the most important programming trends of the 1990s" (Gershon, 48).

"The Most Effective Response Strategy"— The History of International Co-Productions[3]

Although international co-productions increased greatly in number on television in the 1980s and '90s, the process had been used often in film since the late 1940s and '50s. The tensions and uncertainties that surrounded the film industry at this time generated the economic, industrial, and cultural appeal of international co-productions. The parallels between the industrial pressures on the film industry of the 1940s and '50s and the television industry of the 1980s and '90s, and the benefits and drawbacks of international co-productions in dealing with these concerns are significant. Understanding the history of international co-productions in films, then, lays the groundwork for understanding how they later function for television.

Even before the late 1940s, in the period in between the end of World War I and the coming of sound, European countries attempted to work together to fend off the influx of Hollywood films (Kristin Thompson, 105). Many within the European film industries embraced a co-production initiative that became known as Film Europe. While head of Universum-Film AG (UFA), Erich Pommer remarked, "It is necessary to create 'European films,' which will no longer be French, English, Italian, or German films; entirely 'continental' films, expanding out into all Europe and amortising their enormous costs, can be produced easily" (qtd. in Kristin Thompson, 113). In addition to co-producing films, European companies invested in companies in other countries and entered international distribution deals thus ensuring the international distribution of films other than Hollywood productions (Kristin Thompson, 116–117). Although this program only lasted until the coming of sound, we can see early on a mixture of interrelated cultural and economic motivations for international co-productions. Companies wanted to create higher budget productions in order to compete with Hollywood films. At the same time, the desire to compete with Hollywood was at least partly driven by nationalistic and cultural motives.

In the late 1930s, as European film markets either shrunk (in terms of revenue) or completely closed to Hollywood due to the war, the studios attempted to make up some of their lost profits by increasing their distribution in Latin America. Latin America was also a political focus at this time, as Franklin D. Roosevelt instituted the Good Neighbor Policy in 1933, at least in part to prevent the spread of socialism in Latin America (King, 32). The film studios were called upon to present positive images of Latin American locations and characters, which the studios attempted with limited success. The desire to export U.S. films of all types to the Latin American market, however, remained strong. One strategy for this, according to Brian O'Neil, was to block book English-language films with Spanish-language films. Initially, the studios attempted to produce Spanish-language films in Hollywood. Soon, however, the studios realized that they could save money by simply financing films produced in Latin America. RKO Radio, for example, invested 50 percent of the financing for a Mexican film studio in 1945. This mode of co-production allowed the U.S. studios to maintain a presence in Latin America without producing their own Spanish-language films (O'Neil, n. 41).

In Europe, international co-productions resurfaced as a popular mode of production in the period following World War II. This time, however, there were two major differences from the post-World War I period: first, governments became involved by creating co-production treaties, and second, the U.S. film studios participated in international co-productions. Government involvement developed as a result of the creation of a number of incentive programs throughout Europe. To rebuild national film industries that had been devastated by World War II and the following influx of Hollywood films, governments in some countries initiated production subsidies and tax incentives for national films. To qualify for these incentives, productions had to meet specific requirements concerning their content, their personnel, and their financing. As interest developed in international co-productions as a way for European companies to increase the budgets of their films and thus compete with the high budget Hollywood films, companies wanted to be able to continue to tap into the European incentive programs. Co-production treaties became a way for governments to lay out how companies creating co-productions could create a film that would be considered "national" in all of the producers' countries and thus qualify for their incentives. France and Italy were the first countries to sign a co-production treaty in 1949. Treaties between other European countries followed. Such treaties generally spelled out the amount of financing, the number of personnel, the language, and the content required to make a film under the treaty that would be eligible for each country's incentives. The creation of international co-production treaties helped, then, both to formalize the co-production process and dictate terms of creativity within them by prescribing certain conditions necessary in order to create a production that would be economically viable.

International co-production treaties were not the only bilateral film agreements being signed by European countries. In the late 1940s both France and the United Kingdom signed pacts with the United States determining the terms by which U.S. companies could distribute films within and remove funds from particular nations. Along with tax incentives and subsidies, many European nations instituted quotas and other restrictive legislation that made it more difficult for U.S. studios to distribute their films and remove profits from Europe.[4] Although the U.S. studios chafed against such restrictions, in the end they established ways to make money from the funds that they were unable to take out of Europe. These blocked earnings, for example, were used to create subsidiaries in Europe, purchase distribution rights for European films, invest in co-productions, and produce films overseas (runaway productions). One of the most important steps taken by the U.S. studios was to have their European subsidiaries declared national companies. This way, these companies could produce films that qualified for the European subsidies and tax incentives (Guback, 165).

The major studios, according to Thomas Guback, were, in the end, quite content to produce overseas. During this time, the U.S. film audience decreased, competition for leisure time increased, production costs rose, and the Paramount Decision bit into the studios' domestic profits (Guback 164). All of these factors made it more difficult for the major studios to continue their production slates. The lower costs of labor in Europe, combined with the subsidy programs, made European production appealing. Furthermore, the changing tastes of U.S. audiences resulted in an interest in more mature films (Wilinsky, 82–90), a quality that could be assisted by "international" locations and storylines.

Co-production of European films such as Jean-Luc Godard's *Contempt* (1963) and Michelangelo Antonioni's *Blow-Up* (1966) was an additional attempt on the part of the Hollywood industry to tap into the U.S.-based "art house" audience interested in foreign films. Furthermore, production of European films could assist in reaching audiences within Europe. Peter Lev explains, "European markets became a necessity, not a luxury to American film companies in the 1950s, because the American audience for motion pictures was rapidly shrinking" (18). U.S. companies, therefore, not only created runaway productions of U.S. films, but they also invested money in many European art films. Ironically, while U.S. companies were co-producing art films, European companies were co-producing Hollywood style movies. As Tim Bergfelder notes, many of the European co-productions of the 1950s and '60s searched for "generic formulae which had the widest possible appeal across national borders" (2000, 146). The action genre (and its hybrids—western action, historical action, biblical action) became most popular for co-productions (Bergfelder, 2000, 149). The focus on spectacle rather than narrative frequently resulted in co-productions with very high budgets, by European standards (Betz, 23).

Not only did U.S. companies invest in European productions, but as explained above, they did so in ways that allowed them to benefit from the incentive systems that had been created in order to fend them off. According to Guback, *Variety* estimated that in 1966 U.S. subsidiaries would receive 80 percent of the subsidy money distributed by the British Film Production Fund (Guback, 170). Many British producers actively sought out U.S. money in order to fund their films. Not only did U.S. involvement allow for an increase in the production budget, but it also helped ensure U.S. distribution (Guback, 171), a major goal of most commercially-minded producers.

We can see, then, that the subsidy system and the co-production treaties, which had been established with the economic and cultural goals of rebuilding European film industries and encouraging competition with the United States, were in many ways usurped for the commercial purposes of the U.S. majors. As one Italian producer said in the 1970s, "We in Italy can no longer pursue films for the Italian markets. The costs are too high, and we can't get our money back at the Italian box-office alone. We need American capital, we need the American market, and we need American companies to distribute our films globally" (qtd. in Bergfelder, 2000, 141). By the late 1960s and early '70s, the United States' role in European film production was well recognized. Anne Jackel noted that by this time, many of the treaty films were "international" films backed by U.S. money (88). And Guback wrote in 1969, "The British production industry, if one can argue that a substantial *national* one really does exist today, is little more than a branch of Hollywood, dependant upon American companies for both finance and distribution" (172). At the same time, U.S. investment in European art films declined, as the U.S. majors focused their attentions on the American art film movement of the 1970s (Lev, 25). Although the end result appears to be filmic co-productions that use the English language to focus on "international" appeal, for a time the intersection of the cultural and commercial considerations of international co-productions resulted in non-English-language, high budget, U.S.-style costume dramas, European art films, and U.S.-backed "national" films.

Importantly, Europe was not the only place that such conflicting motivations played out in co-productions. In the 1950s, for example, companies in Hong Kong worked with Japanese studios to co-produce films for the Asian market, and in the 1970s the major U.S. studios became involved in co-productions with Hong Kong. For the United States, Hong Kong action films appeared to be a way to reach a young, racially and ethnically diverse audience (in the same way that blaxploitation films reached this audience). The first U.S.-Hong Kong co-production was the classic Bruce Lee film *Enter the Dragon* (1973). The film's Hong Kong production company, Golden Harvest, soon opened up offices in Los Angeles and has been active in the global film market since then (Fore, 46). Certainly these films went a long way to introduce U.S. audiences to Asian culture; however, they were primarily designed for economic reasons.

Around the 1960s, Canada also began to promote international co-productions with plans to use such projects to build its national film industry. According to Michael Dorland, the Canadian government hoped international co-productions would allow Canadian involvement in larger budget productions with international distribution thus boosting the industry economically. Another goal was to expose Canadian filmmakers to more established producers who could teach the Canadians about running a national industry (Dorland, 15–16).

Significantly, when the Canadian film industry faced a serious economic downturn in the 1980s, the industry looked to U.S. companies to help bring in capital and to the U.S. market as a main outlet for its product (Pendakur, 203–213). The Canadian industry wooed U.S. co-production partners and offered strong exchange rates and lower labor costs to encourage production in Canada (Pendakur, 215). U.S. companies took advantage of these benefits and particularly looked for projects that involved both a Canadian and a European company, preferably in a country with which Canada had a co-production treaty. This, according to Manjunath Pendakur, allowed U.S. companies to benefit from the incentives in Canada and the third country and offered an inroad to the European marketplace since the project would count as European product. The turn of the Canadian industry to U.S. partners, despite, as will be discussed below, the tendency of U.S. companies to take over any given project, signals the significance of international co-productions during times of economic difficulties.

In another example, in the 1980s, Latin America suffered from a generally weak economy. Funding and distributing films became a serious difficulty. At this time, discussions began to increase about developing a general Latin American market. While there were certainly partnerships between Latin American countries before this time, the downturn in the economy led commentators like Gabriel García Márquez to become vocal in the need for a united Latin American market to make higher budget and commercially popular films (King, 75).

In Asia, the U.S. film industry embraced co-productions as a way of creating low budget films that could tap into the straight-to-home-video market (Morris, 185). In fact, the relationship between co-productions and the rise of home video is quite significant. As Paul Taylor writes, both U.S. film and television adopted co-productions in their "maturity" as they "fac[ed] rising production costs, audience fragmentation and a new threatening technology on the horizon" (112). For film, this period of growing instability was the 1950s, when shifts in the U.S. market and the pending growth of television viewership threatened the dominance of the motion picture as the main form of mass entertainment. For television these threats came in the 1980s and '90s when the broadcasting industry (both in the United States and in Europe) confronted a similar crisis.

As many scholars have noted, the 1980s proved to be a period of change for the television industry, both in the United States and abroad. Within the United States, the rise of cable and satellite channels (and to some extent the growing popularity of home video) opened up a new demand for programming, and at the same time fragmented the viewing audience and eroded the power of the big three networks. Due to the argument that "air time" was no longer a scarce resource, the opportunities opened up by these new technologies also helped to justify deregulation of the television industry. This deregulation fueled station conglomeration, thus limiting the opportunities for syndicated programs. And, in the 1990s, deregulation led to the removal of the Financial Interest and Syndication Rules (Fin-Syn), allowing the networks to produce their own programming and paving the way for mergers between film studios/television production companies and broadcast networks.

Overseas, privatization worked with deregulation and technological shifts to create not only an increased number of television stations but also commercialization of these stations. The European market, therefore, grew while the U.S. market fragmented. As Simon Olswang explained:

> With the coming of home video and cable and satellite television, traditional American television markets have fragmented whilst costs have risen to the point where increasingly in television the U.S. can no longer go it alone; where deficits for television series, movies of the week and mini-

series grow even larger, and where for the feature films the prospects in overseas markets grow ever more important—the U.S. television networks, cable channels and film studios are forced to look increasingly to foreign markets in the decision making process. (21)

Certainly, co-productions in television occurred before the 1980s. Public broadcasting outlets both in the United States and overseas felt the pressure of increased production budgets and competition with commercial outlets by the 1970s. European public stations worked together to produce programming, and the BBC was a particularly popular co-production partner for the U.S.-based public stations. According to Vincent Porter, by the 1970s, WGBH in Boston already had a bad reputation as a co-production partner for its tendency to make unauthorized changes to the television programs for its home market (8). Cable networks were also early co-producers (Strover, 107), frequently working with the European-based public stations as well as NHK in Japan to create programming.

For the broadcast networks, early participation in the international market involved purchasing interests in international television companies. The U.S. networks also formed early affiliations with broadcasters in Latin America, though, according to John Sinclair, they limited their assistance to technical and organizational advice rather than financial contributions until the late 1950s (38). Direct investment began in earnest in the 1960s when ABC entered a production deal with the major Mexican producer that would eventually become Televisa and Time Life invested in Brazil's TV Globo (Sinclair, 41). By 1965 ABC had financial stakes in 54 television stations in 24 countries in Latin America, Africa, and Asia (Herman and McChesney, 21). By the early 1980s, ABC also held a 49 percent interest in Telemunchen, a Munich-based television production and distribution company (Gershon, 48). And in 1990, CBS and NBC had co-production agreements with British production companies: CBS with Granada and NBC with Yorkshire TV (Gershon, 48).

The move from financial investment to co-production arrangements reflects Carl Hoskins and Stuart McFadyen's statement that by early 1985, industry participants recognized that international co-productions were "the most effective response strategy to the new economic pressures reshaping the television programming environment, in the USA and abroad" (220). The major networks ramped up their international co-productions in the 1990s, particularly as Fin-Syn began to fade away. As *Variety* reported in 1997, "these days being a major player in U.S. television isn't enough. To maintain a spot at the top of the network heap, companies have to conquer the world" (Stuart Miller, M3).

According to Marc Doyle, these deals of the late 1980s and into the '90s were not solely financially driven. Rather, by this time, co-producers recognized the importance of a creative collaboration (Doyle, 12). In 1991 an executive vice president for the Italy-based Berlusconi Communications reported that a company getting involved in co-productions "is not looking anymore just for money for his own production, but for a partner to help create" (qtd. in Glenn and Amdur, 23). At the very least, U.S. television producers needed to look beyond the tastes and interests of the U.S. market. As Ralph Negrine and Stylianos Papathanassopoulos write, "In the end, the liberalization of broadcasting systems leads to an internationalisation of television by forcing broadcasters to operate on the international stage—seeking funds, co-producing, merging and so on" (23). To do this, U.S. producers were challenged to "become more international in outlook and content" (Andrew Neil qtd. in Doyle, 119).

As this brief history of international co-production illustrates, the motivations for international co-productions on television, as in film, have always been a blend of interrelated economic and cultural concerns. Both a form of foreign and domestic media, both privately and publicly funded, both a means of production for the wealthy and poorer media makers, and both an outlet for distributing dominant and peripheral culture, international co-productions have a unique and complex position within the media financial and cultural economies. A more thorough consideration of the benefits and drawbacks of such projects will highlight the specific ways that the process of international co-production interacts with the industrial and cultural contexts in which media are produced.

"Fully Authentic"—The Benefits of International Co-Productions

As their history illustrates, international co-productions have been seen by scholars and industry insiders to have a range of economic and cultural benefits. Undoubtedly, the economic considerations appear to outweigh the cultural considerations. Most likely, without the economic benefits, few companies would engage in international co-productions. Moreover, the economic and cultural benefits of co-productions are frequently intertwined. For example, Paul Taylor writes, "International collaboration is seen as a way of pooling together enough money to produce programming that will provide viewing alternatives to American television" (123). We see in this comment the desire to increase production budgets in order to offer a cultural alternative. We must recognize, however, that different parties involved in co-productions have different primary motivators. For example, while the governments that create production incentives and co-production treaties may be most interested in building up national culture, producers may focus on co-productions' potential to earn more money in the transnational marketplace. Furthermore, these motivating factors can be flipped: some governments may have a primary goal of strengthening a national film industry for economic reasons, while some producers may use international co-production money to make their artistic visions possible. We must be cautious, then, about generalizing motivations and making assumptions about why others act. With that said, however, we cannot fully understand international co-productions if we do not consider who stands to benefit—and to lose—from this mode of production.

The most careful study of the benefits and drawbacks of international co-productions has been performed by Hoskins and McFadyen who, in 1993, examined the trade press for producers' claims about why they engage in international co-productions. Hoskins and McFadyen found that the primary reasons for co-producing were: pooling of financial resources, accessing subsidies and incentives, accessing partner's markets, accessing third country markets, learning from partners, reducing risks, and accessing resources (such as stars and other creative personnel) and locations (Hoskins and McFadyen, 227–229).

Pooling of financial resources has been repeatedly cited by observers as the primary reason for international co-productions. Producers in smaller countries frequently view international co-productions as their opportunity to get involved in bigger budget projects (Paul Taylor, 101). Whereas their own small, domestic markets cannot support high priced productions, when the costs are shared and the potential markets transcend the domestic market, national production companies can invest more money. For many small broadcast outlets, both overseas and in the United States, "co-production may be the only way of participating in the production of large scale fictional programs" (Porter, 7).

Although many of these smaller companies get involved in international co-productions in order to fend off the presence of major U.S. films and television programs, even the major media producers now prefer to lower their risks by working with partners to produce product. These larger companies, however, could work with other domestic companies to lower their costs. The focus on international co-production reflects the majors' interest in increasing their presence in overseas markets. While international co-production essentially guarantees distribution in the partners' countries, the benefits go well beyond mere distribution. For example, international co-production provides the major U.S. companies the ability to enter other markets without setting up subsidiaries (Paul Taylor, 132). By working with companies in Europe or investing money in a project that is already being co-produced under a treaty, producers are able to create television shows with "national" or "European" status, or both, thus allowing the media text to qualify for subsidies and tax incentives and to avoid quotas that might limit U.S. product (Hirsh). Australian co-productions, for example, get local content consideration, tax incentives, and government funding (Cantanzariti, 11). Through involvement in treaty co-productions, the majors lower their risks and the amount of money they must invest in order to create a "quality" production.

Additionally, programs that are co-produced benefit from the insight that the co-production partners bring about their markets. The inclusion of a "cultural collaborator in the creative process" can help produce a more saleable product (Hubka, 2002, 243). Not only will the content be more likely to fit the interests of the various audiences, but the program's format (in terms of length, room for commercial breaks, and such) can be tailored for the markets and various regulatory requirements surrounding, for example, sex and violence (Hubka 2002, 235–37). The programs can be more fully developed so that they will appeal to the co-producing countries' markets and seem more "authentic." Such a process can limit what Carl Hoskins, Stuart McFadyen, and Adam Finn have explained as a media text's cultural discount—the loss of value faced by a cultural product when it leaves its country of origin based on the fact that it will not be fully understood or appreciated by the new, culturally distinct audience. A television program, then, that is produced with a French partner may seem more "French" than if the partner had not been involved and may not suffer as large a cultural discount. After all, as John Frow explains, "under the particular conditions of a globally integrated cultural market it is precisely whatever can be taken to be fully authentic . . . that can most readily be sold on the export market" (17).

The television program *Scene of the Crime*, as discussed by Sharon Strover, illustrates the benefits of co-production for optimizing access to partners' countries. Co-produced by companies in the United States, Canada, and France, the producers were able to get approximately $200,000 per episode from a French network. Typically U.S. exports received only $40,000 per episode due to the cultural discount. Because the program could be billed as French, and because the network could count it within its quota for airing French programming, the producers received a significantly higher sum (Strover, 114).

In addition to gaining access to the partners' markets, international co-productions are often expected to travel well to third markets, simply because they are created to appeal to multicultural audiences. As Leo Eaton said of U.S.-Japanese co-productions, "If the two of us can co-produce together, coming from such wide cultural differences, then we will probably be able to produce a film that is accessible to just about any other audience in the world" (10).

Perhaps the most important market for all co-producers with the goal of global expansion is that of the United States. Regardless of whether a U.S. company is a co-producer, which for various reasons discussed below is only sometimes desirable, many companies hope that by co-producing a project, they will create an "international" program that can sell in the large and powerful U.S. market. Canadian co-productions are particularly aimed at the U.S. market (Dorland, 16). Production companies in Canada, imagined to be closely related to the United States because of geographic and linguistic proximity, are frequently sought out as co-production partners as a gateway to the U.S. market (Hoskins and McFadyen, 232).

Canada is also seen as a country that can easily "double" as the United States. Access to such locations, landscapes, and internationally known actors and actresses are seen as a reason for co-producing (Strover, 112). It is doubtful, however, that an international co-production would be created solely for such access.[5] On the other hand, access to an advantageous exchange rate or lower labor costs could be the basis for an international co-production agreement (Pendakur, 25).

The ability to learn from international partners is another reason for collaborating on international co-productions. Media makers, for example, can learn about international audiences and their tastes, thus allowing them to produce products that will sell overseas (Strover, 112). Additionally, technical skills can be learned when international crews work together. Octavio Getino, a founder of Third Cinema, praised international co-producers for their ability to provide filmmakers with learning opportunities. Getino said about U.S.-Argentina co-productions, "U.S. co-productions are a business and I think that is fine. This helps us because it makes our film crews undergo some technical gymnastics . . . in film production. Some money stayed in the country too, but fundamentally it was in the experience" (qtd. in Falicov, 34). As discussed above, the Canadian government first entered into international co-production treaties at least in part to allow Canadian filmmakers the opportunity to work with filmmakers from around the world and learn about running a national industry (Dorland, 16).

These examples from Argentina and Canada illustrate that there can also be very focused cultural reasons for international co-production involvement. In these cases, the goal of co-productions was to provide knowledge that would allow for the development of a national film industry and thus a national culture. Regardless of whether this resulted, these motivations were taken seriously by many filmmakers and government officials. In addition to developing national industries, international co-productions are also often cited as a way of eliminating national differences and bridging global communities. As Carla Johnston explains in her book *International Television Co-Production: From Access to Success*, "legitimate co-production can serve an important role for the advancement of global understanding and the liberation of people from oppression, and it can be an economic cornerstone for both micro and macro levels of the communications industry" (2). A similarly celebratory reflection on co-productions comes from German media producer Regina Ziegler who says that a "further advantage" of international co-productions "is that national cultures will no longer exist . . . in their pure state within the European countries." At a time when there's a move to a European Community, Ziegler explains, international co-productions can foster a corresponding European culture (Ziegler, 6).

"World Wide Cultural Homogenization"— The Drawbacks of International Co-Productions

The promotion of global or transnational culture through international co-productions is considered by many observers (particularly scholars) to be not a benefit, but a drawback of international co-productions. In their analysis of the pros and cons of international co-productions, Hoskins and McFadyen found that the primary concern about international co-productions reported in the trade press was that "the cultural integrity of the program produced is undermined" through the process (230). This drawback of international co-productions was linked in the press with a loss of control over the project. The other main problems with international co-productions that Hoskins and McFadyen reported were the increased administrative costs and organizational difficulties.

So, while Johnston and Ziegler propose that the ability to create transnational media will be a boon to culture, many other scholars and industry participants worry about the cultural harm that international co-productions may cause. The major concern is that international co-productions will create homogenous programming that models itself on U.S.-style media. Cultural and national issues will be sacrificed to the creation of internationally appealing commercial films and television shows that are actually, as the *Electronic Mail and Guardian* referred to them, "polyglot mess[es]" (Worsdale). This is a problem, many academics claim, on numerous levels.

First, the erasure of national media is of concern. As Dorland explains, Canada's intense focus on international co-productions in the 1970s resulted in decreased funding for national films (Dorland, 16). Pendakur agrees that even later in the 1980s, Canadian companies' "preoccupation with the production of U.S. television series meant . . . fewer films and television projects that had their origin in Canada" (216). In the end, Pendakur argues, the model of international co-production resulted in an abandonment of Canada's stated goal of using the process to build up a national media culture (Pendakur, 221).

Speaking to a group of public broadcasting executives about international co-productions, Eaton said that "the things that go into good films are universal. It's just the styles and the way we approach our subjects that are different" (4). Although Eaton was suggesting the promise of international co-productions (since the elements that go into good media are "universal") his dismissal of national styles and approaches demonstrates why some critics are concerned about the impact of co-productions. As Negrine and Papathanassopoulos observe, "French programmes clearly cease to be 'French' if they adopt North American pacing and production values" (101).

As national media content is overshadowed by internationally co-produced programming, concerns continue to grow about what will take its place. The terms applied to such programming, McTelevision, Europudding, or Euroschlock, illustrate the accusations that these programs lack substance and artistic value. A classic example of Europudding is described by a German television executive:

> I saw a German/Italian/French co-production. It involved three hour-long programs. A German girl went to Italy and met a young Italian. They fell in love. But the daughter of a French banker, who was more attractive than the German girl, eventually ended up with the Italian boy.... It's what they call 'Europudding.' It won't work. To construct a plot that should appeal to all three publics is too artificial. (qtd. in Johnston, 14)

Another more prominent filmic example of Europudding is the 2001 film *Captain Corelli's Mandolin*. Produced by companies in France, Great Britain, and the United States, *Captain Corelli's Mandolin* tells the story of a romance between an Italian officer (played by American Nicholas Cage) and a Greek woman (played by Spanish actress Penelope Cruz) during Italy's World War II occupation of Greece. Set on a Greek island, the film presents characters who all seem to speak English—but with different accents (such as British, Greek, American, Italian). Many reviewers picked up on this assortment of accents, which seemed to contribute to the critique that the film lacked cohesion.

Not only are such productions devoid of complex issues, but they also illustrate a homogeneity that centers around the commercial impulses of Hollywood. On a very basic level, the downside of crews from around the world working together, is that they will eventually begin to create programs that look alike (Paul Taylor, 153). Additionally, time slots and lengths of programs must all be adjusted so that broadcasting systems around the world can share programs (Strover, 116). Furthermore, these programs, produced for international distribution with a special focus on the U.S. market, imitate Hollywood style and content in order to capitalize on the international success of U.S. media. Tamara Falicov noted that the international co-productions made between Roger Corman and his partners in Argentina overwhelmingly resulted in imitation (and exploitation) of Hollywood blockbusters (Falicov, 33). As Bergfelder very strongly states, "Internationalization is exclusively linked to Hollywood's hegemonic, imperialist politics, whose ultimate aim is world wide cultural homogenization" (2005, 323–24).

For aesthetes, less concerned with culture than artistry, this mimicry of Hollywood media leads to concerns about media quality. In her analysis of the relationship between international co-productions and nationalism, Strover writes, "In that coproducing is essentially an industrial response to needs for capital and to newer, wider opportunities for obtaining it, it should come as no surprise that new creativity is not its trademark" (121). The BBC in particular has come under heavy criticism for its use of co-productions, as critics worry that such programs will sacrifice quality in order to obtain funding from other countries and wider distribution (Nossiter, 133).

Questions about the quality of international co-productions also raise concerns for industry participants. While they may not worry about a loss of national culture and increased Hollywood-style homogeneity, they do worry that international co-productions will not sell. Toby Miller et al. explain that producers have "fears of creating the ultimate blandness of 'un Euro-pudding' that works so hard to include multiple linguistic, audience and production norms that it loses form" (92). Mark Betz remarks on the poor reputation of international co-productions, explaining that "the equation of coproduction in Europe with Hollywoodization and U.S. economic and cultural imperialism is ubiquitous" (18). The concern here is that if such media texts are not seen as "good," then they will not get distributed or viewed. Entertainment lawyer Nigel Palmer cautions regarding co-productions that "most dangerous of all, is the (high) probability that the mixture of such disparate elements will inevitably make the sale of the film in the United States of America—still the key to a film's success—extremely difficult outside the art house market" (5). Certainly the same concerns hold true for television co-productions, for which the result of Euro-pudding may also limit a program's distribution potential.

The focus on the U.S. market illustrates the unequal levels of power held by companies in different countries. Control over the script, the creative personnel, post-production, and so forth, are all negotiated between partners. If a treaty is invoked, however, the terms of the partners' involvement are somewhat clearly dictated. For example, for an Australian co-production to qualify as a national product, requirements must be met regarding the source of the script, the financial contribution of the partners, and a certain number of points must be attained, with points being given for the involvement of Australian creative personnel, talent, and crew. Without a treaty these terms are determined by the partners. When a U.S. company is involved, most production executives say that the U.S. partners dominate productions. As one French producer explains, "Co-productions with Americans invariably suffer from identity problems. . . . The American determines the script. There are no compromises" (qtd. in Hoskins and McFadyen, 231).

In her analysis of Roger Corman's co-productions with an Argentine company, Falicov illustrates the problems that arise when the partners are unequal. The Argentine production designer said, "Corman would send down these young arrogant men to work in special effects. They felt uncomfortable working in collaboration with the Argentine crew, despite the fact that many of us spoke English. They essentially gave orders and refused to hear our suggestions" (qtd. in Falicov, 33). As Falicov demonstrates, the production of these films primarily for the U.S. market from the start diminished the power and control of the Argentine production crew (Falicov, 37). One of the main reasons that Canadian companies are so appealing to many European producers as co-production partners is because they offer the North American sensibility without the U.S.-dominated power struggles.

In addition to concerns about media content and control over productions, the number of organizational and administrative incongruities between national media industries is cited as a drawback of international co-productions. Funding sources, regulation, time slots, programming styles, and many other factors vary greatly from country to country leading to confusion and higher costs (Eaton, 7–10). Simply dividing the labor in a way that satisfies necessary treaties often becomes an issue. An example of the division of labor for one Canadian-German animated co-production illustrates some of the complexities. The German partner handled "painting, compositing, and rendering the series with the help of a company in Hungary." The Canadian partner worked on the "script, storyboard, design, art direction and post production." The layout and posing were split between the two companies and the digitally scanned animation was done by a company in the Philippines (Hirsh). This division of the work could undoubtedly lead to confusion, but most certainly created administrative problems in terms of communication (through different time zones), billing, organization, and creative collaboration. Although these concerns may not be primary in keeping companies from co-producing, they are issues that impact the cultural products that result from the process.

"Globetrotting through Convoluted Global Intrigues"—The Content and Culture of International Co-Productions

This book will explore the various ways that these benefits and drawbacks of international co-productions work together to affect the kinds of television programs that get created. Primarily, these chapters tie together the way that the U.S. media—and its reliance on corporate capitalism—impact television programs that are ultimately intended for international audiences. Here, I suggest some of the main issues that will be touched upon in the case studies that follow.

Certainly, one of the main themes that will run throughout all of the case studies is the demise of national culture and the spread of a questionably "global" culture. As Bergfelder observes, "Amidst increasingly international casts globetrotting through convoluted global intrigues, the notions of national and cultural identity became dispersed or reduced to empty clichés" (2000, 150). As he further notes, the significance of the national versus global cultural debate, as it plays out in internationally co-produced media, is related to notions of identity and how people understand themselves and the world in which they live. Is it actually the case that audiences are instead, through international co-productions, being asked to develop a "cosmopolitan and classless identity in a new world made accessible and commodified by tourism, leisure and lifestyle consumerism" (Bergfelder 2000, 150)? As this is so clearly and emphatically explained by Edward Herman and Robert McChesney, "the global media's news and entertainment provide an informational and ideological environment that helps sustain the political, economic, and moral basis for marketing goods and for having a profit-driven social order" (10).

We can also question, however, as Paul Attallah does, whether the consideration of television's "canonical expressions of a national culture" is the most useful way to evaluate media texts (180). Rather, it may be more useful for us to question how international co-productions depict the concepts central to understanding culture. We must examine, then, the global culture being promoted by international co-productions and the ways in which these texts shape the cultural context in which viewers form identities, come to understand the world around them, and think about others.

Most frequently the new global culture is seen as Northern/Western (mostly American) and homogenous. Serra Tinic writes that international co-productions "aim at a form of universalism that homogenizes television content" (175). At a stylistic level, narrative structures follow U.S. patterns. Program formats, pacing, and content reflect the desire for U.S. distribution. There is no denying, however, that U.S. media is also affected by the need to meet demands of the international audience. As early as the 1960s, Guback recognized that "the connections established between the two industries are yielding hybrid films not typical of either the United States or any European country" (176–78). Strover examines the need for U.S. programs to consider European regulations regarding violence and sex, the interest in fewer episodes of any given series per season, the inclusion of international actors and locations, and a story that "operates on some middle ground appealing to both Americans and Europeans" (Strover, 119).

By examining these particulars in international co-productions we can get a better sense of the specific ways that such television programs reflect and impact the globalization of culture. Only through the specifics of television programs can we come to understand any relationship between the globalization of television and issues of national identity and the commercialization of culture.

Language, for example, is an important point of negotiation when trying to determine how to produce an international co-production. It is believed that, in general and for reasons discussed in the next chapter, the programs with global distribution potential—and certainly the only programs that will be distributed in the United States—are English-language programs (Farhi and Rosenfeld, A1). The resulting increased use of English, even when there are no English-speaking partners involved, illustrates a shift in global culture. Additionally, as Strover illustrates, the subject matter of international co-productions represents a need to meet the interests of a varied audience. At the 1926 League of Nations' International Film Congress focusing on intellectual cooperation, a recommendation was made to avoid content that would "arouse a spirit of animosity between nations" and to avoid degrading other nations/races (Kristin Thompson, 115). So, even the 1920s Film Europe movement reflected an understanding that international co-production must influence content. Today, the focus on action, travel, and history, for example, and the avoidance of political and controversial issues, certainly tell us something about the global audience and what it is imagined to find interesting. And, of course, the ways that these "non-controversial" subjects are presented and represented tell us a great deal about the middle ground being laid out for global culture.

Each of the remaining chapters examines a particular type of international co-production. The chapters address the historical and theoretical effects that the industrial mode of international co-production has on television content. Additionally, within each chapter two case studies are used to illustrate and flesh out the relationship between international co-production and television content. Significantly, all of the programs chosen in this book have aired in the United States and all are available for viewing on home video.

The first chapter looks at the genre of historical fiction to consider how international co-productions present the past to international audiences. The chapter considers the representation of concepts such as space and place; nationalism, localism, and globalism; and the role that family plays in these historical dramas. Ultimately, the chapter explores the ways that the past is re-imagined to appeal to audiences around the world while supporting the structures of global capitalism. While the examples in the first chapter illustrate the ways that nationalism can be elided within international co-productions, Chapter 2 focuses on how nationalism can also be constructed to meet particular industrial goals. This chapter focuses primarily on the co-production of "Britishness" by the A&E cable network in order to create programming that promotes its desired brand image. This chapter illustrates how A&E used international co-productions to create distinctive (and distinctively) British television shows to develop an A&E brand while still attracting a large and somewhat diverse target audience. Chapter 3 moves away from the "prestige" British programming of A&E to explore one of the most popular genres of internationally co-produced television: children's programming. This chapter primarily centers on notions of citizenship, primarily in pre-school programming. The goal in this chapter is to consider how programs produced by companies in multiple countries specifically for international audiences can teach children about the function of community and the children's role—and future role—within it. Chapter 4 explores the television documentary and the ways that international co-production shapes these television programs for the international market. Rather than focusing on the content of these "global" documentaries, this chapter analyzes the evidence that tends to be used within them. By looking at the modes of knowledge promoted by internationally co-produced documentaries, this chapter demonstrates how the process of international co-production can support modernity and the ideological constructs that support it. Finally, the conclusion will briefly bring together these separate chapters to discuss the overall implications of this analysis.

Guback, in 1969, perhaps best summed up the complexity of understanding media through the lens of international co-production:

> The finished product will reflect universal idioms at the expense of national ones. These social and artistic features are further enhanced by the economic imperatives connected with the production. . . . While this can yield products which are technically slick, the range of differences among them is reduced considerably—as among loaves of commercial white bread. (178)

The following chapters will offer a more nuanced understanding of whether the comparison of internationally co-produced television to "commercial white bread" is a fair one, and if so, what this means for the television industry and for global audiences arranging their cultural diets around these choices. As this book hopes to demonstrate, internationally co-produced television programs can be quite interesting—in their style, their narrative, their themes, and their ideologies. In the end, however, the corporate capitalist system weaves through and impacts these programs in profound and significant ways.

1 / History without Nation

Global Fiction

P roducers of the growing number of internationally co-
produced television programs on U.S. television in the 1980s
and '90s drew on the knowledge of film producers with experience in international co-production. Ideas about the genres,
narratives, stars, and locations that made international films successful were, in general, reflected in their small screen counterparts.
Although international co-producers in television benefited from the
film industry's presumed knowledge about what "worked" as international material, these media makers were also hampered by the
reputation of low quality "Europudding" that was historically associated with internationally co-produced films.

In a 1990 *Sight and Sound* article, William Fisher offered a recipe
for "Europudding":

> Take a story that crosses the borders of two or more Member
> States in the European Community. . . . Preferably histori-
> cal subjects are recommended. (Take care not to favour
> any single national perspective or choose a subject that
> could offend the national sensibility of any of the other

EC Member States). . . . Add a writer and director from these same Member States then gently solicit investment from their domestic television networks. . . . Fold in the appropriate number of actors and technicians from each country. . . . Yield: Two hours plus of a deal driven fictional 'screen entertainment' devoid of distinctive contour or flavour. (224)

Although this book argues against the notion that internationally co-produced programs are "devoid of contour or flavour," Fisher pinpoints several of the qualities considered significant for the creation of a "successful" international co-production, such as the use of international casts and crews, funding from both film and television sources across borders, and the concentration on historical subjects. The focus on historical topics in order to attract international audiences is somewhat surprising considering the general nationalistic tendencies of history. History, however, is seen as a means of attracting audiences with a pre-sold product. Many major historical "stories" are, after all, considered common knowledge. Furthermore, historical settings can remove narratives from the here and now, allowing media makers to avoid judging contemporary societies and cultures. Historical narratives can also be used to create an exotic cross-cultural environment through elements of mise-en-scène such as architecture, locations, and costumes. Undoubtedly, the desire to appeal to international audiences determines which historical moments are depicted and how they are represented.

This chapter will explore internationally co-produced narrative fiction focusing specifically on how the past is incorporated into these stories and how history is represented. The chapter will concentrate on two specific case studies that illustrate popular international co-production material: the miniseries *The Odyssey* (2001) and the hour-long action drama *Highlander: The Series* (1992–1996). Both of these programs exemplify the ways that international co-production took shape on U.S. television and offer means by which to examine how the recent discourse of globalization helps to form our mediated understanding of our world.

The International Appeal
of History

The participation of international partners as well as the incentive requirements that led to shooting in international locations and hiring international cast and crew members offered U.S. producers the potential to create television programs that perform well overseas and interest international audiences. Although the phrase "international appeal" became a production mantra repeatedly quoted in the trade press by producers in the 1990s, what exactly encompasses or creates this appeal is still relatively uncertain. As explained in the Introduction, the idea is that international co-productions promote the creation of media products that move across national boundaries, not just to the producing partners' markets but also to additional markets since they are created for more than one market.[1] Producers hope that the international nature built into a co-production will allow it to appeal to those people that John Sinclair et al. call the gatekeepers: those who buy and schedule programs for television networks and stations. International appeal is also imagined to help attract audiences in the U.S. market by adding a sense of prestige or glamour that can be promoted. Additionally, overseas locations and international casts might allow these television shows to stand out from the rest of television's congested programming schedule.

International co-production was expected to assist in creating "international appeal" by easing the use of international casts and crews and international settings. Stars such as Christopher Plummer, Isabella Rossellini, Shannon Tweed, Greta Scacchi, Ted Danson, Gerard Depardieu, and Bernadette Peters all helped to create a sense of global inclusiveness with international (though often B-level) stars that were well known to global audiences, if only because of their continued involvement with international television shows. Furthermore, international co-productions frequently made use of global location shooting not only for cheaper labor and tax benefits but also for the locations' abilities to strike a connection with global audiences. As a result, plots involving international travel that narratively explain characters from various countries and multiple locations became popular fare for international co-productions. Additionally, international co-productions were expected to be easily translatable. By using simple stories based on well known material (literature, history, or other forms of popular culture), international co-producers could ease a television program's travel across borders to different audiences. In addition to historical dramas, action-adventure programs also worked well within this schema, allowing for programs with limited dialogue and special effects.

International co-productions could be made additionally attractive to the international gatekeepers by avoiding discussions of current social and political issues. As mentioned above, setting a program in the past is one method by which producers avoid such issues and prevent associating the "bad guys" with any current potential audience. This use of the past may play out in the depiction of a well known historical moment. Other times the past is used as the setting for a new and fictitious story. In both of these cases, a reliance on history allows for a division between any judgments or criticisms that may be inherent in the story (such as the nationality of the villain) and the contemporary audience. For example, a story set during World War II with a German villain is less likely to offend today's German audience. Similarly, a story that criticizes the morals and values of characters in Victorian England probably will not come across as an indictment of current British society. The use of history, therefore, allows for a story that does not offend potential audience members. Additionally, a reliance on the past could also lend a feeling of exoticism to the story. While many people may be familiar with Paris, a story set in Paris during the French Revolution offers audiences a glimpse of a "different" way of life. Finally, historical settings go even further toward creating audience familiarity by relying on a pre-sold story that viewers already know. For example, audiences in Brazil may be confounded by and potentially uninterested in a story set in contemporary Russia; however, a story set during the Soviet Revolution relies on previous knowledge of the well known event to help draw in an audience and clarify character motivation. To be sure, these "historical" works generally diverge quite radically from the "truth" of the past, relying on myth and popular culture to tell their stories. The connection to the past and the attempts to create an illusion of reality, however, illustrate efforts to present these stories as "history" to offer the allure of learning while being entertained.

Of course historical drama is not the only genre employed by international co-producers. As in film, action-adventure, science fiction, and fantasy are also popular genres for internationally co-produced television. Action-adventure does not involve much dialogue or narrative explication and is therefore easily adaptable for international audiences; science fiction and fantasy also frequently rely on special effects and, like historical settings, remove characters from contemporary political and social concerns. As we will see, many international co-producers combine these elements—history, action-adventure, and science fiction or fantasy—to maximize the potential of their television programs with global audiences.

Not surprisingly, creating a program set in the past with elements of science fiction and fantasy as well as action can be prohibitively expensive for some production companies. As discussed in the introduction, international co-productions allow smaller production companies to be involved with high budget programs with "quality" production values. One of the expectations of international co-productions, therefore, is that they deliver the prestige and production values that have increasingly been associated with a program's production budget. Another marker of "quality" television is the style of the program. One of the Hollywood industry's greatest accomplishments has been its ability to establish its style as the "best." Frequently, international co-productions associate themselves with Hollywood quality by mimicking Hollywood product.

One of the most simple and interesting ways internationally co-produced programs align themselves with Hollywood is by literally adopting Hollywood's language: English. The decision to produce in English suggests not only a linguistic preference, but also a connection between such programming and the U.S. media market. These factors will be fleshed out in the following consideration of what it means both industrially and culturally for international co-productions to use English.

English as the Dominant Language

In 2004, Chile began a program called "English Opens Doors." The long-term goal of the program is to make all of Chile's 15 million people fluent in English within a generation. Some concerns were raised about the cultural implications of this program. As one critic said, "We're quite worried about this because it takes an economic hegemony and translates it into a cultural hegemony. Chile's insertion ought to be into the world at large not into the U.S. empire" (Rohter, A4). Meanwhile, the program's director stated that the English spoken in Chile will not "rival Shakespeare's. . . . We'll speak English Chilean-style, because the important thing is to understand English and to be able to use it as a tool in our favor" (qtd. in Rohter, A4).

The discussion surrounding Chile's program highlights the major issues involved in understanding the significance of English-language media production. Some proponents claim that the use of English opens doors to economic opportunities and prosperity. There is apprehension, however, that acceptance of English results in an alignment with U.S. culture and values, such as commercial capitalism and a focus on financial considerations over ethical or cultural concerns. Both sides of the argument associate local language with national culture that is created by the internal cultural industries, while English is connected with global culture and the financial focus of the entertainment business. The difference between those who support the use of the English language and those who critique it is whether the promotion of global English culture over national culture is seen as beneficial or harmful. In addition to the economic benefits, those who believe that using English in order to appeal to an international market is good promote the idea of transculturation, the sharing of cultures or "the fusion of the indigenous and foreign to create a new, original cultural product" (Diana Taylor qtd. in Mahan). On the other side of the dispute, critics argue that the use of English will result in the homogenization of culture and the demise of national and local cultures and values.[2] While both positions contain some truth, most important is an understanding of how English operates within the international market. As Selma Sonntag writes, "Embedded in language use is information about status and identity, as well as cold economic calculations based on efficiency and opportunity. The politics of global English are the politics of globalization, both economic and cultural" (1).

Repeatedly, English-language has been listed as a quality of film and television content that does well in the global market. The reason for the success of such media reveals a circular argument: English-language production is popular because English is the most commonly spoken second language throughout Europe; and English is the most commonly spoken second language in Europe at least partly because it is heard so often in the media.

Certainly, popular culture is not solely responsible for the widespread use of English throughout the world. As has been well discussed elsewhere, the spread of the English language is related to the British colonial power of the nineteenth century and then later to the military, political, and cultural dominance of the United States in the twentieth century (Sonntag, 4; Crystal, 53; de Swaan, 52). Furthermore, the advancements of information technologies (such as the web) in the United States have increased the reliance on English for communication purposes (Crystal, 11).[3] Within the administration of the European Union, for example, English has become the predominant language despite the twenty official languages supported by the EU and despite efforts by the French government to increase the use of French by EU officials.[4]

The French resistance to the widespread use of English illustrates the connection made between language and culture.[5] National or official languages have repeatedly, and not only in France, been tied to the preservation of national identity and used to ward off the threat of an increasingly homogenized culture. As Abram de Swaan explains, arguments in favor of preserving local languages often move from concerns solely about the survival of the language to larger arguments that "indigenous cultural practices and products [are] bound to disappear unless the language in which they are embedded continues to be spoken and understood" (42). From the perspective of those interested in preserving protectionist measures such as subsidies and tax incentives, national culture is pitted again the English language and its "carrier," the United States. The conflation of English with U.S. culture is apparent in comments made by business leaders, bureaucrats, and politicians. The director of the European Centre for Modern Languages, for example, noted that the extensive use of English in Europe is "part of internationalization, on the one hand, and part of American domination of the world in a way" (qtd. in Bita, T06). The reasons for English's association with the United States are rather clear. In addition to the United States' military and economic power, Madelaine Drohan and Alan Freeman explain, "it is also the power of Hollywood and American popular culture. English is the language of T-shirts, rap music, advertising, and MTV. American culture is an export industry that outranks aerospace exports when it comes to global penetration" (D1).

The seemingly accepted connection between English-language media and the United States became increasingly questionable in the 1990s. While the most widely seen English-language films and television shows screened in Europe were—and still are—produced by Hollywood studios (with some from the United Kingdom), more and more of it is produced, at least in part, by European, Latin American, and Asian companies through international co-production. Oftentimes these programs are created in co-production arrangements with English-speaking countries (the United States, Canada, or the United Kingdom). For example, the miniseries *The Odyssey* (1997, United States, Germany, Italy, Greece) and *Fall From Grace* (1994, United Kingdom, Italy, France), and the series *Fly By Night* (1991, Canada, France), and *Counterstrike* (1990–93, Canada, France) are all English-language shows with large investments by non-English-speaking countries. Some European production companies even started to produce English-language product without native English-speaking partners. By 1998, Gaumont had produced *The Fifth Element* (1997) and had begun production of *The Messenger* (1999), *Me, Myself, I* (1999), and *Vatel* (2000) (Williams, 34). Companies in Italy and France collaborated on a season of *The New Adventures of He-Man* (1990–91); and the television miniseries *Diamond Hunters* (2001) was produced by companies in Germany, Italy, Africa, and Denmark. The most obvious question is why a production company would want to create a program that needs to be dubbed or subtitled in its home country. Why would the company forsake possible government incentives for creating "national" product? The simple answer is as obvious as the question: money. Before ending the discussion there, however, we must consider why English-language products make more money so that we can fully understand the cultural impact of this trend.

It is not difficult to understand the appeals of such English-language co-productions for non-English-speaking countries. The desire to reach global markets drives producers to film in English. Industry participants believe that, in general, the programs with global distribution potential, and certainly the only programs that will be distributed in the United States, are English-language programs (Fahri and Rosenfeld, A1). English is also associated with U.S. productions and images of high budget, "high quality" U.S. media products. U.S. media, seen around the world, has become the standard for commercial film and television on an international level. One New York investment banker who is involved in putting together international co-production deals remarked that "America's genius is its ability to make U.S. programs the second most popular in every foreign market" (qtd. in Briller, 72).

The association of English-language production with U.S. media products indicates that there is more involved than just shooting in English. As mentioned above, to compete in the international market, producers also imitate the mainstream Hollywood production style. The use of glamorous actors, high key lighting, U.S.-based formats and genres, and fast-paced action all reflect the influence of the Hollywood aesthetic. The process of international co-production, however, prevents the complete Americanization of such programs on all levels including look, story, and ideology. Because the programs are trying to appeal to global audiences and maintain some element of creative input from several companies, the programs' styles never quite match up to Hollywood's. Additionally, as discussed above, the narratives frequently must accommodate the different needs of the partners through stories that incorporate travel and international characters. And, finally, the programs must develop their own "messages" that are certainly informed by Hollywood and western ideologies but that also integrate the globalizing push that drives their production.

Ideologies for Global Audiences

As illustrated, the production decisions made in order to enhance the international appeal of a television program undoubtedly impact the program's narrative. Beyond that, however, these efforts also affect the "messages" that are embedded within the show. I do not mean to suggest a strict structuralist approach to television analysis; however, I do want to point out some similarities between internationally co-produced fictional programs to indicate that there are particular ideological messages/meanings that either consciously or unconsciously work their way into programs intended for global audiences. These themes and ideologies that are at play in these productions demonstrate the commonalities between international co-productions particularly associated with their depictions of history.

There are three similarities that we can see in many internationally co-produced television programs (as well as other programs created for international audiences). One is the way that space and place are depicted. Another is the position of the community or family as the primary center of meaning in the world. And finally, the representation of internationalism, nationalism, and localism serves as common ground for international co-productions. Each of these clearly interrelated elements will be discussed in general terms below and then within the specific case studies that follow.

The distinction between space and place has been theorized in the literature of many areas of study such as geography, philosophy, globalization, and postmodernism. Although different definitions and ideas have emerged, there have been some consistent usages of the terms. In general, space refers to the three dimensional world—the physical space taken up by objects or a group of people. A place, on the other hand, is more personal than this definition of space. As Barry Brown explains, place is "a particular geographic location (a space, if you will) which has meaningful attachments to the people who pass through it." So while space is abstract and objective, place is local and embodied—space that has personal relevance and resonance. Internationally co-produced narratives tend to exist in many different spaces (whether they actually exist or are created in the realm of fantasy). These are locations that simply exist for the characters in the narrative and which the characters must pass through. Meanwhile, the main characters, particularly the heroes, frequently connect their identities to their places—their communities. The hero's individuality and purpose (for there is usually a single and male hero) stem from his *place* of origin by providing him, for example, with a value system that determines his path or goal for his quest. Space and place, however, are not unrelated. Within international narratives, they are frequently connected through the implication that movement through space(s) is the means by which people achieve the rewards and comforts of place.

A return to *place* is usually the ultimate goal of the hero's travel. And place most often refers to a home or a community that helps to define the hero and motivate his actions. These homes and communities are usually idealized within the programs, depicted as heterosexual, family oriented, ethnic- or religious-based communities that focus on exclusion rather than inclusion. Much of the racial, class, and gender conflict that can be found in the nationally based programs is erased in the internationally co-produced shows. According to Andrew Kirby, the idea of "place" includes not only community but also locality, a concept that acknowledges the political, racial, class, and gender conflicts that help shape the meaning that places have for people (324). So, places with personal meaning are not without discord. The global program frequently ignores the conflict; however, when disagreement does occur, the hero who has experienced global travel can generally overcome it.

In many ways these local communities lay the foundation for the growing fundamentalist movements of the late twentieth century or Benjamin Barber's "Jihad," which, along with more mainstream forces in society, encourage people to find cultural identity in ethnicity during a time of expanding global culture (Barber, 171). The importance of the local, therefore, is strongly connected to the expansion of the global. These programs illustrate, therefore, that it is only by moving through space—by experiencing global travel—that the heroes come to appreciate and deserve their homes and their communities and truly value their places. By moving through space and embracing the global nature of the world, these shows tell us, people can better appreciate their own small parts of the world.

Like global travel and local communities, nations, though often futuristic or historical, are frequently represented in internationally co-produced programs. Nationalism, however, is generally removed from the positive relationship between globalization and local community. Rather, nationalism is frequently a hindrance that must be worked around in order to get back the benefits of one's own place. Mediated representations of the past are often related to and inform how a nation as a social unit remembers itself and understands its place in the global environment.[6] Robert Burgoyne, for example, sees the spate of 1990s' U.S.-produced films about the past incorporating ideas of difference, mainly ethnic and racial difference, to form counternarratives that are then used to expand and support notions of a more inclusive and improved nation. Television programs like *Dr. Quinn Medicine Woman* and *I'll Fly Away* may work in similar ways to reshape ideas about the United States' past. While a film or a television program produced in one country can focus on creating an image of this country's past, international co-productions serve this function for several countries that may want to remember the past in different ways.

Additionally, nationalism is frequently seen as a hindrance for global corporations. As E.J. Hobsbawm writes, "Since World War II, but especially since the 1960s, the role of 'national economies' has been undermined or even brought into question by the major transformations in the international division of labour, whose basic units are transnational or multi-national enterprises of all sizes" (181). Not only does an overall negative representation of nationalism allow global television shows to avoid favoring specific national groups (which may alienate viewers from other nations), but it also promotes the rejection of the concept of nationalism that imposes limits on and works against the values and economic imperatives of transnational capital. It is not surprising then to find nationalism depicted as a threat within programs firmly dependent on multi-nationalism. What emerges from these various forces are representations of the past that attempt to promote the commonalties of various cultures while downplaying their divisions; programs that see the world as one legitimately divided into villages, tribes, and other local groups, yet savaged by nationalism; programs that see not the past but the future in international communities and global ideas. Therefore, at the core of these internationally co-produced programs is frequently a moderate celebration of globalization (though they do not claim that there are not hardships or drawbacks to this process) that allows the heroes to appreciate and deserve the peace acquired from a sense of his place in the world and the community that supports him there.

The remainder of this chapter will explore two specific case studies of internationally co-produced television programs that illustrate these qualities of international co-productions. One program is a miniseries, the other a one-hour action drama. Each of these formats is popular in the world of internationally co-produced fiction. As will be explained below, miniseries were considered to be one of the best formats for international co-producers before the television industry saw promise for co-produced series. And within the field of the regular series, the one-hour action drama program proved to have the most potential for international co-production. These examples will illustrate the ways that internationally co-produced programs, particularly those that focus on historical fiction, shape their representations of global travel, depict the values of space and place as well as international, national, and local communities, and potentially impact how audience members come to understand the world in which they live and the communities of which they are a part.

An Odyssey Through Space and Place

Although the miniseries is frequently discussed as a genre, the term format is more accurate since there are miniseries of different genres (fantasy, melodrama, etc.)—though often miniseries, like modern blockbuster films, are a mix of genres. Essentially, a miniseries is any television program that continues over a series of—but also a limited number of—days.[7] Within the context of U.S. television, the stories usually run from one episode to the next. So, as Margaret Montgomerie points out, the more correct format name might be miniserial. Often these programs are adaptations of both classic and popular books. And, like other television formats, they focus on the family. Industrially, miniseries are the most expensive form of original prime time programming to produce, which is why they are often promoted as special "event" programs (Dempsey, 45). The rise of the miniseries in the United States is generally attributed to three programs: *The Forsyte Saga*, the BBC-MGM co-produced miniseries that aired on NET (the precursor to PBS) in 1969 and received very respectable ratings (discussed in greater detail in the next chapter); *Rich Man, Poor Man*, ABC's adaptation of the novel in the 1976–77 season; and, of course, the enormously successful *Roots*, which aired on ABC in 1977. These three programs helped to define the miniseries in the 1970s as a format that centered on adaptations, family, and melodrama.

This foundation for the miniseries developed into several different strands. The two main categories discussed in the trade press are the high budget, prestige miniseries that are frequently literary adaptations or epic stories, and the more cheaply produced "ripped from the headlines" miniseries that focus on diseases, famous court cases, disasters, and the like. The high budget miniseries began to decline in number in the late 1980s.[8] For the U.S. television networks that were beginning to feel the pressure of the competition from cable, the expense of these programs became a burden. It was at this moment, however, that John Caldwell sees the miniseries taking on the characteristics of what he calls the televisual and serving a particular function for the beleaguered networks.

According to Caldwell, televisuality is a style that developed on U.S. television in the 1980s as a result of particular industrial, economic, social, and cultural conditions. He explains that starting in the 1980s and continuing into the early '90s a number of television programs (such as *Northern Exposure, thirtysomething,* and *Twin Peaks*) focused on stylistic exhibitionism and excess offering distinction to the networks that aired these programs and to the viewers who watched them (3–30). Caldwell argues that at this time, the miniseries was an important component of network strategy for its ability to bring prestige to the networks. The miniseries was, as it had always been, "event" television that, through style, content, and promotion, allowed television to rise above the "mind-numbing flow" (Caldwell, 162–163). Stylistically, like other televisual programs, miniseries were excessive: through factors such as their lavish mise-en-scène, exotic locations, and unusual length, televisual miniseries, at least to some extent, foregrounded style before story. Focusing on the 1988 miniseries *War and Remembrance*, Caldwell examines its excessive style, noting the program's extremely long 20-minute opening, the recurring title sequences that moved the viewer quickly through time and space, and the foregrounding of Herman Wouk as the author of the miniseries (170–172). All of these stylistic characteristics, Caldwell argues, highlighted the constructed nature of the miniseries, requiring that the viewer recognize the miniseries as a story created for television rather than getting absorbed into the story (176). The exhibitionist style of these miniseries also resulted in a particular explosion of time and space. Time was stretched out so that, like *War and Remembrance*, many miniseries focused on one moment in time and its effects on a range of people. By intensely exploring a specific moment in history, the miniseries developed a sense of power and importance. The televisual miniseries also spanned a number of countries and were usually shot in a variety of locations. Setting up the stories to span a number of locations and utilizing on-location production gave these miniseries a powerful sense of worldliness (Caldwell, 187). According to Caldwell this practice helped to "globalize" the characters. I would add, however, that while the characters in the miniseries may have been inserted into the global arena, they were still very much tied to their nations. Most, if not all, of the examples of miniseries that Caldwell cites in his endnotes, such as *The North and the South* (ABC, 1985), *Peter the Great* (NBC, 1986), and *War and Remembrance* (ABC, 1988), are strongly nationalistic.

As Caldwell explains, the worsening recession in broadcast television in the 1990s led to the cancellation of many of the overtly televisual series (292). This recession was fueled by the loss of viewers and advertisers to cable. For financial reasons, the networks had a more difficult time focusing on the prestige that came with the production of high budget miniseries (Caldwell, 292).[9] Leslie Moonves, President and CEO of CBS, said in 1998, "Before, one of the reasons you did a miniseries was the prestige factor. . . . But you can't do something purely for the prestige, not anymore. You need some bang for the buck" (qtd. in Sterngold). According to trade reports, the networks seriously limited their involvement with high budget historical and adaptation-based miniseries and moved to "'contempo' action-adventure mysteries" (Guider, 1).

The increased focus on the global market, however, helped to revive the format. While network interest in prestige miniseries declined, international broadcasters such as Silvio Berlusconi in Italy began co-producing miniseries with plans to air them overseas (Jennifer Clark, 22). As early as 1993 a trade report noted that the potential of the cable and European markets helped make the miniseries "hot again" (Brodie, 1). Increased privatization of television in Europe created opportunities for U.S. producers by opening up new outlets for sales of these miniseries; however, there was also a sense that these programs should better meet the needs of overseas audiences. According to Hallmark Entertainment President and miniseries producer Robert Halmi, Sr., the late 1990s saw a "marketplace where movies with provincial American themes, which once found audiences around the globe, have less appeal for foreign buyers" (Fabrikant, D1). New content needed to reflect less of a national U.S. perspective and more global themes and values—whatever those might be. At the same time that new markets were emerging, though, quota laws to protect "national culture" and "national industries" limited these opportunities. In addition to creating barriers into the markets, in some countries the quota systems led to the rise of national media companies that created television product to compete with the U.S. imports.

The desire for "international appeal" and the need to count as national media in order to get around quota laws led some U.S. producers to work with international partners for their productions. As discussed in the introduction, international partners could assist with funding, guarantee distribution in the partners' home countries, and provide creative insight that could increase overseas popularity. These factors certainly grabbed the attention of producers working in the costly miniseries format. Not only are miniseries expensive to produce, but they also have a very limited aftermarket in the United States since miniseries are rarely bought for syndication and re-runs (Dempsey, 45). Furthermore, miniseries tend to be popular overseas, so this market was rich for those producers who wished to ease the burden of the network system of deficit financing and perhaps even make some money. In fact, four-hour miniseries and television movies were considered the ideal format for international co-productions since it was not yet certain whether a series could work internationally (Guider, 1).

The general popularity of the miniseries format overseas encouraged many producers to search for content with international flavor. Not only would international partners and gatekeepers not be interested in programs that only reflected U.S. culture and domestic issues, but also such programs might not find favor with international audiences. *MediaWeek* reported a decrease in the number of "ripped from the headlines" miniseries and a move toward the more fantastical stories popular internationally. The motto seemed to be that "bigger is better" (Sharkey, 1998, 9). These miniseries, after all, were no longer being bought simply to fill time on a schedule, as some had been in the past. They were being actively produced and purchased at a high cost by international broadcasters and producers. Miniseries producers, like all international producers, were faced with the conflicting needs to represent a global (nationally nonspecific) universe while still appealing to individuals who live their lives on a local level. We see this conflict playing out for the global miniseries in their representations of the global-local nexus.

Like the televisual miniseries discussed above, the internationally co-produced miniseries may also be described as exploding time and space but in a very different way. These miniseries frequently cover a long range of time and focus on only a few characters that move through many spaces (for example, *Gulliver's Travels*, *Arabian Knights*, *Merlin*, and *Noah's Ark*). As discussed above, these geographic locations, however, do not have personal meaning for the heroes. They are spaces that the hero must simply, though rarely easily, move through in order to find or earn his "place" in the world. This reliance on abstract and objective spaces is essential to allow these miniseries to represent and promote many exotic locations. The main character moves through many spaces, presenting viewers with a sort of travelogue, one that is abstract, without personal meaning for the hero (except in that the travels are necessary to find his way back home) or the viewers, thereby avoiding any focus on or assigning meaning to a particular nation that might offend or bore the international audience. These tropes are clearly visible in the example of the miniseries version of *The Odyssey*.

The Odyssey offers an interesting case study for examining the representation of globalism, nationalism, and localism in the global miniseries. *The Odyssey* was not the first or the last or the "best" of this format, but it is fairly typical: an adaptation of a well known epic story designed for an international audience. In many ways, *The Odyssey* exemplifies this trend in television production and illustrates how such miniseries functioned both industrially and textually to negotiate their service of international audiences who still see themselves rooted in their communities. This two-part, four-hour miniseries based on Homer's epic poem premiered in the United States on NBC in 1997. *The Odyssey* was executive produced by Robert Halmi Sr., the president of Hallmark Entertainment, along with Francis Ford Coppola. Although Hallmark and Coppola's American Zoetrope are the two companies that are most frequently associated with the miniseries in the popular press, further research has connected the miniseries' financing with companies in Italy (Mediaset), Germany (Betafilm, Kirchgroup, ProSieben), and Greece (Skai TV). Clearly there was never any question that *The Odyssey* would be distributed internationally, a factor that could not be ignored by producer Halmi, the most hands on of the program's producers, in his conceptualization of the project. Furthermore, Hallmark's position as a transnational corporation with a growing number of cable and satellite channels outside of the United States increased the company's interest in "large scale pieces we think have global appeal" (Hoffman, 18).

That *The Odyssey* was produced as an international co-production is not surprising. The expense of the movie would almost necessitate such a plan. Trade reports place the cost of the miniseries between \$32 and \$40 million.[10] At the time this was reportedly, minute for minute, the most expensive television drama ever produced (Mason, 12). With a crew of three hundred (Mason, 12), a shoot lasting ninety days (most television movies at the time took one month for production) (Bickley. TV3), and a post-production period of ninety days (Liner, 6), distributors were quick to promote *The Odyssey* as spectacular, unique, and important. In fact, the international nature of *The Odyssey* was clearly seen as one of its biggest draws in the United States. Articles about *The Odyssey* and interviews with cast and crew highlighted the international nature of the program.

The international appeal of *The Odyssey* is evident in a number of ways that reflect its role as an international co-production. First, the program was shot in several locations—Turkey and Malta with interiors shot in the United Kingdom—and prominently features travel in its story. The promotional material for *The Odyssey* makes frequent mention of the location shooting in Turkey and Malta, evoking both a sense of exoticism and a connection with ancient Greece that gives the miniseries a false sense of verisimilitude. Most reviews noted the beautiful Mediterranean setting that *The Odyssey* frequently displays in pans and long shots. For example the *Denver Rocky Mountain News* refers to the "breathtaking location scenes" (Saunders). One reporter for *MediaWeek* inquired about the miniseries, "Has there ever been a better commercial for a Greek vacation?" (Grossberger, 30).

In addition to location shooting, *The Odyssey* features a cast (and crew) of different nationalities (Armand Assante, Isabella Rossellini, Greta Scacchi, Irene Pappas, Bernadette Peters, and Vanessa Williams) who speak in a variety of accents throughout the narrative. Director and co-writer Andrei Konchalovsky, though having lived in Hollywood for almost twenty years, has a Russian background that lent him "international" flavor. Even the international legend of Robert Halmi, Sr., which places him as a freedom fighter against the Nazis and a spy against the Soviets, was exploited in promotional material for the miniseries.[11] With homes in New York, Kenya, Spain, and a yacht on the Mediterranean, Halmi was set up as anti-Hollywood, someone who would not turn out the same old Hollywood movie, but would produce something better, something more international (Sharkey, 1996, 25). As *MediaWeek* reported, "Halmi's base in New York and his extended stays in Europe and Africa almost ensure that the perspective of the company will never find its roots in Hollywood" (Sharkey, 1996, 25). Halmi's international lifestyle most likely also impacted not just the publicity surrounding *The Odyssey*, but also its actual production. Halmi's willingness to shoot in places such as Malta is probably related to his comfort overseas. Additionally, Halmi is undoubtedly more aware of the needs of international audiences than a producer who resides solely in the United States.

The decision to adapt *The Odyssey* and the way it was adapted also reflect the miniseries' role in the international marketplace. That this is a television version of a classic literary text that is known throughout the world (and is conveniently in the public domain) is not coincidental. Furthermore, like much international television, *The Odyssey* focuses on the adventure. There are several scenes, such as Odysseus' encounter with Scylla and Charybdis, that use little dialogue and therefore avoid translation difficulties. Furthermore, the movie is certainly fantastical and historical, removing it from any modern national tensions and concerns.

Although the historical setting of *The Odyssey* avoids modern nationalistic biases, the television version of Homer's poem certainly represents globalization, nationalism, and localism, and the significance of place and space in ideological ways. Without depicting currently existing nation-states, *The Odyssey* still offers a picture of nationalism. Here, as in other international co-productions, nationalism is depicted as a sad and dangerous force in terms of its impact on individuals. Nationalism, after all, is responsible for Odysseus traveling to Troy. Odysseus does not go because he believes in the war, but because he has taken a blood oath to protect Greece. Odysseus relates in a voice over "I was forced to leave my home, not knowing if I would ever see my wife and child again." Additionally, this television version of *The Odyssey* actually includes part of the story of *The Iliad* and depicts the ten-year Trojan War. Again, we see the horror of nationalism as the two sides fight without really understanding why. This version also makes Odysseus more sympathetic, so that when we see his point of view as he scans the carnage of war we get a sense of sadness and pity for those dying for an unexplained cause (other than nationalism).

While nationalism may be seen as the motivation for death and despair, globalism has a more productive goal. The trip to Troy begins Odysseus' global adventure. He sees many places and many people. Odysseus moves from space to space; on one island he encounters Cyclops, on another Aeolus the god of wind (played by Michael J. Pollard with a heavy New York accent). He spends time with Circe on her island (where he dreams of Penelope while having sex with Circe) and travels between Scylla and Charybdis.[12] And, while these locations do not have a personal meaning for him, he learns from his travels. The wisdom Odysseus acquires from his journey is an underlying theme in this television movie. When Odysseus goes to Hades to meet Teiresias, the prophet tells him, "You keep your eyes only on your home. Blinded, you do not see that it is the journey itself that makes up your life. Only when you understand this will you understand the meaning of wisdom." Odysseus arrogantly replies that he will find the wisdom alone—and it is this attitude that makes the gods angry with Odysseus who must come to recognize the importance of the global forces in the world. Through global travel—movement through many spaces—Odysseus earns the serenity that comes from returning to his home and his family in Ithaca.

The significance of the local—mainly represented in home and family—is highlighted throughout *The Odyssey*. The focus on home and family as a source of security is foregrounded in publicity materials and reviews for the miniseries. According to one reviewer, "with enduring love at its heart, 'The Odyssey' celebrates the timeless value of commitment. After twenty years of thrills, there's no place like home" (Grahnke, 49). Halmi also described the miniseries as a story about finding something to hold on to (Gritten, 3). And Armand Assante summed up the message of *The Odyssey*: "All that really matters is your home and the life you have established" (Liner, 6).

The miniseries uses several techniques to achieve this representation of the home and community (place) as the source of security and happiness. For example, the miniseries is reordered so that it is not a flashback, and the narrative tension surrounds the question of whether Odysseus will ever make it back home. This adaptation also opens with the birth of Telemachus. Borrowing a scene from 1977's *Roots*, Odysseus holds up his new son to the sky, but instead of telling his son about the greatness of the sky, Odysseus gives his son the land. He asks Telemachus if he sees Ithaca, "your kingdom; do you see how beautiful?" Clearly Odysseus places great importance in his land, so much so in fact that a part of his homeland is built right into the most intimate part of his house. A recurring icon in the miniseries is a tree

Figure 1.1 Greta Scacchi, Geraldine Chaplin and Armand Assante prepare for the birth of Odysseus and Penelope's son in *The Odyssey*. *(Photo courtesy of Photofest.)*

around which Odysseus and Penelope built their bedroom. The tree stands in the middle of the room and symbolizes the life that the two created together and their love for one another. Odysseus dreams of Penelope running around this tree when he sleeps with Circe, indicating not only his love for Penelope but also the grounding of this love in their home, in Ithaca. Furthermore, scenes of Odysseus' travels are intercut with scenes of Penelope at the palace in Ithaca. The significance of Ithaca for Odysseus is marked by Poseidon's words as he decides to punish Odysseus for his belief that he does not need the gods. Poseidon says, "Never again will you reach the shores of Ithaca.... You will suffer." For Odysseus to suffer he must be kept away from his family and his land: his place. Home and family signify the safety, belonging, and peace of mind for which Odysseus, and many people living in the global world, long.

The tears that fill Odysseus' eyes when he finally returns to Ithaca and tastes the food of his home are only part of the story, however. This idealized and nostalgic image of home, family, and place certainly elides some of the more problematical elements that are apparent in the miniseries (and, of course, in the original text chosen for adaptation). For example, it is worth noting that throughout the film, women are tied to their places—in some cases they are literally incapable of leaving. Circe (Bernardette Peters) and Calypso (Vanessa Williams) both use their places to lure and trap Odysseus but they themselves never mention the idea of leaving. Penelope is perhaps the most apparent prisoner of her place as she waits for Odysseus and is practically under siege by suitors attempting to make her forget about her long-missing husband. Odysseus even refers to Penelope as being "trapped in this palace." So, while the men may travel, women remain in their places. And, while these places may be idealized as what is good and worthy in the world, it is questionable whether the women, seemingly incapable of leaving, would feel the same way. This question, however, is not raised in *The Odyssey*, as it idealizes place and equates it with a harmonious community. Instead, the miniseries suggests that those not forced to leave their homes are fortunate because they do not have to earn their place by wandering the world. Of course, the women's places are assigned to them and are not questioned. Women, apparently, already know that there is "no place like home," and have no interest or desire in finding the knowledge and power that might come from leaving "their place." International co-productions, then, while perhaps expressing an interest in place often continue to express dominant and sometimes repressive ideas about the roles of various groups within these places, in some cases simply by adapting texts that embody these ideas.

Who Wants to Live Forever:
Highlander: The Series

As with the miniseries, the increase in internationally co-produced drama series can be linked to several developments within the television industry in the 1980s and '90s. Cable and satellite not only offered competition for broadcast television in their own right, but they further weakened the major networks by making independent broadcast stations more accessible to viewers. These stations, which in many localities had been relegated to UHF channels that were difficult to tune in and sometimes of poor quality, found themselves on a level playing field with all other channels available through a cable system—at least in terms of access and signal quality. The networks, therefore, were in an increasingly difficult position, being threatened both by the narrowcasting of cable and satellite channels and the wider appeal of the independent broadcast stations. As discussed above, this competition along with other industrial pressures contributed to the rise of the televisual style on television. At the same time, however, the rising costs of television production made some programs prohibitively expensive.

Within this environment, the broadcast networks expressed interest in international co-productions, particularly in the early 1990s as production costs continued to escalate. CBS was most active in its pursuit of co-produced product. The network experimented with several such programs from 1991–93 through its "Crime Time After Prime Time" line-up. These programs filled CBS's late night schedule against *The Tonight Show* in between the time that Pat Sajak's show was cancelled and David Letterman moved into this slot. Each night from Monday through Friday CBS aired a different action-adventure program including *Dark Justice, Silk Stalkings, Forever Knight, Fly By Night, Scene of the Crime* and *Sweating Bullets. Sweating Bullets* (first Canada/Mexico and later Canada/Israel), *Forever Knight* (Canada/France), *Scene of the Crime* (Canada/France), and *Fly By Night* (Canada/France) were internationally co-produced. Additionally, in 1992 a number of high-level CBS executives, including then CBS president Jeff Sagansky, went on a tour of Europe visiting potential international partners. Sagansky expressed an expectation that soon network television would include internationally co-produced television programs in prime time (Jennifer Clark, 22). The reason for this was succinctly explained by an ABC executive while discussing the potential of international co-production for his networks: "The car chases are just not affordable anymore" (Harrison, 60). In 1992 MGM and Reteitalia (Berlusconi's media company later renamed Mediaset) co-produced a two-hour action-adventure pilot for CBS about an American woman fighting terrorists in Europe. The plan was that Reteitalia would handle distribution in Europe and MGM would distribute in Latin America and Asia

(Freeman, 1992, 33). There is no evidence, however, that CBS ever picked up the pilot and without network support the program was not produced.

Although the networks explored the idea of internationally co-produced series, and CBS even aired a few of these programs during fringe times, for the most part the networks focused on internationally co-produced special event programs like the miniseries. Cable networks and independent stations, however, had a significant amount of time to fill and looked to independent producers, many of which operated through international co-productions, to help them acquire original series. Independent stations picked up internationally co-produced programs that included *Hercules: The Legendary Journeys* (United States/New Zealand), *Xena: Warrior Princess* (United States/ New Zealand), *Kung Fu: The Legend Continues* (United States/ Canada), and *The Secret Adventures of Jules Verne* (Canada/United Kingdom) in first-run syndication. Among the newer cable networks, USA was particularly involved in airing internationally co-produced series, especially in the mid to late 1990s as the network looked to increase its profile with original programming (a strategy that will be discussed in greater detail in the next chapter). Programs like *Counterstrike* (Canada/France), *TekWar* (United States/Canada), and *La Femme Nikita* (Canada/France/United States) aired on the USA network.

While all of these programs fit into the action-adventure genre, many of them also contain historical elements—especially those that were picked up by independent stations. The focus on one-hour drama series is easy to explain using conventional wisdom about what kinds of programs "travel well." Comedy programs are considered too culturally specific with a high cultural discount as they travel across borders. Creating a comedy program that would appeal to international audiences has consistently seemed like a monumental task. Comedies, and later the increasingly popular reality programs, are considered to be better suited for formatting, by which the same program is recreated for different markets using local talent and languages.[13]

Drama programs and specifically action-adventure and historical shows, are seen to have potential with international audiences. Of course certain conditions must be met. For example, although "quality dramas" were being created for U.S. television in the 1980s and '90s, international co-productions did not, and could not fall into this category. Quality dramas, such as *Hill St. Blues*, *NYPD Blue*, and *Northern Exposure*, tend to be writer-driven, focusing on dialogue and character development. Internationally co-produced programs, on the other hand, focus on action and style. The reasons for this necessity relate to the difficulties in dubbing programs with a large amount of dialogue and the cultural specificity that usually comes along with this. In his examination of the quality dramas of the 1980s and '90s, Robert Thompson describes them as "national drama" (17). As "global dramas," international co-productions still frequently reflect elements of the excessive, televisual style that Caldwell associates with this time period (as discussed above), but these programs do so through the use of special effects, high concept imagery, music, and fashion. Internationally co-produced dramatic series did not appeal to the quality audiences of nationally produced programs, but instead sought international audiences interested in distraction and entertainment.

By the late 1990s the outlets for internationally co-produced series had decreased in number. Independent stations began to disappear as their newfound accessibility led them to mergers and eventually affiliation with new television networks (Fox began in 1986; UPN and WB in 1995), thus limiting their need for first-run syndicated programs. The creation of UPN and WB also marked the decline of the independent producers who were so heavily responsible for these co-produced programs. In 1995 the Federal Communications Commission repealed the Financial Interest and Syndication Rules (Fin-Syn) that had kept networks from producing their own prime time fictional programs. The new permission for broadcast networks to create their own programming led to a wave of mergers that found the networks united with production companies (such as ABC/Disney, Viacom/CBS, and later NBC/Universal; 20th Century Fox's Fox Broadcast Company, Time Warner's WB, and Viacom's UPN were vertically integrated from their inception). In the aftermath of the mergers, the broadcast networks were not only connected with television production companies, but also several cable outlets. FX (owned by Fox), USA (owned by NBC/Universal), and ABC Family (owned by ABC/Disney), needed fewer independent programs since they now had access to off-network hits from their "sister networks." Independent producers, including those who focused on international co-productions, have, overall, suffered since the repeal of Fin-Syn has decreased the market for independent programs.

Although the number of internationally co-produced drama series has decreased on U.S. television (except perhaps for the number of co-produced formatted programs), the early to mid 1990s suggested a great deal of promise for such programs. One of the most successful programs that made television producers and station owners take notice was *Highlander: The Series*, a show that combined elements of fantasy, history, and action-adventure to become one of the most popular and well known internationally co-produced dramatic series.

The idea for *Highlander: The Series*, by all accounts began with Davis/Panzer Productions, the owners of the *Highlander* films. Because these films were successful in Europe (more so than in the United States), they were thought to be a strong basis for an international television program. Peter Davis and Bill Panzer, who had no experience producing for television, connected with the relatively new Gaumont Television, a subsidiary of the French conglomerate (Sherwood, S30). The initial funding package developed for *Highlander* divided the show's production costs of approximately $1.1 million per episode between companies in five countries: Gaumont, the program's producer and TF1, a French broadcasting company, invested 25 percent of the show's cost; 30 percent came from Germany's RTL-Plus, a private television channel; 15 percent from Reteitalia, an Italian broadcasting conglomerate; Rysher Entertainment, which distributed the program in the United States, contributed 25 percent; and the remaining 5 percent was invested by Amuse Video, a subdistributor in Japan. When *Highlander* was picked up for syndication in the United States in 1992 with a 93 percent clearance, it became the first commercial series on U.S. television to have the bulk of its financing come from outside the United States. Although the U.S.-based Davis/Panzer was still strongly involved in the production of the program, *Highlander* was, technically, a French-produced program which, to reap the benefits of a Franco-Canadian treaty, shot

half the season in Canada and half the season in France (which is why
the characters picked up and moved to France in the middle of each
season).

One of the central questions about *Highlander* regarded why
Gaumont, a celebrated French production company, would produce
a U.S.-style, English-language, program. Gaumont is one of the oldest
film companies in the world, which started in 1895 as a manufacturer
of film projectors. The company began producing films the next year
to help sell projectors. Gaumont quickly reached out to the international market branching out into Britain and the United States. The
company opened theatres in France in the early 1900s. World War I
seriously harmed Gaumont as it lost most of its market to U.S. companies. Despite declaring bankruptcy in 1935 and problems around
World War II, by the 1990s Gaumont was a successful public company controlled by Nicholas Seydoux, the president and primary
stockholder (Cohen, 175). Gaumont was, and is still, a diversified
conglomerate, owning a major theatre chain in France as well as
theatres in other countries such as Switzerland, Belgium and the
United States. Gaumont produces films and multimedia for its national and for international markets. Although the company produced
for television on and off for many years, Gaumont officially formed the
subsidiary Gaumont Television in 1992.[14] As we can see, Gaumont
grew in the 1990s, becoming an increasingly large, vertically integrated, transnational corporation. The 1990s also brought significant
changes in the company's outlook toward the international market.

Gaumont International started in the 1960s and attempted to
become a major player in the international arena when Nicholas
Seydoux became president of Gaumont in the late 1970s. Seydoux
opened up production and distribution facilities in Italy, Brazil, and
the United States (Garcon, 79). The company produced and distributed films by international auteurs for international audiences.
Gaumont specialized in European art films, concentrating on this
niche as its means of international expansion. In the late 1970s and
into the '80s Gaumont produced and distributed films for Federico
Fellini, Ingmar Bergman, Andrzej Wajda, Andrei Tarkovsky, Joseph
Losey, Franco Zeffirelli, and Hans-Jürgen Syberberg[15] (Garcon, 80).
A 1983 *New York Times* article reported, "In the United States,

Gaumont now has what it calls a 'cultural approach' to the movie business. After several failed experiments, it has discovered that Americans will not go to see European family entertainment films. Gaumont now wants to promote Europe's cinema d'auteur, a type of artistic film that appeals to a smaller, more sophisticated audience" (Lief, 13). These auteurs, who were frequently associated with their national cinemas yet comprised the international art film culture, offered the prestige that would provide long term financial success.

However, Gaumont's projects in Italy, Brazil, and the United States failed financially by the mid 1980s and Gaumont pulled back to focus on its national market (Garcon, 86–87). The realization that the quality image of European cinema would not attract the U.S. mass audience reportedly concerned Gaumont executives and it was not until the late 1980s that Gaumont again tried to go after the international market. This time, however, Gaumont's approach was quite different. Instead of focusing on films by auteurs, Gaumont re-entered the American market with films like *The Professional* (Besson, 1994) about the relationship between a hit man and an orphaned girl and *The Fifth Element* (Besson, 1997), a futuristic action film starring Bruce Willis. For television, Gaumont co-produced the television shows *Fly By Night*, starring Shannon Tweed as the adventurous owner of a private air jet company, and *Counterstrike* with Christopher Plummer as the head of an anti-terrorist group.[16] These programs allowed for travel, international locations, and international casts. On both shows, Gaumont worked with Canadian companies, which helped get the programs into the United States. It was not until the formation of Gaumont Television and the *Highlander* series project that Gaumont sold its own program into the United States.

For reasons discussed above, English-language co-production offered Gaumont a useful opportunity to increase distribution potential, production budgets, and profits. These kinds of productions, however, also raised concerns within France. The question of whether French-produced, English-language programming could fulfill national programming quotas became a point of contention in France in the 1990s. French broadcasting rules require that 60 percent of television programming be European with 40 percent being "original French expression" (Hart, 7). Complicated regulations instituted in 1991 required that a certain percentage of French origin programming be in French. Though the concept of French expression was carefully, and some say strictly, defined, later negotiations allowed stations to air more English-language programming in exchange for increased investment in national production (Charret, 50). Gaumont had a mixed reaction to the quota regulations. While the company favored the quotas limiting non-European productions on television, executives of the company spoke out against the restrictive legislation defining a work of French expression. Gaumont, along with other production companies and broadcasters, complained that the requirement that French broadcasters air programs in French severely limited the international distribution potential of French television shows (Amdur, 37). Simply, the companies believed that French programs would not sell overseas unless they were in English; however broadcasters, who are important sources of funding for film and television in Europe, could not help fund English-language productions because they had to fund French-language programs to fill their airtime. The investment in French-language programming left broadcasters little money to invest in additional English language productions or co-productions (Godard, 98). The easing of the restrictions on French works indicated the government's growing interest in promoting the overseas sale of French programming—whether or not it was in French (Mattleart, 81).

Before the weakening of the French-language regulations Gaumont lost part of its funding for *Highlander: The Series*. TF1, the most financially successful broadcast station in France, co-produced the show in its first season. However, the intensifying French-language regulations caused TF1 to drop *Highlander* so it could fund French-language programming. Gaumont went to M6, a less financially successful station that did not have to meet the same requirements as TF1 (Sherwood, S30). But M6 could not invest as much money as TF1 so Gaumont ended up selling off some of its distribution rights to Rysher Entertainment, the show's U.S. distributor, and bringing in the Canadian co-producer Filmline to benefit from the Franco-Canadian production treaty.

Gaumont's commitment to *Highlander: The Series*, despite the financing difficulties, illustrates one level of the two-tier production plan envisioned by Christian Charret, the head of Gaumont Television in the 1990s.[17] Charret realized the importance of the European market for Gaumont's expansion and he saw the company producing two types of products: international productions—which centered around English-language international co-productions—and Franco-European productions (which would focus on French society) (Popper, 1). Charret expected the international market, including Europe, to be more interested in the English-language products. These were the programs produced for profit while the Franco-European programs fulfilled Gaumont's responsibility to its local market and its duty to promote national and European culture. Marla Ginsburg, then head of Gaumont Television's international co-production division, who is an American and a former executive at Columbia Tri-Star Television, worked to, as she said, "blend European craftsmanship and an understanding of the American market" (qtd. in Sherwood, S30). Ginsburg repeatedly emphasized the importance of English language projects for the Gaumont co-production division. She explained, "We'll see more cross-border production in Europe because Europeans will be producing programming in English and selling it to the United States. The United States will become our secondary market" (qtd. in "European Television Production Not Unified").

The 1990s saw a change, then, not only in Gaumont's actual practices, but also in how Gaumont conceptualized the international market in its self-promotion. These co-productions, and Gaumont's commitment to future English-language co-productions, indicated a shift in Gaumont's approach to the international market. While as late as the 1980s, "international" product at Gaumont referred to films by European auteurs, in the 1990s international media programming referred to those works that were easiest to distribute globally: English-language co-productions.

The international co-production arrangement of *Highlander* offered its producers many benefits, particularly since, at least in its first year, production partners did not just invest money but also received equal votes, along with the executive producers from Gaumont and Davis/Panzer, regarding the creative content of *Highlander*. This was an important factor for media companies wanting to create an international television product that would appeal to a global audience but also to their own local markets. Ginsburg stressed the importance of respecting each partner's cultural differences. But, she noted, "I have often had to make several rounds of phone calls to arbitrate differences or fight for my creative vision in an effort to avoid what has commonly been dubbed 'Europudding'" (Ginsburg, 130). Although this production utopia was streamlined after the first season (probably as a result of changes in the program's financial backing), a concern was still expressed about integrating the different cultures into an artistic unity.

Although some critics might consider *Highlander* to be Europudding that failed to find this unity, we can see that the values of place, community, and global travel do offer the program ideological underpinnings. And all of these issues coalesce around the program's complex representations of history and the past.

The show's hero, and the lens through which we understand this fantasy universe, is Duncan MacLeod. MacLeod, a Scot born in the 1500s, has over the years loved many women, fought in many battles, and lived in many countries, including Japan, India, England, France, and the United States—spaces we see through flashbacks that the show uses to give viewers backstory. The sequences in the present are fairly typical action-adventure stories in which MacLeod faces some dilemma. During these adventures MacLeod (or another Immortal) "remembers" something that happened in his past and we see it play out. MacLeod's memories—going back over four hundred years and including his travels in Verona in the 1600s, his years as a military strategist in Turkey in the 1700s, and his study of flamenco dancing in Spain in the 1800s—are interwoven into *Highlander*'s basic action format.

While MacLeod certainly has strong connections to his national, Scottish background (ties that, as will be discussed, are questioned throughout the show), when he introduces himself to other Immortals, he does not identify himself as a Scot, but he says, "I am Duncan MacLeod of the Clan MacLeod." MacLeod identifies with his clan not his nation. This method of identification illustrates the program's concentration on the local, the groups and communities that operate underneath and within the nation. The focus on such social organizations makes a good deal of sense for an international co-production anticipating audiences in different nations. These kinds of familial and communal local groups are general enough to allow a point of identification for people in many different countries. Therefore, subnational communities such MacLeod's clan, a community of Roma, a Bronze Age village, or a Native American tribe are formally and narratively privileged within *Highlander*. The program, generally concerned with illustrating how the past can be used to move forward, comes closest to nostalgia when focusing on the local. As mentioned, even after four hundred years MacLeod still feels connected to his clan. In flashbacks to his life among the MacLeods (before Duncan knew he was an Immortal),[18] Duncan is happy and secure (in general). When he is killed in battle and then "rises from the dead," he is exposed as "different" and the clan banishes him, with Duncan's own father saying that his son must be possessed by the devil. Duncan is then lonely and devastated. The clan in this case, though certainly superstitious, is also connected with a sense of family and belonging that MacLeod rarely experiences again.

Several episodes of the series flash back to a time when MacLeod does almost reconnect with a community and a family, when he finds a way to create a *place* for himself. This is when MacLeod is living with a Native American tribe in the American West in the late 1800s. MacLeod is happily living with a widow, whom he is soon to marry, and her son as part of a community. MacLeod returns from a ride away from the tribe to find everyone slaughtered by the U.S. cavalry (led by an Immortal working for the cavalry). In a guest role in the series pilot, French actor Christopher Lambert playing Connor MacLeod (Duncan's clansman and fellow Immortal, as well as the main character in the first three *Highlander* films) comforts Duncan. Warm, red lighting envelopes the scene as the camera pans across images of dead Native Americans strewn across the ground. One of show's theme songs, "Who Wants to Live Forever," by the rock group Queen, plays: "There's no time for us, there's no place for us, what is this thing that fills our dreams then slips away from us, who wants to live forever who dares to live forever?" We hear Duncan sobbing off screen before we see him sitting on the ground holding his dead lover. Talking to Connor, Duncan cries for more than the loss of his loved ones, "All the

Figure 1.2   Adrian Paul as Duncan McLeod finds love within a community of Native Americans. *(Photo courtesy of Photofest.)*

names, all the grasses, the wildflowers, the songs that told where her people came from, how they lived, what they believed in." MacLeod is thinking about the death of the tribe and its culture. Connor further highlights the Immortals' sense of longing, asking MacLeod in a voice over as they look sadly at the bodies of the Native Americans, "Do you think we ever lived like this? Like a tribe? Together with a common language. A reason and a name for each living thing. Did we once belong somewhere? A time, a place; however briefly."

In this flashback, Connor and Duncan MacLeod express their still-present desire for a sense of belonging and a sense of community in the form of nostalgia for a time when communities, tribes, and villages existed. This strong connection that MacLeod has with his clan and with his immortality has both a positive and a negative influence on his life: MacLeod's clan identity grounds him and gives him a moral code throughout his world travels, while his association with immortality limits his access to certain social groups. That the peace and inclusion of community consistently elude Duncan (he is also forced out of a Roma community for superstitious reasons) reinforces the impossibility of MacLeod ever being part of a community that is not based on his own kind (Immortals).[19]

While MacLeod's connections with local groups end sadly, these are the connections he misses, the ties he regrets losing. On the other hand, MacLeod's affiliations with national groups tend to be the ones he regrets ever having. MacLeod's national attachments often take the form of military service and are associated with pain and suffering. Government service, such as his work for the British government in India, exposes potentially dangerous national prejudice. The two wars most frequently represented in *Highlander* are the Jacobite rebellion against the British in the 1700s (in which MacLeod fights with the Highlanders against the British and, at the Battle of Culloden, sees his friends die, witnesses the British massacre of Highlanders even after the battle ended, and goes himself after British soldiers for revenge) and the Napoleonic Wars (when MacLeod now fights for the British). On a snowy battlefield of the Napoleonic Wars (made to seem even more cold by dark, blue lighting) MacLeod meets Darius, an Immortal who was once a conqueror but is now a priest who advocates for peace.

When MacLeod asks Darius how the battle is going, Darius asks, "Why does that matter to you? Napoleon may lose a campaign, [the British] may win a great victory but what have they really won or lost? Their reputation? These men [referring to the dead on the battlefield] have been robbed of their most precious possession." We are shown a long shot of the battlefield with explosions in the background. A point of view shot shows us MacLeod's view of the dead soldiers as Darius tells him, "You shouldn't be taking part in this tragedy." MacLeod explains, "I was raised a warrior. I choose battles I believe to be just." Darius replies, "Oh, I'm sure. You're quite loyal to your convictions and compatriots. But I wonder what these men think about that, about conviction and compatriotism." Scenes such as these reinforce *Highlander*'s message about the futility of war (even wars individuals believe to be just) and support the value of human life. While wars between individuals may have value (MacLeod is generally in the right when he seeks justice for an evil Immortal), fighting to expand or free nations is not considered, in the world of *Highlander*, to be worth the loss of life.[20]

MacLeod's experiences in the Jacobite rebellion not only illustrate the tragedy of war but also the difficulty of living with one's actions afterward. In an episode from the last season of *Highlander* titled "Forgive Us Our Trespasses" MacLeod is hunted by an Immortal, Stephen Keane, who wants revenge on MacLeod for killing Keane's British friend after the Battle of Cullodin. MacLeod explains that he has already paid, and continues to pay, for what he did because he "live[s] with it every day, but I also live with the fact that revenge doesn't make anything better." Keane recalls that he had another friend who also believed in leaving the past alone and we see a flashback to Keane's discussion with the Immortal Sean Burns set in "England 1779."[21] Burns tells Keane to forget about trying to hunt down MacLeod because "In every century that I've lived there's been a war that kings and generals said would end wars, there's been a people ground down in the name of peace, and there have been men like you . . . and MacLeod fighting on one side or another always believing in their hearts that theirs was the side that God was on. . . . Until one day they look around and they're sick and they retch with the pain of it and they ride and ride until they can ride no more, hoping they'll find something different across the steps or across the Atlantic. Hoping, praying that they won't have to keep killing."

This quotation, along with Darius', illustrates the idea that nationalism is created by those with power, not by the people, to sustain their control and wealth. The nation, though, is still depicted as a powerful force and each individual chooses whether or not to get caught up in nationalistic feelings and wars. While *Highlander* certainly illustrates that the past impacts our present by using flashbacks to illustrate why MacLeod feels or acts a certain way, the program also establishes the individual as the ultimate actor within history; history affects our situations but individuals determine their actions. In the end, MacLeod wants to accept responsibility for his actions in war. He wants to be judged by Keane. MacLeod's readiness to be accountable for his past marks him as a concerned and "good" Immortal.

Certainly, characters considered better warriors or more virtuous peacemakers than MacLeod appear on *Highlander*. Darius the priest, for example, is frequently held up as a wonderful person.

Darius, however, is not the hero of *Highlander* whom viewers are encouraged to think of as the potential ruler of humanity.[22] What makes MacLeod more worthy than Darius? MacLeod, as the main character of the show, has a different past and potential future than Darius. Because Darius does not want to kill anymore, he takes refuge on Holy Ground on which Immortals cannot kill one another. For 1400 years Darius has remained on his church grounds in Paris; he is grounded in the local. And while local communities are valued in *Highlander*, the program frequently suggests that more is necessary for one (particularly one Immortal) to survive. Importantly, MacLeod also travels through many varied spaces and learns about global cultures. MacLeod, a man who yearns for his communal past, also offers an idealized example of the benefits of having global experiences. MacLeod's temporal and spatial shifts through the narrative establish him as a true transnational man backed by global cultural and economic capital. MacLeod has traveled in many countries and known many people, instilling in him a respect and an understanding of different cultures. This knowledge accumulated through his global past helps make MacLeod a hero. His knowledge of languages, antiques, wine, different cultural and religious beliefs, and various fighting techniques all save his life at some point during the series and also mark MacLeod as superior to both mortals and other Immortals. *Highlander* glorifies the benefits of being part of a global community—the same global community that *Highlander*'s producers and other multinational companies are part of and need audiences to participate in by watching their programs—and illustrates MacLeod's past as an ideal for our developing transnational future.

Immortals, then, are enlightened through their global travels and they find their ideal communities in local groups. While national associations do as much as global and local ties to form Immortals' identities and understandings of the past, the program clearly represents their experiences with nationalism as sad and many times regrettable. As MacLeod matures he moves further and further away from any national affiliation and as the program develops MacLeod increasingly locates his identity in his immortality, not any national connection. Immortals' identities, in fact, remain, essentially, most strongly shaped by their immortality.

By focusing on the immortality of the characters, *Highlander* returns to the more traditional view of group belonging through blood and origins that is perhaps most strongly tied to past, local cultures of tribes, clans, and villages. As discussed above, Burgoyne examines films that demonstrate a more inclusive view of the nation that represent "a form of belonging conceived not on the narrow, ethnic model of blood and origins, but rather on the model of a civic pluralism" (11). While *Highlander* generally suggests a multicultural, politically correct attitude toward diversity, the program also expresses nostalgia for a time when Immortals may not have been spread out around the world fighting against each other but living together in a community; when they were united as a people. The Immortals' incorporation into national issues is seen as an unfortunate outcome of their lack of local culture. And if Immortals live long enough and gain enough insight through their global experiences, they can come to recognize the futility of national alliances. Unlike many U.S.-produced films, then, *Highlander* does not attempt to reconfigure nationalism but rejects it.

The positive spin put on global and local culture and the downplaying of national allegiances was a useful representational strategy for a program that aired in over seventy countries. With the various producers of *Highlander* concerned about their individual markets (sometimes national, sometimes regional) it was important to create a product with appeal for different local markets all over the world. In both *Highlander* and *The Odyssey*, by downplaying nationalism and instead idealizing local and transnational identities and histories, by foregrounding the importance of moving through spaces to find your place, the television programs found common ground for people in different nations, and at the same time reflected ideologies that support transnational capital.

Perhaps it is this lack of national association, the freedom to question the foundations and usefulness of nationalism while bolstering globalism and localism, that has the potential to provide internationally co-produced television fiction the "distinctive contour and flavour" that *Sight and Sound* found lacking in Europudding (Fisher, 224). Certainly we should not immediately celebrate the rise of historical texts produced internationally. We must still consider what this strategy of historical representation is covering up, the kind of local culture it idealizes (i.e. heterosexual, paternalistic, family-based communities), and the ways producers exploit and commercialize history to connect with the global audiences. By looking at these international co-productions and their depictions of the past, however, we can begin to recognize the differences in representation that can potentially emerge from the growing trend of international co-productions on television and the impact of the globalization of television culture. We can also see the potential these depictions have to shape our understandings of the world in which we live by creating fictional worlds that stress the benefits and values of globalization and world travel; the importance of local communities; the ubiquity of the English language; the superiority of the U.S. media aesthetic; and, of course, the dangers of national allegiances.

2 / Clear, Strong Brands

British Television as a Marketing Tool

The internationally co-produced television fiction discussed in the previous chapter was strongly influenced by the increasingly competitive environment of the television industry. The rise of cable and satellite in the 1980s and '90s along with deregulation led to an erosion of the audience. Narrowcasting and niche audiences became the industry's new buzzwords as broadcasters saw their shares of the mass audience decline. The need to differentiate networks from the growing competition became overwhelmingly important particularly for the new cable networks.

The expensive proposition of starting a new network and marketing it effectively led some programmers to rely increasingly on international co-production as a means of reducing costs while creating the desired programming. While the last chapter examined the trend of creating programs "without nation" in order to satisfy international co-production requirements, this chapter looks, in some ways, at an opposite trend: co-producing nationalism, specifically Britishness, in order to brand a television network. Exploring the concept of branding, the significance of the "British" brand, and two case studies of how this brand was mobilized will illuminate reasons for the U.S. co-productions of what Jeffrey Miller called in the title of his book "something completely different." This chapter will specifically consider the example of the A&E Network and its connections to and co-production of the British brand by examining two A&E co-productions, the mystery series *Cracker* (1993–1997) and the miniseries *Pride and Prejudice* (1995).

Branding

The application of the marketing jargon of "branding" is relatively new to the entertainment industries, though, as we will see, many of the concepts and practices are not. A brand can be defined as a "the totality of the thoughts, feelings, associations, and expectations a prospect or customer experiences when exposed to a company's name, trademark, or to any design representing the company or product" (Chan-Olmsted and Kim, 77). Branding is the creation of associations between these names, trademarks, and designs and certain qualities on the part of the consumer (Keller, 4). The expectation is that these associations will contribute brand equity or added value to a product (Farquhar, 24). In other words, when a consumer sees a pair of shoes with the Nike "swoosh," she will, Nike executives hope, associate that shoe with athleticism, freedom, and strength. Then, of course, she will purchase the shoes, which she believes will make her faster, stronger, and freer. Or, a consumer looking at a new Apple computer will think of the new machine as hip, sleek, and secure and then buy the computer in part for its functionality but also because of the symbolic value that resides in being a "Mac person." In television terms, the logo of CNN connotes, for many people, accuracy, timeliness, and respectability. These associations, CNN expects, will encourage viewers to get their news from CNN.

The growing significance of branding within the television industry can be tied to the increased competition of the 1980s. According to the "production of culture" model summarized by Richard Peterson and N. Anand, specialty organizations (or specialty brands) are made possible, and in some cases necessary, by the competition between generalist organizations trying to reach a mass audience (323). As these organizations compete with one another, space opens up for the creation of niche groups that serve specific audiences. The competition between the mainstream broadcast television networks in the United States, which intensified in the 1980s, can certainly be seen as a catalyst for the creation of the niche stations on cable, as these station owners attempted to reach audiences who felt they were not being served by the general entertainment networks. Cable brands centered on sports, news, weather, and music have all stemmed from the major broadcast networks' inability to program for specific target audiences.

An ongoing challenge for the niche networks is to convince their target audiences that their programming will meet particular needs of viewers in ways that the broadcast stations cannot. In the case of cable, the network owners need strong identities not only to expand viewership but also to convince cable operators to include particular networks on their cable systems. Creating positive associations with the network helps to establish superiority for the specialty channels.

Although brand associations do emerge from the actual product (CNN is often timely, Nike shoes do provide good support, Apple computers contract fewer viruses), we must remember that these are qualities that the brand has chosen to reinforce—not only with the products created but also through marketing campaigns that associate the brand with particular attributes, benefits, and attitudes. Brand *attributes* are simply features that consumers connect to the brand. These attributes can be product related or non-product related. Product related attributes are those that are essential for the product performing its intended function. In television these may include the genre, format, and length of programs associated with the brand (The Weather Channel gives information about the weather; Nick at Nite offers primarily half-hour situation comedies from the past). Non-product related attributes are those traits of the product that do not directly relate to the ability of the product to perform its function. For example, whether a network is on broadcast, cable, or digital cable is an attribute of the brand but does not affect the network's ability to provide its service. In another example, the cost of receiving the network is an attribute that does not directly impact its functionality but is often important to consumers.

Brand associations are also formed by the perceived *benefits* connected with the brand's products (or programs). Brand benefits involve what viewers believe they will gain by watching this network. These benefits can be functional, meaning that viewers will gain something concrete that will help them do something or make a decision: watching The Weather Channel helps me decide whether to bring an umbrella today; watching PBS will make my children smarter; watching Home and Garden will teach me how to decorate my new home. Benefits may also be experiential, meaning that the benefit to be gained is in the event of watching: watching the Cartoon Network will make me laugh; watching ESPN with my friends will be fun; watching Lifetime will make the night go faster. And benefits can also be symbolic, providing some kind of cultural value to the viewer: watching Comedy Central will make me seem hip and young; watching FX will make me seem edgy and raw; watching Turner Classic Movies will make me seem cultured and intelligent.

These brand benefits inform a third element of brand associations, *attitude* associations. Essentially this refers to the way that viewers, in the end, evaluate the brand. For example, MTV is trendy; CBS is for old people; E! is silly and frivolous. These attitudes are generally formed in conjunction with the brand's perceived attributes and benefits, and together generate the associations that the consumer establishes with the brand. All of these different kinds of brand associations are managed by marketers to promote one brand over another. In the case of cable, the network owners need strong branding not only to expand viewership but also to convince cable operators to include particular networks on their cable systems.

As mentioned above, brand associations are not completely reliant on marketing, but usually do have some basis in the existing products that are part of the brand. Companies make careful choices about these products, thus steering their brands in particular directions. The concept of television network branding is perhaps additionally complicated by the fact that the programs that are on the networks can themselves be seen as brands (for example, the *Law and Order* brand or *The Simpsons* brand). Individual programs may create their own brand images since the real value of the program, at least for the show's producers, lies in its sales *after* its network run, in syndication. While a Nike shoe will never have to be sold without the Nike brand behind it, *The Sopranos*, *The Shield*, and *Monk* all have to go on the market on their own, without any brand associations that may come from HBO, FX, and USA. It appears, therefore, that television network branding is particularly reliant on the secondary associations between the network brand and the qualities of the programs that are available on the network (since these programs have a vested interest in creating their own strong images). If a network airs a number of programs that are perceived as hip and young and relevant, then the network brand itself may be associated with those qualities. Programming choices, therefore, are extremely important in the branding process for television networks. Network programmers look at all the qualities of the programs, including the producers, actors, studio, genre, and national origin, which may help particular shows bolster the network brand.

Nations certainly work to develop their own brand images in order to promote tourism and trade. According to Chris Powell and Peter York, "National branding matters in the international competition for markets, investment and people" (28). Marketing research has further shown that, for consumers, a product's heritage does matter. Allyson Stewart-Allen explains that "the synergy of the country's values and the brand's values can deliver an even more compelling and differentiated brand experience in the increasing sameness of the global brand" (7). John O'Shaughnessy and Nicholas Jackson O'Shaughnessy consider, however, the complexities of the national brand. Because nations are multifaceted, marking them with one brand may be difficult. O'Shaughnessy and O'Shaughnessy write, "Different parts of a nation's identity comes into focus on the international stage at different times, affected by current political events and even by the latest movie or news bulletin. Moreover, national images exist at different intellectual and cultural levels, and for different audiences, they have different meanings according to class, demography, and so forth" (58). The difficulty in branding a nation, then, is to connect the brand to the desired target market at the correct time. The difficulty of achieving this, leads O'Shaughnessy and O'Shaughnessy to suggest that, rather than relying on a blanket national brand, marketers should tap into the "reputational capital" of particular products and particular product categories associated with a nation (59). Not all products from a nation, then, would rely on the same national branding process. Additionally, not all products from a nation would use national branding to encourage consumption.

Within television specifically, C. Lee Harrington and Denise Bielby found that a nation's reputation can certainly influence decisions to pick up a program for international distribution and that "national images are used by some distributors as a marketing tool" (911). Undoubtedly, the idea of reputational capital encourages the distribution of particular genres from particular nations. The presumed expertise of certain nations for making specific types of programs also plays a role in determining international co-production partners. Companies will work with those production partners that are known for being able to deliver a particular product. Canadian production companies, for example, as will be shown in the next chapter, are well respected for the quality of their children's programming. While international co-productions are presumed to create a cultural product that can generate interest across national borders, this is not always the case. In some circumstances, such as those discussed in this chapter, production partners seek out the national brand; the process of international co-production is used not to create international appeal but to generate a very specific *nationalism* that is intended for an international audience. This representation of nationalism may be highly questionable, both culturally and ideologically, but the idea that international co-productions may not always strive to erase nationalism is significant. Rather, in the attempt to create a unique and identifiable brand, international co-productions may strive to develop a particular notion of nationalism that can be sold to global audiences. We will see that the British brand in particular offers U.S. television programmers a rich source of material with international co-production potential, that can shape brand associations and encourage viewership.

The Brands of Britain

The complexity of understanding "British" as a brand of visual media is tied to the intricate role of British film and television in the United States. Historically, within the U.S. market, British films benefited from their use of a common language. Simply on the basis of English-language production, British films could achieve a level of distribution in the United States that was not possible for French, German, and Italian films, which were squarely relegated to the art film circuits (with a few notable exceptions such as *The Bicycle Thief*). British films, therefore, had the benefit of being generally comprehensible to a mainstream audience while still maintaining a sense of cosmopolitan appeal. As Sarah Street explains, the cultural role of British films (as early as the 1930s) was to offer an alternative to Hollywood, but one that was not too radically different. Street writes, "What emerges [in the 1930s] is not a desire for British films to be indistinguishable from American but the advocacy of distinctive films which conformed to classical conventions, particularly in terms of pace and editing" (88). At the same time, the use of unknown actors (with accents) and unfamiliar cultural references has created a cultural discount for British films, making them less economically valuable in the United States. Additionally, their relative similarity to Hollywood films has led to comparisons between the two. Frequently when British filmmakers attempt to make straight genre films (without a sense of clear British distinctiveness), these comparisons hurt the films. In some ways, British filmmakers who desire international distribution are required to make something like Hollywood films, *but still a little different*. The means of differentiations cultivated by British filmmakers for international distribution helped to create the "British" brands, of which, I argue, there are primarily two: the "heritage" brand and the "mod" brand.

"British Television with a British Accent"— The "Heritage" Brand

What I am calling the heritage brand associates Britain with the qualities of elitism, high culture, classic literature, and orderly society. This brand of Britishness has continued to be surprisingly popular with U.S. audiences. Stewart-Allen suggests that U.S. consumers appreciate the quality of British products that have been around for a long time and are part of a set of existing customs and conventions, writing that "Americans appreciate the tradition and history that underpins these brands" (7). Andrew Sullivan sees the U.S. fascination with British society stemming from the erroneous but pleasant misconception that British society is founded on tradition and standards that make the British more cultured, educated, and civilized than people in the United States. Focusing on U.S. consumers' fascination with class structure, Sullivan adds, "There are few things more dear to Americans than the notion of Britain...as a halcyon place of tea, crumpets, and generations of aesthetes who went to tony private schools and know much of Shakespeare and Milton by heart" (19).

The British media exported to the United States has promoted this image of British society. The category of heritage films first received major scholarly attention in the 1980s. Heritage films have been defined in a number of ways, but for the most part they include films that are primarily costume dramas (though not all costume dramas are heritage films), based on literary classics, focused on characterization and conversation over action, presented at a leisurely pace, steeped in a pictoral visual style, and promoted as historically "authentic." These films, as John Hill argues, are marked as different from Hollywood films in their style and content but are not connected with the more traditional style of European art films (Hill, 78). These films, then, enjoy the prestige of art cinema, however they remain accessible to audiences who might shy away from more aesthetically innovative films.

The success of these accessible yet different films in the United States has had a long history. By the 1940s, Street illustrates, the appeal of literary, historical, and satirical films about the British nation emerged as some of the most popular British films in the U.S. market. Films such as *The Private Life of Henry VIII* (1933), *Henry V* (1944), and *Great Expectations* (1946) proved successful with U.S. audiences and critics. Additionally, films like *Brief Encounter* (1945) and *The Red Shoes* (1948), which offered particular views of British culture and class, were also popular with specific audience segments in the United States. In the 1980s and early '90s, however, the current wave of heritage films were the subject of harsh scholarly criticism. The new heritage cycle, which included *Chariots of Fire* (1981), *A Room with a View* (1985), *Howard's End* (1992), and *Shadowlands* (1993), were critiqued for their conservative politics. Along with a larger heritage culture, film scholars associated heritage films with the Thatcher government and its attempts to promote a conservative agenda. Film scholars argued that heritage films, through their creation of a particular type of national identity, promoted conservative ideas. These films, critics claimed, used pictoral splendor and images of country homes to provide a "compensatory fantasy of a stable and ordered British past at the very moment when the economic and social policies of the Thatcher government were not only eroding stability and order but also utilizing a rhetoric of national greatness in order to justify doing so" (Davies, 121). Such films, and their producers, were further lambasted for catering to the American market by providing a false image of the British nation that would appeal to U.S. audiences and for overshadowing the popularity of more contemporary British films such as *My Beautiful Launderette* (1985), *Sammy and Rosie Get Laid* (1988), and *Naked* (1993) (Davies, 121).

The success of heritage films within the U.S. market has been explained by several factors. Certainly the beautiful imagery of lush countryside and large, historical mansions within the films is considered to be one factor that creates pleasure for the viewer, particularly those in the United States not accustomed to such sights. Additionally, Martin Hipsky argues that what he calls "Anglophilic" films are an accessible form of art cinema, as discussed above, and thus provide an opportunity for middle class audiences to increase and illustrate their cultural capital. The generally conservative values displayed in these films are also believed to hold appeal for U.S. audiences. While issues of class are addressed, most critics agree that, in the end, these films re-inscribe the class structure of traditional society without suggesting any subversive alternatives. Heterosexual romantic love, while questioned, is generally also idealized. For U.S. audiences, then, "these historical films function to efface the very social history they purport to portray; they provide North American viewers with a kind of sanitized, guilt-free nostalgia. . . . They can enjoy being transported through time and space to a gorgeous space of high society, a cultured alcove that appears hermetically sealed off from the ugly contamination of real history" (Hipsky, 106).

Not surprisingly, the popularity of the heritage films as early as the 1940s led to the brand's relatively quick inclusion on television.

In fact, some of these earlier heritage films noted by Street were among the first British films on U.S. television. Although many U.S.-produced B-films had been released to television in the 1940s and early '50s, the major studios, for a variety of industrial reasons, were not yet ready to release films to the new medium. British producers, however, did distribute to television. When seen next to the B-films that were primarily available on television, these movies reinforced the high quality image of British film. As television matured, the major U.S. networks focused on attracting *all* audiences and avoided programming that was "too British." The British heritage brand soon found its place on U.S. television, however, outside of the major networks on a service that had the benefit of aiming at a niche audience and the necessity of differentiating itself from the mainstream networks: public television. On this network, U.S. and British media makers worked together to create (and often co-produce) the heritage brand of Britishness.

In the 1960s and '70s, quality British programming most regularly appeared in the United States on the Public Broadcasting Service. Mobil's Masterpiece Theatre highlighted the cultural quality of British programs, while profiting from the cheaper costs of importing or co-producing British shows. The beginning of Masterpiece Theatre is most closely associated with the relative success of *The Forsyte Saga*, which aired on the PBS precursor NET in 1969. Interestingly, *The Forsyte Saga* itself was a co-production between the BBC and MGM, although publicity for the miniseries rarely, if ever, mentioned the connection between the program and the major Hollywood studio.

The Forsyte Saga was a 26-part series of 50-minute episodes that were based on John Galsworthy's 1920s novels. The program was produced in the United Kingdom in 1966 for an estimated £260,000 (about $720,000), which was considered a very large budget for the time (Feretti, 70). In fact, according to some reports, the budget for the program was controversial within the BBC, particularly because it was being shot in black and white (actually one of the last black and white productions at the BBC) (Feretti, 70). When the program's production was reported on the front page of *Variety*, it was labeled the BBC's "biggest ever drama project." There were to be 120 speaking parts and 100 sets in the costume drama that followed the Forsyte family from 1879 through 1926 ("MGM-BBC," 1).

Although its position on public television limited the popularity of *The Forsyte Saga* in the United States, the serial was certainly one of the more popular programs ever to appear on NET. The serial began airing in the United States in 1969 and received a great deal of coverage in magazines and newspapers, much of which centered around the ability of the British to produce upscale soap operas that are better quality than U.S. daytime soaps (Gould, 94). The image of quality surrounding *The Forsyte Saga* was further confirmed when the series was, in 1970, nominated for Emmy Awards for Outstanding Dramatic Series and Outstanding New Series, and actress Susan Hampshire won the Emmy for Outstanding Continued Performance by an Actress.

The Forsyte Saga illustrated the potential for public broadcasting to appeal to a "quality" audience with representations of highbrow British heritage. With the creation of PBS in 1969, Mobil Oil chose to capitalize on this connection by sponsoring Masterpiece Theatre. As Mobil Oil became increasingly active in financing British programming, both Mobile and its broadcast partner WGBH became more hands on in their dealings with British producers. The U.S. organizations let British producers know which titles they would be interested in financing and also had input into cast, script, producer, director, and other creative decisions (Jarvik, 118–19). One Mobile executive explained, however, that he was not interested in "Americanizing" the British programs, but rather in making sure that the programs remained clearly British (Jarvik, 120). Mobile and WGBH participants helped to define this Britishness in their selection of titles and cast.

Concerns about U.S. involvement in the production of British (particularly publicly owned BBC) productions circulated in British society. In fact, Mobile's participation in the financing of British programs potentially violated BBC rules about corporate sponsorship. According to conservative critic Laurence Jarvik, the BBC was able to accept Mobile's money by claiming that these productions were primarily made for export since such programs were permitted to have corporate sponsorship as long as the connection to the corporation was not apparent when the program aired on the BBC (117–18). One means of allowing U.S. funding of the British shows, then, was to openly acknowledge their intention for the U.S. market.

So, while many Masterpiece Theatre programs reflected British history and British culture, to some extent this Britishness was a mirage created for the international audience. This critique of U.S. involvement in British film, incidentally, continued through the 1990s. A 1998 article in *Electronic Media* questioned whether the BBC was producing so many costume dramas, at the expense of contemporary dramas, because such productions sold well to the United States and could garner co-production dollars (Kavanagh, 86). Although the BBC denies these accusations, it is probable that, at least to some extent, co-financing potential draws British producers to particular representations of their heritage, what Jarvik describes as "British television with a British accent" (9).

The heritage brand of Britishness, as reflected in British film and television, then, became associated with particular attributes, benefits, and attitudes that bolstered British producers' reputational capital in the creation of historical costume dramas. The heritage brand of Britishness evokes the attributes of costume dramas that recreate a beautiful and seemingly more simple past. These media texts are often slow paced, visually lush, and based on literary classics. In terms of non-product attributes, heritage dramas tend to be, but are not exclusively, available for screening at art cinemas or, as we will see below, on "quality" television stations. The functional benefits of seeing a heritage drama include learning about the literary text as well as the historical period in which it is set and seeing the places depicted in the film. Experientially, a viewer may benefit from the escapism the program offers as well as the enjoyment of watching a beautifully filmed, slow paced narrative. And, of course, the symbolic benefits include the cultural capital that will be gained by having watched a "high quality" drama. The attributes and benefits connected with the heritage brand of British media combine to associate this brand with particular attitudes. These texts are sophisticated and mature programs for intelligent viewers. British historical costume dramas are often assumed to be high quality, high culture, and simply better than U.S. media. These attitude associations positioned such productions well for continued success in the United States.

Mid-Atlantic Mod: The "Mod" Brand

While the British brand of heritage relies primarily on the United Kingdom's past, the second brand, what is referred to here as the "mod" brand of Britishness, is decidedly contemporary, highlighting the current and modern elements of British culture. This brand includes internationally minded films and television programs that focus on trans-Atlantic topics, some of which were discussed in the previous chapter. The mod brand of Britishness in film and television can be tied to the rise of the British new wave in the late 1950s and into the '60s (Street, 170). While, according to Street, the earlier films in this "angry young man" movement (such as *Look Back in Anger* [1958] and *Saturday Night and Sunday Morning* [1960]) were not overwhelmingly successful in the United States, they helped to shape later films and television programs that were often at least partially financed by Hollywood studios and well distributed throughout the United States. Films in this category include *Tom Jones* (1963), *Hard Day's Night* (1964), and the James Bond movies. The motivations for U.S. co-production of these films include many of the reasons for co-production discussed in the introduction, such as the cheaper labor costs in the United Kingdom, the need to use money that could not be taken out of the country, and the desire to benefit from the British mod brand. Some of these films, particularly the Bond movies, certainly differed from the British new wave films of the late 1950s and early '60s. As James Chapman discusses, the Bond films, with their focus on wealth and escapism, were, to some extent, the complete antithesis of the "angry young man" films (68–69). Chapman does note, however, that both the Bond movies and the British new wave films touched on a desire to escape the traditional, working and middle class life of family and work (69). Similarly, both the British new wave films and the Bond films rejected the "traditional image of the English gentleman hero" (Chapman, 81).

The later British films, most notably the Bond series, did succeed internationally. These films contained themes with "international appeal" and were thus ripe for international distribution and world-wide profits. The Bond films included an amalgamation of various elements of fashion, style, commodification, international politics, and sexual politics that resonated with contemporary and youthful audiences around the world. Paul Stock wrote, "Bond is performed for global consumption. Following this, Bond remains a capitalist commodity, and one that has the advantage of a globalizing economy, and a global commercial media system" (39) International appeal remains important for the mod brand. The popularity of films like *The Commitments* (1991), *Trainspotting* (1996), and *The Full Monty* (1997) illustrate the continued U.S. interest in stylish British films about heroes who break with tradition and strive for a different life.

Although splitting with the true "mod" movement in its commercialization and its ignoring of real political and social critique, the commodified image of British mod culture transferred to television quite well. As Jeffrey Miller discusses, programs such as *The Saint* (syndication, 1962–67; NBC, 1967–69), *Secret Agent* (CBS, 1964–66), *The Avengers* (ABC, 1966–69), and *The Prisoner* (CBS, 1968) were picked up by the U.S. networks and aired during prime time. Jarvik describes these programs as "mid-Atlantic," illustrating qualities of both U.S. and U.K. television. These shows combined elements of the British mod culture—with their focus on contemporary settings, somewhat anti-authoritarian heroes, and glossy style—with traditional qualities of U.S. television genres (spy, police, sci-fi dramas) to create familiar yet distinctive programs. These shows reflected interplay between U.K. and U.S. cultures. Discussing imported British culture of the 1950s and '60s, Jeffrey Miller writes that "popular British imports to the United States could be seen as by-products of Americanization: British remaking and remarketing of American genres that had already made their way to Britain, frequently with the assistance of American money" (12). By 1970 the U.S. networks began replacing the obviously British programs with U.S. reworkings of similar themes and with remakes of British formats. In the 1970s, the mod image of the United Kingdom gave way, at least on U.S. television, to that of public television's focus on heritage.

The attributes, benefits, and attitudes associated with the mod brand of Britishness, then, are clearly different than those associations made with the heritage brand of Britishness. In terms of media, the brand refers to texts that include heavy elements of sexuality, fashion, style, pop culture, and irreverence (though generally while still working within the system). These films and television shows frequently include elements that are believed to have international appeal (such as travel). Often, these texts are expected to offer something alternative in terms of style (such as fast paced editing, low key lighting, or handheld camera work). In terms of a non-product attribute, these media texts are sometimes seen as coming from outside the mainstream commercial system and, therefore, being "different" from the mainstream. The functional benefits of the mod brand include the ability to keep up with latest trends and fashions and to see sites from around the world. Experiential benefits may include the sense of joy that may be evoked from watching something that is fun and playful or a sense of discomfort from watching a television program that is alternative and dark. Symbolic benefits include the casting of oneself as hip, young, modern, and trendy by watching these films and television shows. Certainly there is cultural capital to be gained from the mod brand, though it is different cultural capital than that offered by the heritage brand. The mod brand offers the benefit of feeling hip and current while the heritage brand provides a sense of proper and upper class culture. Although the attitudes associated with the mod brand of Britishness are somewhat different than those associated with the heritage brand, there are also some similarities. The attitudes of hip and trendy differentiate the mod brand from the heritage brand. However, the attitude association of high culture, high quality, and difference apply to both the mod brand and the heritage brand. These similar brand attitudes will help us later to explain why A&E would co-produce two very different British programs in order to create a cohesive brand for a network.

In the mid-1990s the mod brand of Britishness was adapted into the concept of "Cool Britannia" promoted by New Labour as a way of distinguishing itself from the stodgy, old-fashioned image of the United Kingdom that was associated with Thatcherism and to some extent the "old" Labour party. As Ken Urban explains, this re-branding of Britishness was meant create a connection between New

Labour politics and younger voters (355–56). To this end, "New Labour looked at Britain as a brand, a commodity, to be managed and marketed." (Urban, 356) To counter, in many ways, the heritage brand of Britishness, Cool Britannia focused on all that was hip and modern about England. John O'Sullivan describes the concept pejoratively as a re-branding of Britain as "a new, young nation that rejected the traditional symbols of national continuity and would now impress the world with its style, fashion, pop musicians, dress designers and celebrity chefs" (19). Connected to the mod brand through a focus on style, fashion, (limited) social commentary, contemporary culture, and "coolness," Cool Britannia was not a complete reimagining of England, but, rather the promotion of an already-existing brand that was often seen as a more crassly commercial, U.S.-influenced strand of British culture. Although the concept of Cool Britannia fell out of favor by 2000, New Labour attempted to use this brand to reshape the way the global community viewed the United Kingdom and its exportable products. This recasting of Britain worked particularly well for U.S. television in the 1990s.

A Clear Strong Brand

At the same time that liberal academics questioned the British heritage brand and New Labour attempted to update the global brand of Britishness into Cool Britannia, the television industry within the United States was undergoing significant shifts that made these brands of Britishness useful for cable programmers. The 1980s saw the rise of cable systems across the United States, as well as a revitalization of independent stations, which, on cable systems, could now compete with the networks despite UHF allocations. The rise of the Fox network and the growing popularity of the VCR contributed to the volatile and confusing state of the television industry in the 1980s. Cable stations, first gaining popularity with viewers, primarily relied on programs from the broadcast networks to fill their airtime. While off-network syndication provided a good portion of the cable stations' line-ups, foreign shows offered an opportunity for "new" programming—or at least programming that was new to U.S. audiences (Mullen, 138). British programming was particularly useful for cable stations since viewers were already somewhat familiar with British shows from public television, which, as discussed above, had infused these programs with an air of "quality."

As Megan Mullen explains in her book *The Rise of Cable Programming in the United States: Revolution or Evolution?* the new cable stations focused heavily on niche broadcasting strategies and brand creation to attract audiences. The art of cable programming was in choosing the off-network programs that would support the brand. Eventually, in the 1990s, cable stations "were operating at a profit, receiving widespread carriage, and selling time to major advertisers" (Mullen, 182). Successful cable stations soon looked to produce, or at least co-produce, programming that would help support their brands and attract their target audiences.

A&E was one network that emerged as a strong contender within this competitive environment. The collapsing cable networks ARTS (owned by ABC and Hearst) and Entertainment (owned by RCA) combined to form the Arts and Entertainment Network in 1984, as a co-venture of Hearst (37.5 percent), ABC (37.5 percent) and NBC (25 percent). From its inception A&E's goal was to target a select audience of affluent and educated viewers (Burgi, 1995, 26). To do so, A&E identified four main "program themes": comedy, drama, documentaries, and performing arts (Burgi, 1994b, 12). Many of the actual programs that were used to flesh out these themes were off-network re-runs or acquired programs, frequently from British producers. Like most new cable networks, A&E produced some, but not much, original programming. In 1987, A&E began to show a profit and continued to make money (Davatzes, 55). By 1993, the network's revenues were estimated at $147 million, up 27 percent from 1992 (Burgi, 1994a, 24). A&E executives attributed the revenue jump to the increased advertising that A&E's upscale demographic attracted.

With the larger profits, A&E developed an increased interest in original programming ("Necessary For," 6). As the prices for off-network re-runs rose, A&E followed other cable networks that had started by airing programs with "pre-sold recognition factor" then moved to original programming (Burgi, 1994a, 24). Original programming offers several benefits for a cable network. It gives the network a library of programs that can be cheaply re-run in the future.

Original programming also provides material that the network can sell for additional profits in secondary markets such as home video and international television. A&E has particularly benefited from video releases, with its A&E Home Video line that includes titles such as *Cracker*, *Emma*, *Pride and Prejudice*, and the "Biography" series[1] Finally, original programming serves as a way for the networks to stand out from one another (Parsons and Frieden, 245).

While original programming is important for the development of cable networks, it can also be quite expensive. Co-productions, therefore, are frequently used as one way to increase original programming while limiting the financial investment in the programs. The need for original programming to build a brand image was particularly important for A&E and other cable networks at this time when the number of cable stations was growing and competition from satellite systems and telephone companies loomed (Burgi, 1994a, 24). A&E was especially active in co-productions with a tendency to invest about 25–50 percent of the cost of the shows (Johnson, 92). Co-production with British producers for documentaries and dramas became a staple for A&E (Dempsey, 1999, A3).[2] A&E could then maintain control of these titles in the U.S. media. British programs also fit well into the brand image that A&E worked to foster.

With its original programming, A&E set out to increase ratings, and thus advertising revenue, by creating a more distinct image for the network. Branding for A&E was not easy. As Whitney Goit, the executive vice president of sales and marketing, said, "We knew we needed a clear, strong brand. But for a horizontal network like ourselves, that's not easy. We don't have a critical noun in our name" (qtd. in Ross, S1). Unlike the Weather Channel or American Movie Classics, there was nothing in the name "Arts and Entertainment" that helped define the network. In the early 1990s, the network sought to alter this. In 1994 the network changed its name from Arts and Entertainment to A&E to avoid the pretension of "arts" and the vagueness of "entertainment" (Burgi, 1994c, 9). The network reduced its focus to three program themes: original biographies, mysteries, and specials (Burgi, 1994c, 9). To reach the "selective, discerning, better educated viewer" that Brooke Bailey Johnson, the executive vice president in charge of programming, described as the network's target audience, A&E tried to "do television that's a little more intellectually challenging than the norm" (qtd. in Mifflin, 1996a, 55).

The main area of expansion for the network and the focus for creating its brand image was in the area of original biographies with the program *Biography*, which was also the cheapest to produce. In 1994, A&E increased its showing of *Biography* from one night a week to five and focused on this show as a way to create an identity for the network as something unique and intelligent. The expansion proved successful for A&E's ratings and its advertising (Dempsey, 1998, 1). A&E did not, however, want to rely solely on *Biography*, and some critics noted, as did the *New York Times* in the mid-1990s, that A&E "is as much the 'whodunit?' network as the biography network" (Mifflin, 1996a, 55). Although A&E focused on two types of drama—mysteries and specials—mysteries were selected as a potential additional brand identity (Davatzes, 55). The network occasionally promoted mystery nights or mystery months (such as the "Tuesday Night Mystery Movie" or the "July to Die For" in 1997) and programmed, in 1996, for example, four hours of prime time mysteries (two hours of which were original). A&E associated its brand with what it considered high quality, upscale mysteries. Although A&E has more recently expressed an interest in U.S.-based mysteries, many of those programmed in the 1990s were British, such as *Poirot*, *Lovejoy*, and *Cracker*. Johnson concretely associated the co-production of British drama with the network's brand and target audience when she explained, "A&E produces a lot of drama with the UK because our target audience is better educated, affluent adults" (92).

Johnson does not explain the connection she makes between British television and upscale audiences, making it seem common-sensical. Significantly, however, A&E did not show British programs from all genres. Rather, the cable network relied on the reputational capital of British television producers to create "high quality" costume dramas and mysteries. A&E then helped to create specific programs that could capitalize on two well known brands of Britishness: heritage and mod. Creating programs that could be associated with these brands allowed A&E the opportunity to appeal to a diverse Anglophile audience by presenting two different visions of Britishness. Both of these brands associated A&E with quality and high culture, but did so in very different ways, perhaps allowing A&E to, as *Variety* explained, "bridge intellectual programming with the desire for a large audience" (Bernstein, 27).

Pride and Prejudice and Austenmania

The A&E/BBC co-production of *Pride and Prejudice* aired in the United States in January of 1996 in the midst of what was being called "Austenmania." The 1995 theatrical releases of *Persuasion* and especially *Sense and Sensibility* proved critically and commercially successful. For reasons discussed below, Jane Austen novels had become hot properties for film and television producers, with the six-hour miniseries version of *Pride and Prejudice* serving as the ultimate example of what could be done with the combination of a British heritage drama and U.S. financing.

Pride and Prejudice aired in the United Kingdom in December 1995. Production costs for this lavish, three part (two hours each) miniseries were reported to be £6 million or $9.73 million (Kavanagh, 86). These costs seemed justified when the program received the BBC's highest ratings ever for a costume drama. Reports estimated an average audience of 10 million people in the United Kingdom (Kavanagh, 86). The last episode supposedly attracted 40 percent of the television audience in the United Kingdom (Dean). Additionally, by January 1996 the home video of the miniseries had sold 100,000 units and the companion novel had sold out in bookstores (Dean).

By the time A&E aired the miniseries in January 1996, it had already received a fair amount of press coverage. Articles on the newfound popularity of Jane Austen abounded, and the success of the *Pride and Prejudice* miniseries in the United Kingdom was repeatedly mentioned. The miniseries also received rave reviews from British and U.S. critics and from Jane Austen fan clubs that gave the miniseries a very decided seal of approval. A&E scheduled the miniseries for three consecutive evenings Sunday, January 14 (8–10 P.M); Monday, January 15 (9–11 P.M); and Tuesday, January 16 (9–11 P.M).

The ratings for the miniseries proved to be the highest for any A&E movie with an average of 3.7 million homes tuning in to the show.[3] *Pride and Prejudice* also proved very successful for A&E in the home video market, with the special edition of *Pride and Prejudice* selling, by April of 1997, 125,000 units at $99.95 (Sherber, 59).

The decision by A&E to co-produce a classic literary work with the BBC is not difficult to understand. For the most part, classic adaptations do well in the United States and this project offered A&E a means to create a prestige miniseries that would attract its core audience of upper class, highly educated viewers—particularly women. The selection of a Jane Austen novel, however, was somewhat unusual, although it did not appear so once Austenmania became evident.

Moving away from the Merchant-Ivory productions of the 1980s and early '90s, the heritage genre of the mid to late 1990s seemed to center on the works of Jane Austen. According to Madeline Dobie, these adaptations of Austen actually represent a post-heritage movement in which the filmic versions of the novels take on political and social issues (the evils of capitalism in the 1995 BBC/WGBH version of *Persuasion*; slavery in the 1999 BBC/Miramax *Mansfield Park*; and poaching in the 1996 adaptation of *Emma* co-produced by A&E and Meridian). These post-heritage films, Dobie argues, illustrate the different kinds of materials that can be produced when niche audiences are targeted. So, while the 1980s heritage films were aimed at a mass audience, the rise of cable and the "major-independent" film distributors in the United States made possible the production and distribution of films aimed at upper class, highly educated women. Furthermore, these films could include an element of social and political commentary (even if slight). Dobie points out, however, that while films and television programs aimed at niche audiences may be possible, most distributors and television channels still have hopes of crossover success, and, therefore, usually include elements of a more familiar genre—such as romantic comedy—in order to increase the potential audience for the product. The A&E/BBC *Pride and Prejudice*, Dobie writes, mixed an investigation of social hierarchies with elements of romantic comedy (252).

Dobie's analysis of the popularity of Jane Austen in the 1990s, brings to light many of the industrial shifts that made *Pride and*

Prejudice attractive for A&E: the prestige, the quality audience, and the branding that the program would cultivate. Dobie does not, however, consider the implications of the miniseries being a co-production. Carol Dole, for example, examines the differences between U.S. and British adaptations of Jane Austen novels. Dole argues that U.S. versions of Jane Austen's works tend "on the surface to ridicule class snobbery but on a deeper level to ratify class divisions" (60). British versions, on the other hand, generally address the class divisions in a more direct and questioning manner. Of course, Dole's primary example of a "British" Austen adaptation is *Persuasion*, a co-production of the BBC, WGBH Boston, and two French production companies. Even more significant than country of origin may be target audience. *Persuasion* was originally produced for television but then released into theatres. In the United States, *Persuasion* primarily ran in art houses. *Persuasion*, therefore, was not necessarily intended for a mass audience. For A&E, however, a crossover audience was definitely a goal.

In addition to a particular representation of class, depictions of gender, social manners, and morality also inform Austen's popularity in the United States. Much of the popular press analysis of the Austen revival of the 1990s focused on why Americans enjoyed films based on Austen's novels. According to Edward Rothstein in the *New York Times*, "It is no accident that her novels' finely detailed accounts of moral and social education should inspire such interest at a time when conservative criticism of American culture is increasingly concerned with failures in those areas" (1). Writing in the *Washington Post*, Patricia Brennan agrees: "This is a story about morals and values, not just high position and wealth" (Y07). Austen's novels, critics observe, allow people in the United States to visit a time when manners ordered people's lives and clarified their place in society. In the 1990s, when the world seemed disordered and family values were being presented as a means of organizing this disorder, Jane Austen replaced the chaos with a very British sense of order and precision.

This heritage brand of Britishness linked civility, manners, and class structure to Britishness. By offering a story placed in the British past, the producers established two levels of removal—historical and national—that mitigated any discomfort that might be felt by the U.S.

upper middle and upper classes, the intended target audiences for the miniseries. Still, A&E could not risk presenting a hypercritical view of class divisions, which are undoubtedly still part of U.S. society. Co-production on the part of A&E allowed the cable network a hands-on opportunity to choose a text and then create a program that would tap into this British brand of heritage, while at the same time limiting the social commentary in order to increase the possibilities of crossover appeal.

The A&E/BBC version of *Pride and Prejudice* clearly links these industrial needs in its representation of gender, class, and manners. Numerous academic and popular articles have examined Jane Austen's depiction of social status and the place of women in British society. The rather faithful adaptation of the A&E/BBC version of *Pride and Prejudice* includes, throughout its six hours, many clear illustrations of the way that class and gender are governed by proper British manners. Sue Britwistle, the program's producer, explained that she wanted to highlight the importance of economic status in Regency England. She explained, "There isn't a character in the novel who's introduced without his income being mentioned in the next sentence" (qtd. in Grimes, 3). The miniseries, unlike the 1939 film, also foregrounds issues of economics, class, and social status. The program, however, does not significantly question the power of social rank. Darcy is, in fact, superior. His main flaw is that he knows it. Jane and Elizabeth are congratulated for marrying into the upper classes. Class, therefore, while an issue is not, in the end, a real concern; and, as the end of the novel dictates, this television version refuses to question the correctness of the class system.

In the attempt to appeal to both Austen fans and unfamiliar viewers, the miniseries emphasizes, as Dobie's analysis predicted, the romantic comedy aspects of the story. When the BBC first announced the miniseries, Britwistle commented that this version of *Pride and Prejudice* would focus on the main points of the novel: sex and money. Many fans in the United Kingdom expressed great concern that the program would "update" the story with nude scenes and historically inappropriate innuendo (Grimes, 3). Britwistle explained that she was actually referring to long looks across a room, not explicit material. The miniseries does, however, add a few scenes that draw attention to the romantic qualities of Mr. Darcy. For example, at one point we see Darcy taking a bath. He sits in a tub full of water while a servant pours water over his head. A bathrobe (being held by the servant) blocks his naked body as he stands up and moves to a window, from which he watches Elizabeth outside playing with a dog. We also see Darcy at a fencing lesson. The miniseries clearly explains that he is using the exercise to try to forget his love for Elizabeth. Darcy says to himself after the lesson, "I shall conquer this. I shall." Perhaps the most famous added scene that underscores sexuality is that of Darcy returning to Pemberley, taking off his jacket, and swimming in a lake. He then walks to the house, dripping wet, and runs into Elizabeth who is touring the house with her aunt and uncle. Although these scenes of Darcy may be justified as a way to attract more male viewers by adding more material about men, clearly these scenes are actually about creating Darcy as a sexual object for women. The popularity of Colin Firth's Darcy as a romantic hero can be seen in the numerous letters sent to the program's producer—including one woman who told of how, after the final episodes, she went to the hospital with shortness of breath, sweating, and a racing pulse. The doctor's diagnosis was that she was in love with Darcy (Grimes, 3). The miniseries invited women to identify with Elizabeth as she fell in love with Darcy. Significantly, in the program's faithfulness to the original text, it did not update *Pride and Prejudice* to include any material that would be considered subversive regarding women's roles in society. While the miniseries makes clear the fact that women's places in society depended on their fortune, family, and marriage, it does not suggest that this was in any way a real hardship for women of proper breeding and intelligence. Again, by sticking closely to the original text, *Pride and Prejudice* was able to make a claim to quality and avoid including any material that might be considered subversive by the upper class, primarily female viewing audience that might not want to question its own values.

Perhaps less overtly discussed, but equally as important for understanding *Pride and Prejudice* as an example of the heritage brand of Britishness, is the use of the British countryside and images of tourism to introduce viewers to Regency England. The importance of tourism in this adaptation of *Pride and Prejudice* plays out in the

Figure 2.1 Colin Firth as Darcy looks out over his estate in *Pride and Prejudice.*
(Photo courtesy of Photofest.)

numerous scenes that are set outdoors, allowing the viewers to get a glimpse of the beautiful and rich countryside. Most powerful, and narratively important, is Elizabeth's trip with her aunt and uncle to Derbyshire, the county that is home to Darcy's estate of Pemberley. She makes this trip after refusing Darcy's marriage proposal, but also after reading a letter from him explaining the truth behind his dealings with Wickham. So, while Elizabeth still dislikes Darcy, she is perhaps beginning to think him less dishonorable.

The trip through Derbyshire begins with a slow pan of the green hills that make up this part of the country. In voice over we hear Elizabeth's uncle describing the land as "nature and culture in harmony," thus setting the tone for the viewers' awe. Before getting to the highlight of the trip, Elizabeth's visit to Pemberley, we see Elizabeth walking through high peaks and looking down at the breathtaking valleys. The trip to Pemberley, which comes after the brief scene of Darcy's fencing lesson, is built up with great suspense. As Elizabeth and her aunt and uncle ride through the woods of Pemberley, Elizabeth jokingly asks, "Will we reach the house itself before dark, do you think?" When the house is revealed, the suspense pays off. That the house is breathtaking is seen on Elizabeth's stunned face. Her aunt asks, "Perhaps the beauty of the house renders its owner a little less repulsive?" We are asked to see the beauty of the English countryside and architecture as a virtue of those who own it.

Elizabeth and her aunt and uncle then tour the inside of the house guided by the housekeeper. This walk through of the house is very similar to present day tours of large National Trust homes, without the ropes keeping tourists away from the furniture. This personally guided tour invites the viewers to experience the spectacle of wealth that eventually leads Elizabeth to reconsider her feelings toward Darcy. Toward the end of the miniseries, after Elizabeth accepts Darcy's second marriage proposal, she jokingly acknowledges to her sister Jane that she first began to love Darcy after seeing his beautiful grounds at Pemberley. By tying together the beauty of England, the spectacle of historical mansions, romance, and class status, *Pride and Prejudice* capitalizes on the heritage brand of Britishness to create a miniseries that promotes a romantic view of Regency England, perfect to appeal to A&E's target audience.

The A&E/BBC version of *Pride and Prejudice* offers a strong example of the heritage brand of Britishness. It is a historical costume drama, slow paced and visually breathtaking. The benefits of watching *Pride and Prejudice* are clearly in line with the functional, experiential, and symbolic benefits of the A&E brand. In terms of functional benefits, the program returns (or introduces) viewers to a major literary work. Additionally, the program is "historically accurate" in its recreation of Regency England, thus giving viewers something of a history lesson. And *Pride and Prejudice* certainly allows opportunities for the viewer to act as a tourist by seeing the countryside and visiting historical homes. The experiential benefits are also significant. *Pride and Prejudice* offers romance, comedy, and beautiful settings to allow viewers to escape to another time. The symbolic benefits of watching *Pride and Prejudice*, particularly a six-hour miniseries, are somewhat self-evident. Viewers could claim cultural capital from watching a television adaptation of one of the most light-hearted and romantic literary classics in circulation. All of these attributes and benefits, especially at this time of Austenmania, helped to concretize the attitude associations that this longer, more faithful version of an Austen classic is a high quality, culturally sophisticated, and superior way to pass one's television time.

By staying generally true to the novel while adding some connections between Britishness and virility (through the added scenes of Darcy) this version of *Pride and Prejudice* provided A&E with a strong branding opportunity. Audiences, particularly older, female audiences, would recognize A&E as a network of quality. A&E, however, also wanted to reach younger audiences—and men. To solidify its connection with this audience, A&E would turn to a different brand of Britishness: the mod brand.

Cool *Cracker*

Co-produced by A&E and independent producer Granada Television, *Cracker* aired on ITV stations (some of which were owned by Granada) beginning in 1993. A&E began showing *Cracker* in the United States in 1994. If sometimes controversial,[4] *Cracker* was quite successful with critics and audiences, appearing throughout the 1990s not only on British and U.S. television but also in international markets such as Iceland, Poland, Israel, and Japan (Victoria Clark, 7).

New episodes of *Cracker* were produced from 1993–1996 (another two-hour episode was produced in 2006 without A&E's participation).[5] The program starred Robbie Coltraine as the psychologist Dr. Edward Fitzgerald (Fitz), who is excellent at working his way into the minds of criminals but is, himself, a wreck. He is an obese compulsive gambler who smokes too much and drinks too much. His family life is a mess and he is frequently estranged from his wife, Judith, whom he periodically cheats on. This is not a conventional mystery program and Fitz is not a typical leading man for a recurring television series in the United States—either in terms of the stereotypical, proper British detective or the stereotypical, infallible U.S. detective. *Cracker* is darker and angrier.

Over the course of *Cracker*'s four-year run in the 1990s, ten different series were produced (with names like "Mad Woman in the

Attic" and "To Be a Somebody") each consisting of approximately two or three 60-minute episodes. The first and third seasons had seven episodes (and three series), the second season nine episodes (and three series) and the last season only two episodes (one series). In total, 25 episodes of *Cracker* aired. This kind of program structure is certainly different than that in the United States where television programs run for anywhere from 13-22 episodes per season. The stories may connect from one episode to another, but there are rarely individual story arcs that can be separated out as stand-alone pieces.[6] Furthermore, the running time and structure for each episode differed from U.S. shows, as *Cracker* was made to accommodate fewer commercial breaks than the number permitted in the United States. Furthermore, the sexuality and language in *Cracker* also reflected variations in British and U.S. standards and practices, with British television being more accepting of narratively motivated sex and explicit language.

Nevertheless, A&E helped to create and then aired *Cracker* as part of its attempt to associate itself with high quality television. Unlike *Pride and Prejudice*, *Cracker* clearly does not rely on the heritage brand of Britishness. Rather, *Cracker* is more closely connected with the mod brand associations that tie Britain to style, contemporary culture, anti-authoritarian heroes, and social commentary. More specifically, *Cracker* may be connected to the legacy of "in-yer-face" theatre that helped to forge the Cool Britannia concept in the 1990s.

Plays connected to the in-yer-face British theatre movement of the 1990s attempted to shock audiences with on-stage violence and sex in order to encourage people to react and perhaps take up social and political activism. The home of the in-yer-face movement was the Royal Court Theatre (not coincidentally the place where many of the original theatrical versions of what would become "angry young man" cinema such as *Look Back in Anger* were first staged). In an attempt to attract younger audiences, the theatre's management decided to produce the work of young unknown artists. Stephen Daldry, the artistic director at the Royal Court at the time, explained, "The writers who grew up under Thatcher experienced two things: they were disempowered and simultaneously empowered. On the one hand, the state was strengthened at the expense of the individual; on the other, the only way of achieving anything was to do it yourself.... Thatcherism provided a climate of anger and the motivation to do something about it" (qtd. in Sierz, 39). Many of the in-yer-face plays focused on contemporary British culture and the cultural divisions that existed there, such as the war between the sexes, the crisis of masculinity, violence, terrorism, ethnic cleansing, homelessness, cruelty, and drugs (Sierz, 238). Representing the anger and confusion of the times, in-yer-face theatre emphasized moral ambiguity.

Urban connects in-yer-face theatre to the Cool Britannia movement promoted by New Labour in the 1990s. Cool Britannia relied on Britain's achievements in the cultural fields to re-brand the nation as someplace hip rather than stodgy. Music, fashion, and the culinary arts were also part of British society that helped to create Cool Britannia. Theatre, therefore, Urban argues, was part of the cultural reawakening within Britain that helped to shape Cool Britannia (Urban, 355). Like Cool Britannia, in-yer-face theatre represented the drive to reach younger audiences. In-yer-face theatre, however, did so by emphasizing the moral ambiguity, anger, and cruelty that existed in current society. Urban writes "that such 'in-yer-face' work could become part of a marketable cultural identity may seem odd at first, but, in truth, the 'nineties were all about peddling the provocative" (357). In some sense, in-yer-face may be more closely connected with 1960s culture and the original mod brand than the 1990s Cool Britannia.

Cracker can be seen as an attempt to modify in-yer-face theatre for television and make it more palatable for (U.S.) television audiences prepared to think of Britain as hip and modern. By combining elements with the themes of in-yer-face theatre, *Cracker* offered A&E a different brand of British television, while still appealing to the "high end" demographic the network targeted.

The resonance of art cinema can be seen in *Cracker*'s form and content. The show's narrative structure is at times intricate, with the narrative moving back and forth between Fitz, the police, and the criminals, creating connections between the various characters through crosscutting. Long takes and close-ups are also used to convey character emotions as well as to make viewers uncomfortable. For

Figure 2.2 Robbie Coltraine as Eddie Fitzgerald interrogates a suspect in *Cracker*. *(Photo courtesy of Photofest.)*

example, in the episode "To Say I Love You," Fitz tries to calm down Sean, a young man who is ranting in his holding cell. A medium shot of Fitz and the man is held for a long take as the man, loudly, urgently, and repeatedly insists that his girlfriend must be notified of his whereabouts. This shot effectively informs the viewer of how upset the man is, while also unsettling the viewer who is left to hear the repeated ranting of the disturbed man. Lighting is also utilized to promote ambiguity within the narrative. *Cracker* is shot dark and flat. The lighting underscores the dark nature of both the crimes and Fitz's own personality. Story lines are frequently left ambiguous or unresolved. Also, episodes oftentimes begin en medias res, requiring viewers to pick up quickly on what is happening, and the endings of the episodes can lack normal televisual closure. In the same episode, "To Say I Love You," Sean turns out to be a murderer, part of a Bonnie-and-Clyde-like team. At the end of the storyline, the woman is arrested for the two murders they committed, but the final shot is of the man—who has been set free—on a dark street, carrying a bag and running away. The episode ends in a freeze frame, not unlike the ending of *The 400 Blows*, leaving the viewer unsure as to what the future holds for this clearly unstable man. Another episode, "One Day a Lemming Will Fly," focuses on Fitz's and the police's efforts to prove that a teacher murdered and raped a young boy. In the end, we learn that the man actually did not commit the crime, though he is going to be charged and probably convicted anyway. We never do discover who is actually guilty of the crime.

Cracker also includes incredibly complex characters that are often unlikable and morally questionable. Fitz himself is a hub of mixed values and characteristics. Glen Creeber sees Fitz as a "complex anti-hero who seemed both to encapsulate and explore many of the ambiguities and contradictions inherent in contemporary British masculinity" (169). Fitz's drives and impulses, particularly his gambling addiction, center on the very "mod" desire to stave off the boredom of traditional middle class life. While attending a gambler's anonymous meeting led by his estranged wife Judith's therapist (whom she is now dating), Fitz cannot stop himself from seducing all of the attendees to gamble with him. He does this in part because he truly believes that gambling is fun and in part because he wants to make a fool out of the therapist. As viewers watch this scene we both enjoy the upending of the meeting while we recognize that Fitz is pathetic.

Although Fitz seems capable of intense compassion and frequently seems to care deeply for the people in his life, he is also incapable of displaying that love or of harnessing his selfish impulses. Fitz's relationship with Judith is extremely complex. While they both appear to want to save the marriage, and Fitz insists that he loves his wife, they do not always treat each other accordingly. Fitz, for example, forged Judith's signature in order to increase the mortgage to get money for gambling (leading her to leave him). Judith appears particularly fed up with the marriage. After she tells him the terms by which she would get back together with him, Fitz asks a waiter for a very sharp knife because "my wife would like to cut off my balls." Judith responds angrily, "I used to enjoy that sort of thing Fitz. . . . But now it's boring. The way you probe is boring. The way you analyze is boring. Your search for the bloody pure motive, it's as boring as living with a bloody poop." Judith's statement does not illustrate a yearning for lost love, but an intense anger and a desire to hurt Fitz. This element of anger and pain, which sometimes manifests as cruelty, is an integral part of *Cracker* that ties the program to in-yer-face theatre.

The *New York Times* observed that *Cracker* "looks at the contemporary urban scene with ferocious anger and grim humor" (O'Connor, C18). *Variety* noted that the "unrelenting camera work underscores the grimness of the game" (Scott). And the *Village Voice* described the show as "melancholy" and "packed with ambivalence" (Taubin, 45). As with in-yer-face theatre, moral ambiguity and cruelty are at the heart of many *Cracker* episodes. The cases on *Cracker*, as with many other police shows, explore issues of cruelty. Since Fitz is a psychologist, however, *Cracker* tends to examine the psychological causes of cruelty in more detail than other programs. *Cracker* is interested not only in the cruelty demonstrated by the villains but also the cruelty in their lives that shaped who they are. In the episode, "To Say I Love You," discussed above, we not only see the devastation caused by Sean and his girlfriend Tina as they kill people, but we also see the pain that they experience as Tina is rejected by her family and Sean is teased for stuttering. Additionally, the "good guys" are also capable of cruelty as they try to solve their cases and, in some instances, in their everyday lives. One of the police detectives, for example, mercilessly teases Sean for stuttering, causing him to get angry and violent.

Fitz himself is full of anger and capable of cruelty, particularly when he interrogates suspects. In the first episode of *Cracker*, "The Mad Woman in the Attic," a man is arrested as a suspect for a very violent and bloody rape and murder of a young woman on a train. The man says he cannot remember anything, not even his name. The police do not believe the man and try to break his claim of amnesia by bringing in Fitz to interrogate him. In the process Fitz is both cruel to the man, berating him for lying about his amnesia, and, in a later interview, cruel to the female detective D.S. Penhaligon (an eventual friend and lover of Fitz's), by using her as an example of the kind of woman who is begging to be a victim. As she is sitting in the room watching the interrogation, Fitz says some truly painful and mean things about Penhaligon's childhood—guessing that she was a lonely girl rejected by the popular kids at school, who lost her virginity to a boy who did not really care about her. Whether or not what Fitz said was true, his ability to humiliate Penhaligon is overwhelmingly uncomfortable—to the point that even the suspect asks Fitz to stop.

Perhaps even more disturbing is Fitz's sad view of the world and the cruelty found within it. During his first interrogation of the amnesiac, Fitz tells the man that he understands his desire to hurt women, because after all, sexual attraction for the sake of reproduction is natural. Fitz describes sex crimes as "natural." But, he tells the suspect, "They'll crucify you for it of course. Know why? Cause you've gone and done exactly what they've always wanted to do deep down in their hearts. Murdered. Butchered. Raped. They'll look at you and they'll be looking deep into their own hearts and it will terrify them. They'll crucify you out of fear. Not out of decency or justice or anything like that. Out of fear." This view of society and humanity, whether Fitz truly believes it or not, is disturbing and uncomfortable for the viewer. Throughout the episodes, *Cracker* demonstrates an anger and disaffection with the world that ties the program to in-yer-face theatre. At the same time, however, the program's format and style connects the program to more traditional art cinema, marking it as "different." By labeling the program as something "unusual" and "quality," we are not necessarily asked to question the world in which we live, but we are left to comment about the quality of British drama and how unique and edgy it is: very Cool Britannia; very mod.

Cracker's connection to the mod brand of Britishness is evident in the attributes, benefits, and attitudes associated with the program. *Cracker* is a television drama that is alternative in style and format. It focuses on sexuality (through the crimes committed) and appeals to young audiences in its focus on a dark, angry psychologist who works on the fringe of the system. Like other texts within the mod brand, *Cracker* questions the appeal of a "normal" life, particularly through its examination of masculinity and family relationships. *Cracker* is also seen as a program that comes from outside of the mainstream system. Not only is it a British program, but it is also set in Manchester, and the people in the program have distinctly northern accents that are sometimes difficult to understand. In terms of the program's benefits, *Cracker* allows viewers to see a side of England and a side of the justice system that they may not normally see on television. Viewers may learn about psychological issues. And they may also (seemingly) learn about contemporary society. As an experiential benefit, the fascination of watching *Cracker* is not necessarily joy, but the program is fascinating and intellectually stimulating. The program may also be seen as a voice for a viewer's anger and sense of injustice. In terms of symbolic benefits, viewers of *Cracker* can, like the viewers of *Pride and Prejudice*, gain cultural capital by watching something alternative. Viewers may feel edgy and "in the know" from watching a complicated British mystery (as opposed to *Poirot*, which would probably fall more easily into the heritage brand of Britishness). In the end, while the attitudes associated with *Cracker* would include trendy, hip, alternative, and complex, they would also include terms that may be associated with *Pride and Prejudice*: high quality, intelligent, and superior.

Cracker's story, incidentally, continues in the process of formatting and additional co-productions. In 1996, ABC (one of the owners of A&E) commissioned Granada's newly formed Granada Entertainment USA to create an Americanized version of *Cracker* starring Robert Pastorelli, best known for his comedic role as Eldin on Murphy Brown (Culf, 6). Granada co-produced the program with the U.S. company Kushner-Locke, creating yet another co-production, which was seen by many as an international co-production despite Granada Entertainment's U.S. base (Stanley, 22). ABC, like all networks that rely on formats from other countries, was drawn to the idea of benefiting from a program with a pre-sold name that already proved successful. The U.S. version of *Cracker*, however, did not last in the United States. The show went on the air in 1997 at 9 P.M. on Thursday nights—opposite *Seinfeld* (an interesting example of counterprogramming) (Gallo, 40). The program was well received by critics, although many pointed out the differences between the U.S. version and the original. According to critics, the U.S. *Cracker* made Fitz more sympathetic and less of a wreck. The show itself was sunnier, as it was relocated from Manchester to Los Angeles. The *Guardian* noted, the "grime and grit of Granada's original are gone" (Glaister, 7). Despite positive reviews the show did not find a large enough audience to suit ABC programmers, even after it was moved to Saturday night. Although 22 programs had been commissioned, 16 were produced and only 12 aired on ABC before the show was cancelled ("Production Deals"). Regardless, the program sold quite well in secondary markets. Not surprisingly, A&E bought the 16 existing episodes of the program that were made (showing four that had not been aired on ABC) ("Anglo-American 'Cracker,'" 70). The ITV network also bought the rights to the U.S. *Cracker* (Clarke, 1997a, 10). Interestingly, Granada's distribution company, BRITE, found that the U.S. version of *Cracker*—which it called *Fitz* for overseas buyers so as to avoid confusion with the original—was, at the time, its fastest selling program (Clarke, 1997b, 15). The U.S. version sold to approximately seventy territories by August of 1997 (Clarke, 1997a, 10). The reason that *Fitz* sold so well, according to Nadine Nohr, Granada's managing director of international distribution, was that the U.S. version had the "more flexible one-hour format" (Westcott, 79). The international familiarity with U.S. programming undoubtedly also benefited the U.S. version of *Cracker*. Not surprisingly, Granada soon increased interest in producing more shows in the United States. One Granada executive explained that "the overseas market is very used to buying U.S. programming. So if we can make high-quality, volume series for them, that is a powerful force for our distribution arm . . . in driving international sales" (qtd. in Fry, 74).

A&E, in the meantime, announced plans to move away from British co-productions to create more U.S.-based mysteries.[7] Johnson explained that "the higher level more intelligent American–based mystery" would be produced and programmed by A&E (qtd. in Mifflin, 1996a, 55). A&E would co-produce one-off movie versions of Nero Wolfe, Gene Wilder's *Murder in a Small Town*, Robert Parker's Spenser mysteries, and later the television series *Nero Wolfe* and Sidney Lumet's *100 Center Street*. In the end, the move away from the British programming, while perhaps necessary for industrial reasons (including the creation of BBC America), left A&E without a brand image. The U.S. mysteries that A&E created did not succeed. Without the secondary associations of the British brand, the programs did not help to create positive associations for A&E. Additionally, A&E executives determined to go after a younger audience, even if it meant giving up some of the upscale viewership (Frutkin, SR56). Focusing on non-scripted series, such as *Dog the Bounty Hunter*, *Airline*, and *Growing Up Gotti*, A&E has attempted to balance its audience with both "common denominator" and upscale shows (Frutkin, S58). The network's abrupt cancellation of the recent BBC co-production *MI-5* (*Spooks* in the United Kingdom) and its replacement with re-runs of *CSI: Miami* illustrated the network's turn from British international co-productions to more domestic ratings grabbers.

A&E's relatively strong position within the television industry has made this revisioning of the network possible. A&E had a loyal base of viewers from which to grow; a base made possible, at least in part, by the secondary associations of the British brands that allowed A&E to target a quality television audience. Significantly, by co-producing British programming, A&E assisted in the creation of the British brand and utilized two different brand images to broaden its audience appeal. Programs that built on the brand of heritage, like *Pride and Prejudice*, attracted an older, more traditional female audience. *Cracker*, with its in-yer-face mod styling, on the other hand, was expected to appeal to a younger, male audience. While both brand images retained the attitude associations of high quality and superior British culture, they appealed to different demographic groups, so that A&E could, while still targeting its audience through branding, cast its cultural net as wide as possible.

3 / The Three C's

Children, Citizenship and Co-Production

As discussed in the previous chapter, branding provides television programmers a means to target audiences in a fragmented viewing environment. International co-productions thrive in this more competitive environment where viewers select programs based on a number of different criteria and interests. One of the basic premises underlying the industrial growth of international co-production is that nationality is not a primary basis for people's media choices. Viewers do not require that films and television programs—at least not in all instances—speak to them as members of a given nation-state. The assumption is that nationality, while perhaps a contributing factor, is not the sole (or perhaps the most significant) factor determining a person's identity. Other elements of a viewer's make-up, such as gender, economic status, age, ethnicity, or race, are seen as more significant and can potentially allow for the development of "universal" themes so that global viewers can enjoy the same programming. At the same time, international co-productions, for the most part, create programming that de-centers nationalism and in some cases condemns nationalism, as illustrated in Chapter 1. International co-productions might, then, create a cyclical effect in that they assume the limited importance of nationality for viewers and then help to foster the limited importance of nationality through their "global" content.

Industry participants, of course, benefit from international co-productions in many ways. As discussed in the introduction, the creation of programming that does not foreground nationalism or speak to the people of a particular nation has numerous benefits in the increasingly international media environment. For example, global broadcasters can use such programs to fill air time on their stations around the world. And producers can share resources to create higher quality programming. Culturally, co-productions have the potential to usher in the "global village" in which programming with universal themes unites people around the world. More critically, the international programming of co-productions can lead to cultural homogenization. While viewers in different countries certainly read the same programs in different ways, thus limiting their homogenizing potential, global audiences are increasingly starting their readings with the same material. Cultural identities are being generated from many of the same media products.

Many scholars have examined the role of television in creating cultural identity. Quantitative and qualitative research has shown that people are affected by what they see on television: televisual representations shape how people understand themselves and their places in the world. If, as many have argued, identities are created from a person's understanding of his or her position in society, then increasingly the electronic communities that are shaping our lives are informing how we think of ourselves and the world in which we live (White and Preston, 254). Technology and globalization are two elements that have complicated identity formation since at least the end of the last century. Arlene Dávila writes that "the new diversities ensuing from transnationalism and the flow of populations and cultural goods have not only opened possibilities for new pluralities and hybrid identities, but, most significantly, created new demand for establishing 'belonging'" (11). This sense of belonging that Dávila and others have written about centers on the changing conception of citizenship and what it means to belong within a community. Citizenship, scholars argue, must be reconsidered during an era when transnational corporations increasingly overshadow nation-states, and concepts of community and belonging are shaped not by national media companies but by global media intended for international audiences. International co-production, which brings together different understandings of citizenship, community, and belonging from companies in different countries, offers an interesting perspective on how television "teaches" citizenship. Most interestingly, we can explore this arena by focusing on one of the more popular forms of international co-production: children's television.

The relationship between children and television has been the subject of a great deal of analysis. Explorations of the impact of televisual violence and gender roles frequently focus on the negative effects of television as a tool for shaping children's identity. An increasing number of recent studies have examined the commercial nature of television programming and the ways that children are being taught the wonders of consumerism through their interaction with media and the corresponding licensed merchandising. As Matthew P. McAllister and Matt Giglio write, "Children face waves of images of themselves and things they love that are increasingly connected together by a dominant message: 'you should buy/watch this as a part of being a kid'" (42). Whether the effect of television on children is seen as positive or negative, most scholars agree that television influences the way that children build their own identities—how they understand who they are, what they like, their place in the world, and their goals and desires. Hannah Davies et al. explain that "children's assertions of their own tastes necessarily entail a form of 'identity work'—a positioning of the self in terms of publicly available discourses and categories" (21). Television and the decisions to view particular programs, then, offer children a mechanism by which both to develop and demonstrate their individuality.

This chapter will explore how internationally co-produced children's programs contribute to the "identity work" of children, primarily through a consideration of how such programs illustrate and teach citizenship. Due to the growth and subsequent segmentation of the children's television market, this chapter will concentrate primarily on pre-school programming to examine how television lays the groundwork of citizenship for some of its youngest viewers. Programming for this young age group is generally expected to be "educational," with producers careful to illustrate that children will gain some benefits from watching the program, or at the very least that children will not be harmed. Often, producers laud pro-social pre-school programming for its ability to shape children into better people. One study illustrated that children who watch these kinds of television shows have more positive social interactions, are more giving, and are less likely to rely on stereotypes when dealing with others (Shochat, 82). Values of childhood, however, must also be recognized as differing from nation to nation. The ideologies that are promoted within the programs, the values that will make children into good people, may not be universally accepted. As with other forms of programming, internationally co-produced children's shows must serve the interests of programmers, as well as parents and children, in a variety of markets. Looking at internationally co-produced programs for their potential, and perhaps requirement, to move beyond categories of nationalism, this chapter will focus primarily on what these shows tell children about citizenship. What kinds of citizens are created through internationally co-produced programs? How do these notions of citizenship position U.S. children to participate in society?

To explore these issues, this chapter will consider two case studies, both of which emerge from U.S. co-productions with its American neighbors. The first is a commercial example of the Disney Channel-Nelvana (Canada) co-production of the animated program *Rolie Polie Olie* (1998–2001). This pre-school program, based on a poem by William Joyce, illustrates the important role of international co-productions and the Canadian production industry in the mainstream animation market. The second example is a bit more complex. *Plaza Sésamo* (1972–present), a co-production of the U.S.-based Children's Television Workshop (now Sesame Workshop) and Televisa (Mexico), is the Spanish-language version of *Sesame Street*. This program began airing in the United States in 1995 on both Spanish-language television and PBS. These very different programs, which emerge from very different co-production arrangements, offer examples of the potential of children's television to teach pre-schoolers how to be a part of a community and how to be a citizen but also how this potential is often constrained by the requirements of consumer capitalism.

Outpacing the Demand: Children's Television in the 1990s

Many histories have been written about children's television, and this chapter will not offer a summary of all of this research. Rather, here I will focus on the major industrial issues that impacted children's television since the 1980s. Factors including increased competition, shifting conceptions of the children's market, and elevated production costs helped to develop the co-produced programming surge of this time period.

The 1980s was a special time for the children's television industry. Drastic deregulation allowed children's programmers to focus on the profit potential of the youth market rather than on the "public interest." Children's television is not considered to be a highly profitable field. Until recently advertisers had not been overly interested in reaching the children's audience as this market does not have extensive expendable income. Profit from children's programming, however, was seen to come from selling toys and other goods that feature the programs' characters. The 1980s is noted for the growth of merchandising, licensing, and program length commercials (shows based on pre-existing toys and licensed characters primarily designed to sell merchandise). In 1981, for example, $14 billion worth of licensed goods were sold, more than double the same figure for 1977 (Langway, 56). Shows such as *Strawberry Shortcake*, *The Care Bears*, and *He-Man and the Masters of the Universe* relied on successful greeting cards, stuffed animals, and action figures to fuel their popularity. Many of the programs of this time period, as well as the early 1990s, were also criticized for their intensely violent content. *Teenage Mutant Ninja Turtles* and *Power Rangers* offered high profile examples of television shows that encouraged children to copy violent acts (even if in the service of good over evil). The resulting programs featured what was considered low quality animation and special effects and a high quality sales pitch. By the end of the 1980s, however, audiences, particularly parents and children's rights groups, grew weary of these programs and began to seek alternatives.

Within the traditional broadcast media, opportunities in the children's market led to competition. In 1986, Fox started its television network and moved heavily into children's programming. The broadcast networks traditionally only showed children's programs on Saturday mornings. Programmers avoided scheduling afternoon slots with kids' shows because of concerns that these light hearted shows would provide awkward lead-ins into the more serious network nightly news programs. Fox, however, had no network news program and began programming a Fox Kids block in the afternoons. Fox then used its afternoon timeslots to promote its Saturday morning shows, so that, by 1996, Fox was the highest rated Saturday morning broadcast network (Carvell and McGowan, 100).

While Fox relied heavily on low budget, violent, merchandiser-friendly programs (such as *Power Rangers*), other producers saw an opening for quality programming that would appease parents' concerns and offer children a higher quality product. Disney began producing a strip of programs which it syndicated as "Disney Afternoons" (including shows such as *Chip 'N Dale* and *Duck Tales*), raising both expectations and production costs for what would be considered quality children's television. Half an hour of *Duck Tales*, for example, reportedly cost $300,000 to produce. And by 1991 Disney was spending an average of $400,000 for each animated half hour of programming (Hubka, 1998, 162).

Additional competition for viewers came from cable television. David Hubka writes, "As child viewers turned away from animated toy tie-in programs in the late 1980s, they turned towards alternate distribution formats such as all-children cable services" (1998, 246). Although many children still did not have cable in their homes,[1] networks like Nickelodeon, Cartoon Network, and to a lesser extent the premium Disney Channel, made their mark. Nickelodeon proved exceptionally successful, focusing on high quality programming designed to appeal to kids. As Heather Hendershot writes, "Nickelodeon succeeded because the product-based shows, which owed their existence to deregulation, had drastically lowered the standards of children's TV. There was a vacuum waiting to be filled" (2004, 9). Nickelodeon, which started in 1979 and began accepting advertising in 1983, was branded as a channel for kids. The network developed an "Us v. Them" strategy that allowed the network to promote itself as speaking not *to* children but *for* children. The success of Nickelodeon was truly astounding. By the summer of 1996 Nickelodeon's Saturday morning line-up beat all of the broadcast networks in the ratings despite the fact that it only reached 70 percent of U.S. homes with televisions (Mifflin, 1996b, C18).

The abundance of children's programming coincided, not coincidentally, with a rethinking of the children's market in general. The merchandising boom of the 1980s, however, brought with it a realization that children bought goods with their increasing amounts of personal money ("Too Much of a Good Thing," 97). Throughout the 1980s and especially into the 1990s, the amount of money spent on children's advertising soared. In 1998 over $1 billion was spent on advertising during children's television (Preston and White, 116). Advertisers not only promoted children's products during children's shows, they also advertised adult products, as new studies indicated that children influenced adult decisions about major household products such as computers and cars (Preston and White, 117). The children's market was also seen to have the potential to build brand loyalty. Recognizing children as their future users, advertisers became interested in attracting children earlier and earlier (Preston and White, 117).

Like advertisers, television networks recognized the significance of attracting children as future markets. Geraldine Laybourne, the president of Nickelodeon from 1980–1996, said "we recognize that if we start getting kids to watch us at this age [pre-school] we have them for life" (qtd. in Pecora, 31-32). The interest in the pre-school audience was helped along by the success of *Barney and Friends*, the PBS phenomenon that began in 1992. The merchandising success of *Barney* prompted both Nickelodeon and Disney Channel to appeal to the pre-school audience (Hendershot, 2004, 10). Despite advertisers' limited interest in pre-schoolers, who generally do not have their own money to spend (Elizabeth Jensen, B3), this market developed as an important component for children's programmers. In addition to their potential as future loyal viewers, an appeal of the pre-school audience is its attentiveness to television. Unlike older children, the pre-school audience has not been lured away by videogames, the internet, and mobile phones (Patrick, A1). Overall, pre-school shows designed to attract young audiences to a network and build brand

loyalty rely little on advertising, generally using program sponsorships that bookend the programs rather than including commercials
within the programs, and primarily on merchandising (Jensen, 1996,
B3). One short-lived 1999 CBS program, *Rescue Heroes*, produced
by Fisher Price, was based on the pre-existing toy (Snyder, 3). Intended to increase sales of the action figures, *Rescue Heroes* illustrates
the use of pre-school programs to connect young children to toys.
The existence of *Rescue Heroes* in 1999 also demonstrates the suc-
cesses and failures of the regulation of children's television in the
1990s.

The decade began with the passage of the 1990 Children's Television Act. A rollback of the deregulation of the 1980s, the Children's Television Act placed limits on the number of minutes of
advertising time for children's television[2] and banned program length
commercials. Program length commercials, however, were very nar-
rowly defined as shows that actually contained paid advertisements
for the merchandise associated with the program. In other words,
Rescue Heroes would not be considered a program length commercial
as long as no paid advertisements for the Rescue Hero toy aired
during the program; the fact that the whole half hour was unpaid
commercial time was considered irrelevant.

Most significant for this discussion, the Children's Television Act
required local stations to air children's programming that is "educational and informational." At this time Congress and the Federal
Communications Commission (FCC) did not define "educational" or
"informational" and allowed broadcasters to count public service an-
nouncements and short interstitials within these categories. With these
vague rules in place, broadcasters began to search for programming
that could be defined as educational if necessary, resulting in broadly
pro-social programs with nice messages or in which the good guys beat
the bad guys in the end. The real boon for educational programming
came later in 1996 when, by order of Congress, the FCC determined
an exact number of hours of educational and informational children's
television a station was required to air. Beginning in 1997, the FCC
determined that stations must broadcast weekly at least three hours of
programming that "demonstrate[d] that educating or informing children is 'a significant purpose,' not an afterthought. Generally that

means having curriculum goals written out and employing educators to review scripts" (Mifflin, 1996c, D1). Furthermore, to count toward the three-hour requirement, programs had to be at least 30 minutes in length and they had to air weekly (Levinsky, 7).

These numerous changes within children's television that coalesced in the 1990s—including increased competition from new broadcast and cable outlets, new conceptions of quality children's programming, growth and segmentation of children as consumers, and changes in children's television regulation—profoundly affected children's television production. Increased costs and specific content requirements put additional pressure on program producers at a time when the television industry was already experiencing significant shifts. After all, these changes were taking place within the larger framework of the television industry in which conglomeration and globalization dominated.

Increased competition within the children's market, in the United States as well as in Canada and Europe, led networks to produce fewer programs and pay less for programs bought from outside sources (Daly, 38). According to Toper Taylor, the president of Nelvana, a leading Canadian animation production company, the growing number of outlets for children's programming and "the growth in advertising time is outpacing the demand for the same" (33). As a result, Taylor notes, license fees that broadcasters are willing to pay for shows decreased and the production of programming became more expensive. In this environment, along with merchandising, international sales took on an increasingly important role for children's programs (Toper Taylor, 33).

The changing landscape of children's television convinced many television programmers to look outside of the United States for programming, and television producers to look overseas for financing. Nickelodeon, for example, co-produced early programs such as *Count Duckula* and *Dangermouse* in order to keep costs low (Hubka, 1998, 128). Importantly, children's programming travels well internationally. These programs tend to have simple plots and, if animated, are easy to dub with little to no cultural discount ("Too Much of a Good Thing," 97). Additionally, animated programs lend themselves to an international division of labor, thus easing the co-production process as different tasks are farmed out to workers in different countries (Hubka, 1998, 144). Interestingly, the United States did not necessarily dominate the field of children's television. Although U.S. children's programs continued to sell internationally, the violence of some of the programs did not sit well with many international programmers. In fact, as will be discussed below, Canada, rather than the United States, emerged as one of the most popular sources of children's programming—and one of the most sought after co-production partners.

As with all other genres, co-production within children's television was certainly not new. The widely popular *Smurfs* program was co-produced in 1982.[3] In the early and mid 1980s, however, co-production was not considered essential. Oftentimes, these arrangements were motivated by the desire to gain the rights to internationally popular characters such as Asterix, the Smurfs, or Babar. The need for co-production in the 1990s, however, was motivated increasingly by the need for financing and market access. In 1996, France's national film board, Centre National de la Cinématographie (CNC), found that international financing, both through co-productions and pre-sales of programs, "represent[ed] the main financing source for animation programming" (Paoli, 64). French domestic broadcasting rights reportedly funded only 16 percent of an animated production, while the rights for live adult drama funded 60 percent of production costs (Paoli 64). Active co-producers of animated programs, French companies received the majority of foreign financing from the United States (26.6 percent) while Canadian partnerships accounted for a close 25 percent of funding. Partnerships with other European companies provided less than half of France's animation co-production funding (Paoli, 64). North American co-production partners were particularly desirable because they would ostensibly pave the way for distribution in the United States. Certainly a U.S. co-producer would have a stronger chance of forging a distribution deal in the lucrative U.S. market. As discussed in the introduction, however, European production companies increasingly sought to co-produce with Canadian rather than U.S. companies, because they could benefit from Canada's cultural proximity with the United States without having to kowtow to U.S. producers' demands.

Canadian companies, like some European companies, were also attractive co-production partners because the government provides funding for the production of children's programs. The Canadian government, for example, dedicated $73 million to children's television production in 1996, just as the U.S. educational television rules were going into effect (Crary). Production costs are then significantly lower, allowing the producers to sell the shows for less money, thus increasing the chances of the show being bought. Since the goal of the producers is really to sell merchandising and licensing rights, getting the show on the air is quite important. Before merchandized products can be sold, the television program must be aired. According to one Australian children's television producer, international shows that have high merchandising potential are often given to broadcasters for little money, and sometimes broadcasters are even given a percentage of the merchandising profits (Matthews, 36).

Not surprisingly merchandising and licensing rights are frequently, if not always, an important part of co-production deals for children's television. The Canadian company Nelvana, for example, produced CBS's Saturday morning line-up for the 1998–99 season. Although the company worked with CBS executives on the content to make sure the programs would satisfy the three-hour educational requirement, Nelvana retained ownership of the programs and all of the non-U.S. distribution rights. Nelvana was also responsible for licensing and merchandising the shows. CBS got a percentage of international sales and merchandising revenue. Meanwhile, CBS handled U.S. off-network distribution, of which Nelvana got a cut (Spring, 3). This unconventional co-production deal between these two companies was clearly designed to maximize their profit potential and meet their corporate needs.

Furthermore, as in the United States, children's television is an area that is often regulated by national governments with particular requirements. Co-producing partners must be careful to accommodate different content prerequisites to make sure that programs conform both to regulations for national content (in order to receive government subsidies, tax incentives, or both) as well as to regulations about children's television (Daly, 38). The regulation of children's programs frequently aims to provide children with educational, pro-social messages that will allow them to grow into strong and well-adjusted citizens. With their anti-nationalistic tendencies, international co-productions perhaps offer an unpromising means by which to meet these goals. As Cindy White and Elizabeth Preston explain, in contemporary children's television shows "landscapes are often featureless territories, unmarked by familiar landmarks that would tie them to a specific location. Characters are carefully crafted and animated in such a way as to maximize the potential for identification in a global market, ironically by stripping them of any specific cultural identity" (239). With their universal themes and culturally ambiguous characters, the ability of global programs to teach citizenship of any kind must be questioned.

Empowering Citizens?

When interested parties—be they politicians, academics or television producers—talk about creating citizens, we must question how the term is being used and to what ends. Toby Miller proposes three interrelated means of conceptualizing citizenship: the political, the economic, and the cultural, each of which will be briefly reviewed here (2001b, 1). Most popularly, citizenship refers to the political realm—belonging to a community that is associated with a nation-state. Citizens have certain rights as well as responsibilities within the nation that meld to form a functioning society and government. More recently, this political definition of citizenship, with its focus on nation-states, has been posed as only one type of citizenship that defines the lives of people today.

Economic citizenship, Miller explains, refers to particular economic rights and responsibilities, such as "a promise of full employment in the First World and economic development in the Third" (2001b, 2). Miller argues that economic citizenship is in decline, as people are increasingly expected to rely on the private sector to meet their economic needs. The concept of economic citizenship and its decline can be linked to the rising discourse of consumer citizenship. In *Consumers and Citizens*, an English translation of his 1999 book, Néstor Garcia Canclini argues that the failure of national citizenship has opened the door for other forms of citizenship and belonging.

Canclini sees consumerism as a form of participation that helps to shape people's identities. Viewing this shift in a positive and potentially political light, Canclini writes that "we should ask ourselves if consumption does not entail doing something that sustains, nourishes, and to a certain extent constitutes a new mode of being citizens" (26). As people increasingly understand themselves in terms of their habits of consumption, Canclini argues, market power shapes our participation in and contribution to society.

In her study of Nickelodeon, Sarah Banet-Weiser uses Canclini's concept of "consumer citizenship" arguing that the recognition of a group of people as a significant market segment marks them as full participants within society and worthy of recognition and consideration. Banet-Weiser points out that in today's consumer society, "we are recognized as meaningful citizens depending on both an economic and a cultural recognition of our purchasing power" (223). She concludes that it is the "*intermingling* of political rights and consumption habits that most profoundly characterizes citizenship" (Banet-Weiser, 230). Despite Canclini's suggestion that governments regulate consumption in order to make it more "fair," his concept of the consumer citizen has been highly criticized for its acceptance of consumerism as a basic form of identity. The idea of legitimizing consumer identity as a meaningful and empowering means of accessing citizenship might assist in prioritizing consumerism at the expense of political and economic power.

Cultural citizenship, the third and final discourse of citizenship proposed by Miller, stems from the idea that "genuinely 'cultural' dimensions of citizenship can no longer be assumed to be peripheral within modern mediated, globalised and post-modernised societies" (Stevenson, 331). Miller writes, "Cultural citizenship concerns the maintenance and development of cultural lineage through education, custom, language, and religion and the positive acknowledgment of difference in and by the mainstream" (2001b, 2). Rather than defining citizenship primarily in terms of judicial rights and responsibilities, cultural citizenship foregrounds the values, norms, and ideologies that create a sense of belonging among a group of people. The rights associated with cultural citizenship include the right to express a particular lifestyle or identity, the right to have this lifestyle/

identity treated with respect, and the right to be heard within the community (Stevenson, 333, 334). Nick Stevenson explains, "Cultural versions of citizenship need to ask who is silenced, marginalized, stereotyped and rendered invisible" (336). Access to and representation in the media is a significant right of a cultural citizen (Miller, 2001a, 183).

Understanding citizenship requires that we consider all three of these areas of cultural, economic, and political participation. As Miller explains, "Citizenship is no longer easily based on soil or blood. Rather, it is founded on some variant of those qualities in connection with culture and the capitalist labor market. And the state is no longer the sole frame of citizenship in the face of new nationalisms and cross-border affinities that no single governmental apparatus can contain" (2001b, 4–5). To comprehend the role that internationally co-produced television plays in creating children as citizens we must, then, connect this multidimensional approach to the discourses of children, citizenship, and television.

That children's television potentially teaches children how to be part of a community—whether global, national, or interpersonal—cannot be denied. Writing about children's programming in Ghana, Carla Heath found that children's television set the parameters for how children understood nationhood. She writes, "Children's television programmes . . . are concrete realizations of ideas about modernity, in particular ideas about what children should be taught in order to become useful, self-sufficient citizens of a modern African nation" (269). Much has been written about children's television as "empowering" children (or groups of children such as girls). We can consider the extent of this empowerment by examining how it plays out on the three levels discussed by Miller: the political, the economic, and the cultural.

While pre-school children may not be (overtly) political, the groundwork for their political beliefs and participation are certainly laid at a young age. David Buckingham explains that "children develop 'political' concepts at a very early stage, through their everyday experience of institutions such as the school and the family: notions of authority, fairness and justice, rules and laws, power and control, are all formed long before they are required to express their views in the form of voting" (177). Children, then, learn about political citizenship not only through explicit concepts of politics (voting, democracy, etc.), but also from more subtle ideas about leadership, parity, rules, and responsibility. Jean Northam examined British pre-school shows to consider what they "tell" children about community participation and citizenship. Comparing programs (*Trumpton* and *Chigley* from the 1950s and *Bob the Builder* from the 1990s), Northam looked at elements such as how the programs depicted characters in relation to their communities and how characters in trouble received assistance (from community members, community officials, or individual persistence). Northam found that the two different time periods presented different models of community—each closely resembling the dominant political ideology of its time. The earlier shows illustrated more public assistance and greater reliance on community members as opposed to the more recent program, which focused on individual responsibility and assistance from a small group of friends. The shift to global and co-produced programs undoubtedly necessitates such an ideological move, as any program that references specific political or public institutions may be considered too culturally specific for an international audience. As illustrated in previous chapters, international co-productions frequently eliminate particularities of place while trying to shape generalized physical spaces into emotional places. The use of "universal" values such as friendship, love, cooperation, and independence serve the interests of both international co-producers who wish to create culturally non-specific programs and purveyors of dominant ideology by presenting a form of political citizenship that shifts responsibilities from specific national governments to individuals and the private sphere.

There are tensions of course between the ideological goals of contemporary capitalist democracy and the financial prospects of children's television. Rugged individualism, for example, is not profitable for children's television. Individualism may be a "pro-social" trait, but it does not create an extensive set of action figures or stuffed animals that children can purchase. Small and private communities of friends and helpers (such as the team of builders on *Bob the Builder* or the "family" of tools in *Handy Manny*) both illustrate to children that problems can be solved within a small group of friends without the need for public or official assistance, and they provide children with a line of merchandise to purchase.

The connection between the forms of children's empowerment and the capitalistic interests of the producers is always evident. On a very basic level, each show (whether on commercial or public television) begins and ends with a sponsorship, reminding children that there is a benevolent company responsible for the program. As with most television shows, economic responsibilities are rarely addressed. Characters on children's shows, especially pre-school programs, live in a world in which money seems non-existent. While characters may hold jobs, the economic benefits and imperatives are rarely acknowledged. Empowerment, in the realm of economic citizenship for children, falls primarily within the recognition that children are important consumers. Banet-Weiser suggests that Nickelodeon's representation of girls as pro-active agents is an important form of empowerment—even if it is done in order to create consumers. She further argues that the recognition that girls are important consumers has granted them a certain amount of power and has made them visible within society. The same can be said of Latinos, who became visible on television only after they were marked as a growing group of potential consumers. The rise of child consumers, as discussed above, certainly led to an increased number of children's programs on television. We must question, however, whether this really does offer children rights and responsibilities as citizens. Does this limited type of recognition afford children status as important participants in society, or does it limit their possible roles within society as they are placed into categories based on their habits of consumption? Does their value become prescribed and their identities limited by their ability to support a brand?

As opposed to consumer citizenship, cultural citizenship seems to offer more empowering opportunities for children's programming. By including characters of different nationalities, races, genders, ethnicities, and socioeconomic realms, children's television has the opportunity to normalize difference, give "others" a voice, and tell children that alternative identities and practices are okay. Unfortunately, international co-productions are not the best means by which to create these kinds of inclusive messages. With their effort to stay within generalized and universal standards of international appeal, a wide embrace of difference potentially limits the program's appeal in international markets and creates shows that will not travel well. With their generalized, prosocial messages, international co-productions illustrate the value of acceptance without demonstrating any real differences with which children can identify. The push toward globalization as embodied by the international co-production in effect limits the cultural empowerment of citizens by fostering the creation of "safe" shows that promote a homogenous middle ground.

As we can see, then, the empowering potential of children's programs in terms of citizenship, while great, is for economic and industrial reasons unlikely to be fully mobilized. In many ways internationally co-produced programs are in a prime position to create shows that support ideologies that are dominantly useful—politically, economically, and culturally. Their need to move away from nationalistic approaches to citizenship while still sending pro-social messages, leads such programs to politically correct, yet non-threatening representations of what it means to be a citizen in today's world. Communities are private and self-contained. Public assistance is rarely necessary. Consumer citizenship is supported through programming and sponsorships. And cultural acceptance is limited and superficial. In the end, children's programs are seen less to empower children than to inculcate the values of capitalist democracy.

The role of international co-productions in helping children develop as citizens, in terms of politics, economics, or culture, must be suspect. After all, as Cary Bazalgette and David Buckingham write, "It is likely, for example, that within a given national culture girls and boys or working class and middle class children will be defined differently (and will define themselves differently) in relation to the categories of 'child' and 'adult' " (5). The idea that there are universal qualities of childhood that can empower children to be responsible and strong citizens, and that the process of international co-production will elicit these qualities in television shows, requires examination. To explore specific examples of internationally co-produced pre-school programs and their representations of citizenship, the remainder of this chapter will focus on two such programs. The first is *Rolie Polie Olie* (1998–

2001), co-produced by Nelvana and Metal Hurlant for Disney Channel. The second is *Plaza Sésamo* (1972–present), the Spanish-language version of *Sesame Street*. A co-production of Children's Television Workshop and Mexico's Televisa, this version of *Sesame Street* began airing in the United States in 1995. The program's availability in the United States complicates our understanding of international co-productions and requires a different conceptualization of the way that children's cultural identities are shaped by co-produced programs.

Familial Citizenship: Life in Polieville

Based on a poem by writer-illustrator William Joyce, *Rolie Polie Olie* was co-produced by the Canadian company Nelvana and France's Metal Hurlant "in association" with Disney. The show was created using advanced 3D digital technology that had not been used for a children's program before this time. With a target audience ages two–five, the program premiered on Disney Channel in 1998 airing on Saturdays and Sundays at 8:30 A.M. (By 2000 the show had moved into daily rotation and it was off the schedule by 2001.) Each half-hour episode of the Emmy-winning series consists of three seven-minute segments that tell stories about a little robot boy named Olie who lives in a world in which everything is round. The show focuses on Olie's interaction with his family and a few close friends.

According to Joyce, one of the main goals of the program was to depict a close nuclear family in which everyone is treated with respect. He explained in an interview, "I do think that there's too many cynical shows out there, which are aimed at the collegiate crowd. The other day, my kids and I were watching TV together and I saw so many anti-parent messages in the show that I just had to get up and turn it off. I began to wonder if I let my kids watch this stuff, when are they going to get some shotguns and decide to take care of their parents?" (qtd. in Zahed, 20). Joyce's interest in creating a show that was respectful of children and parents fit well with Disney Channel's brand in the 1990s.

Disney Channel started in 1983 as a premium channel for which viewers paid anywhere from $6 to $12 a month (Walley, S10). The network began to grow in popularity in 1985 and eventually moved to basic cable in a process that started in 1996 (some homes still receive Disney as a premium channel). That year Disney had approximately 15 million subscribers in the United States while its main competition, Nickelodeon, reached about 60 million homes (Lieberman, 2B). The switch to basic cable increased viewership of Disney, which by 2000 reached 61 million homes (Zbar, S12). Despite moving away from the subscription format, Disney remained non-commercial until 2002 when the network began to accept sponsorships to appear before and after programs (Friedman, 1).

The mid 1990s saw not only an increase in viewership for Disney Channel, but also a re-branding. In 1996, after merging with ABC, Disney hired Geraldine Laybourne to head its cable networks (which included Disney Channel and partial ownership of A&E, Lifetime, and The History Channel; ESPN, while owned by Disney/ABC, was not part of Laybourne's division). Laybourne was considered a powerhouse of children's television because of her previous work at Nickelodeon where, as president, she spearheaded the branding of the network as a kid's channel that spoke for and to kids. Laybourne then hired (away from Fox) her former assistant at Nickelodeon, Anne Sweeney, to run Disney Channel. Laybourne and Sweeney understood Nickelodeon's brand and chose a path for Disney that would differentiate it from the competition. To better serve, and segment, its viewers, Disney, like Nickelodeon, partitioned its day to cater to different age groups. Playhouse Disney (ages two–five) ran from early morning until 2 P.M.; at 2 P.M. programming switched to Zoog Disney (primarily designed for ages nine–14, but also attracting ages six–eight). Overnight, Disney ran repeats of both Playhouse Disney and Zoog Disney shows.[4]

Disney ultimately became a "family" channel that parents and children could watch together. Sweeney explained that Disney research showed that "kids said what they wanted most was more quality time with parents" (qtd. in Robertson, 16). Rich Ross, head of Disney Channel World Wide, further said, "You can empower kids without disempowering families" (qtd. in "Too Much of a Good Thing?," 97).

Disney focused, then, on creating programs that children and parents could watch together and that empowered families, not just children.

Of course this Disney programming was created within the larger context of the Disney Company and its own ideologies about children's entertainment. Much criticism has been leveled at Disney for its racist and sexist content as well as for its focus on merchandising of children's products. According to Mike Budd, Disney is a "global leader in the transformation of people into consumers and low-wage workers" (6). Furthermore, many scholars have contended that Disney's films create an ideology that supports global capitalism—"an ideology at odds with democracy and creative, participatory social life" (Artz, 76). Lee Artz argues that Disney's focus on individualism and globally marketable characters (such as "animals, aliens and monsters") "do not encourage healthy communities or democratic societies" but rather help to spread global capitalism (81). According to White and Preston, Disney Channel fit well within this corporate ideology. By branding itself as a "place" where children could go to feel part of a community, Disney emphasized individuality, honesty, and hard work, rather than the fun-loving kids' place promoted by Nickelodeon (White and Preston, 249). White and Preston write, "Rather than relying on oppositions between children and adults, Disney Channel portrays children and adults as partners united by their allegiance to these values, values that permeate and define Disney as place" (249).

Rich Ross explains that this family brand had strong international potential, saying that children in America and Britain think of themselves as independent, but in Latin America, continental Europe, and Asia families are more involved with one another's lives ("Too Much of a Good Thing?" 97). This concern about the international market was not insignificant. By the mid 1990's Disney Channel (and, of course, the Disney Company) had interests in the international marketplace. In 2000 nine Disney Channels existed around the world—in France, Germany, United Kingdom, Spain, Italy, and the Middle East; channels were in the planning stages for Latin America, Scandinavia, and Asia (Wasko, 20).

Disney Channel's appeal to international markets to promote the family-unifying values of global capitalism not surprisingly led Disney to seek out international producers and partners. *Rolie Polie Olie* emerged from a partnership with the Canadian company Nelvana, which emerged as a leading children's television producer in the 1980s. Nelvana, like many other Canadian companies, benefited from Canada's reputational capital as a producer of "high quality" children's programming. Canada, in fact, is well known for its export of children's television programs (Ingrassia, 20).

Canadian companies' skills for producing children's television emerge from the industry's regulatory requirements, government support, and social values. As discussed above, the Canadian government invested money into the production of children's programming. This monetary commitment may have been in response to a Canadian law that took effect in 1994 requiring special attention be paid to children's television. This law prohibited the depiction of violence as a means of problem solving or violence without consequences (Quill, A1). As a result Canadian stations cancelled U.S. programs like *Teenage Mutant Ninja Turtles*, *GI Joe*, and *X-Men* and replaced them with more "positive programming" that was frequently nationally produced (or co-produced). The Canadian Broadcast Corporation operated according to this code since 1984 (Bawden, E5), and so had already invested in the production of many pro-social children's programs. In fact, by 1998, the CBC aired three and one-half hours of children's programming each morning (8:30 A.M.–12 P.M.). These programs, according to an executive at the CBC, were chosen to reflect Canadian "values and ideals as a peaceful nation" (qtd. in McKay, F7). This meant that the programs would not be violent or contain excessive merchandising. This combination proved internationally successful. By 1999, according to Toronto's Alliance for Children's Television, Canadian animation studios produced approximately 24 series for the U.S. television networks and exported children's shows to two hundred countries (Regan, 6).

Nelvana certainly benefited from and contributed to Canada's strength in children's television. Started in the 1980s, the company faced financial trouble in 1983 but was saved by the success of *The Care Bears Movie* in 1985 (Walmsley, 54). By 1991, Nelvana was the third largest animation house in North America, co-producing *Babar*, *Tin Tin*, and *Rupert Bear* (Adilman, B1). Nelvana continued to grow throughout the 1990s, producing programs based on popular children's characters. In the late 1990s, Nelvana aimed to own programs rather than produce shows for hire. In other words, Nelvana wanted to own the merchandising and licensing rights for its shows as well as the actual productions (Ebeling, 166). At this same time, U.S. broadcasters urgently needed educational and information programs that would allow them to meet the three-hour children's television requirement established by the FCC.

Nelvana's most high profile arrangement came when CBS hired the company to produce its entire Saturday morning line-up for the 1998–99 season. After attempting a similar deal with Children's Television Workshop (CTW) the previous season, CBS suffered in the ratings. CTW's live action children's programs proved unpopular with viewers. CBS hoped that Nelvana's experience making educational and entertaining animated programs would help improve the network's Saturday morning ratings. Additionally, CBS reportedly paid very little for the programs (around $10,000–20,000 per episode— significantly less than the usual cost of an animated program), because Nelvana, along with various French co-production partners, received government subsidies and national license fees that helped to offset the costs (Schmuckler, 5). Both CBS and Nelvana stressed the importance of the partnership between the two companies. One CBS executive said, "we will work with them very closely on the development of the shows. With it all coming out of one shop, the upside advantage is working together on a marketing and promotional plan" (Schneider, 120). Nelvana's president, Toper Taylor, agreed: "The deal is unique . . . we're partners in the truest sense of the word, in execution of programming to profit participation all across the board" (qtd. in Schneider, 120).

During this time, Nelvana expanded to further become a self-sustaining children's entertainment company. Nelvana purchased two publishing houses, Kids Can Press and Klutz, as well as the U.S. 3D digital animation studio Windlight located in Minneapolis, Minnesota. The purchase of Windlight, which physically produced the animation for *Rolie Polie Olie*, for $2.2 million was designed to jumpstart Nelvana's plan for a Toronto 3D CGI facility (Kelly, 8). Nelvana's strength as an animation company allowed it a great deal of freedom within the market. Most particularly, Nelvana could create programs with pre-sales in the international markets but without necessarily having a U.S. broadcaster on board (Toper Taylor, 33). For a program like *Rolie Polie Olie*, however, which would launch Nelvana into digital animation, the cost would be too high to produce without U.S. support. According to one report, Nelvana spent tens of thousands of dollars just to create samples of the show's animation that worked for both Disney and Olie's creator, William Joyce (Zahed, 20). Disney's importance to the project is illustrated by the fact that Nelvana uncharacteristically agreed to give Disney the merchandising rights to the show (Ebeling, 166). Clearly then, Nelvana needed to create a program that fit with Disney's brand and accommodated the needs of the international market (including those of the show's French co-producer). Uniting Joyce's desire to create a program that would not make his children want to kill him with Disney's interest in "family" programming, Nelvana produced *Rolie Polie Olie*, a show that centers on the nuclear family as the ultimate community where membership comes along with particular rights and responsibilities.

As mentioned above, *Rolie Polie Olie* focuses on a young robot named Olie who lives with his mother, father, grandfather, younger sister Zowie, and dog Spot. They live on another planet where all things are round and curved, and many typically inanimate objects (like tables and bowling balls) have eyes and can move around (though they are clearly still objects to be used by the Polie family). Although the program is animated using computer technology, the feel of the program is surprisingly retro. The nuclear family, in which the father goes to work and the mother stays at home, is strong and structured. The children obey their parents and the parents never raise their voices. Characters use old-fashioned phrases like "okey dokey," "woopsie daisy," and "swell." This old-fashioned style might lead viewers to expect storylines that focus on community and social responsibility. More closely connected to the sitcoms of the 1950s, however, *Rolie Polie Olie* retreats into the nuclear family, rarely leaving the site of the home, resulting in interesting and limited messages about what it means to be a citizen.

Not surprisingly, there are no overt references to political citizenship within *Rolie Polie Olie*, a program designed for pre-schoolers. As Buckingham suggests, however, the show still offers viewers strong messages about what it means to be part of a community, about "notions of authority, fairness and justice, rules and laws, power and control" (177). These notions further reflect the Disney ideologies of individuality, honesty, and responsibility. The family within *Rolie Polie Olie* is clearly hierarchical, with Mr. and Mrs. Polie the dominant figures in the home. There is no question about who is in charge. In the episode "Mom's Night Out" (1999; which actually centers on Dad and the kids making dinner while Mom is out—not on Mrs. Polie's experiences out of the house), after making a mess baking a cake with the children (and hearing his wife drive up to the house), Mr. Polie says it is time to clean up and the children clean up. There is no whining or dawdling—only helping.

Mr. Polie remembers that he must clean up because he *promised* that he would not make a mess. This sense of responsibility is clear and unwavering within the show. He promised he would not make a mess, so he must clean up. Another episode, "Top Dog Fish" (1998), highlights the responsibility that family members have for one another. When the children help to take care of Olie's class fish, they ignore Spot to watch the fish. By the time the children realize that a dog is more fun than a fish, Spot has run away (though he does not actually leave the backyard). Mrs. Polie tells her children that there's "more to taking care of pets than feeding them and changing their water." The children quickly realize that they have a responsibility to Spot. As members of a family, they must pay attention to him and include him. Children, then, are prepared for citizenship by clearly highlighting their responsibilities and rights within their nuclear families. The notion of responsibility to the community, however, is limited to being nice to friends (such as a new neighbor who comes to town). There is little or no sense of social activism and participation.[5]

Economic citizenship is also only indirectly expressed. The Polie family does not suffer from want. They are able to make a 17-layer chocolate cake from ingredients in the house without going to the store or thinking about the resources being used on one dessert. The

Figure 3.1 Olie and Zowie care for Olie's class fish in *Rolie Polie Olie*. *(Photo courtesy of Photofest.)*

home is always spotless, kept up by the stay-at-home mom in this one-income family. Olie has a range of toys with which to play. In the episode "Looove Bug" (1998), Olie and a friend try to impress a new neighbor, Pollie, by playing a variety of games with her, all of which require them to have specific toys (like a pogo stick or a basketball). In the end, the boys end up competing to see who can make Pollie the better "Gooey Hearts Day" card, ignoring Pollie in their quest to give her something good. Having "things"—whether they are certain toys, a fish, a dog, or a fast vacuum cleaner—comes in handy in *Rolie Polie Olie*, and these things, some of which are even anthropomorphized, are as much a part of the family as the "people."

The family also takes center stage in the lessons of cultural citizenship within *Rolie Polie Olie*. Olie does have one good friend, Billy, who is marked as different by being square rather than round. Primarily, however, the voice within this show is ultimately limited to family members. In the "Looove Bug" episode, after being bitten by a literal love bug, Olie and Billy compete for Pollie's affections. Interestingly, however, they do not actually spend any time with Pollie. Instead they play together, having fun seeing who can pogo stick higher or make the nicer card. Pollie is left out. Rather than getting upset, Pollie simply tells Mrs. Polie that she is going home. After calling the boys "goofy," Mrs. Polie tells Pollie to give them time and sends Pollie on her way. We see Pollie pass Mr. Polie as he returns home from work. Although the boys realize that Pollie has left, by this time the effect of the love bug bite that has worn off and they go off to play by themselves. Pollie is gone without a single word about how she felt or Olie's responsibility to be a good neighbor.

Perhaps this treatment of Pollie should not be surprising considering the traditional roles given to girls and women in this show. Olie's mom takes care of the home and the family in a way reminiscent of *The Donna Reed Show*. She is frequently seen in the kitchen, cooking, and cleaning. While she does go out bowling in "Mom's Night Out," the action of the show remains focused on what is going on inside the house and awaits her return to the domestic sphere where she belongs. The girl who gets the most lines in this show is Olie's little sister Zowie. Zowie appears to be around two years old and she is seen frequently wreaking havoc in the household, simply because of her enthusiasm to play with her brother. Like her mother, however, Zowie does not often leave the house (as does Mr. Polie when he goes to work or Olie when he goes to school). And, while Zowie is accepted for who she is (a mischievous two-year-old), her exuberance frequently disrupts the stability of the home. The cultural citizenship afforded girls in this show is limited by their function within the family. Similarly, Pollie, as an outsider, does not receive a voice with which to express her feelings. She accepts that she does not fit in and she leaves. Lack of acceptance within the Polie house does not mean that you play by yourself—it means that you leave.

In its "family focus," then, Disney Channel helped to create a program that not only empowers the family but also, to some extent, isolates them. Citizenship within *Rolie Polie Olie* refers to familial citizenship. There are rights and responsibilities but they are nuclear. There is little if any reference to life outside of the Polie home (although some episodes do show Olie at school). The process of international co-production undoubtedly supports this kind of micro-citizenship. References to specific places, community structures, or public events are eliminated, allowing the program's popularity in Canada, France, the United States, and any other country that wants to take a step back in time to Polieville.

Planetary Citizens: Living on *Plaza Sésamo*

Plaza Sésamo also offers children a place to "go" where they will begin to shape their identities and learn about their roles in the world. This show, produced in Mexico by Televisa and Children's Television Workshop (CTW),[6] began airing in the United States in 1995. Giving Latino children an opportunity to see Spanish-speaking adults, children, and Muppets working together and playing together offers great potential for the development of citizens. We must examine, however, what *Plaza Sésamo*, as an international co-production designed primarily for Latin American audiences, tells U.S. children about their rights and responsibilities in society.

When *Sesame Street* first aired in the late 1960s little thought was given to the show's international distribution. This was, after all, a television program designed to help pre-schoolers in the U.S. learn basic reading and counting skills. Quickly, though, in what Michael Dann referred to in *The New York Times* as "one of the more delightful and fortuitous accidents of the television medium," a number of international broadcasters expressed interest in importing *Sesame Street* (D13). Dann observed, "A lot of us who had been looking for McLuhan's 'global village' found it populated by pre-schoolers" (D13). Others, however, were not quite as optimistic about the educational benefits of the international distribution of *Sesame Street*. Critics argued that *Sesame Street* enmeshed children outside of the United States with U.S. values and U.S. culture. In other words, *Sesame Street* was seen as a tool of cultural imperialism. As a result of these criticisms and the desire to increase the potential reach of *Sesame Street*, CTW began to co-produce international versions of the program with overseas production companies. The first foreign-language versions of *Sesame Street*—in Spanish, Portuguese, and German—attempted to create programs that focused on the specific educational needs of the foreign markets. The idea was that, despite copying *Sesame Street*'s format and educational ambitions, these local language versions would better represent the values and ideals of their national or regional cultures. These initial international co-productions of *Sesame Street* were, then, sparked by the desire to avoid cultural imperialism (or at least charges of cultural imperialism). As one group of CTW insiders explained, "Exporting television programs to countries requesting them may seem to produce an inevitable uniformity of television content around the world. Our effort, however, is to produce an opposite effect—to encourage diversity to meet the needs and interests of children in different countries" (Edward Palmer et al., 122).[7]

Plaza Sésamo was, in fact, one of the first international co-productions for CTW, which now produces 21 foreign language versions of *Sesame Street*. In 1972, CTW and Televisa gathered a number of educators and researchers to explore the specific needs of Latin American school children and how to address these needs using the *Sesame Street* format. Significantly, despite Televisa's role in the co-production, not all of the members of this initial team were Mexican. The inclusion of representatives from Argentina, Colombia, and Venezuela, and later Costa Rica, Chile, Peru, Panama, and Bolivia, illustrates that the producers of *Plaza Sésamo* intended to use the program to reach audiences throughout Latin America (Diaz-Guerrero et al., 7). In fact, initial research on the part of CTW found that the countries in Latin America actually preferred to pool their resources to create one program rather than produce several versions separately (Edward Palmer et al., 112). *Plaza Sésamo* went on the air in Mexico (on one of Televisa's four commercial television stations) in 1972 supported by funding from Xerox Corporation, which received sponsorship recognition before the program (Edward Palmer et al., 112). Broadcast stations in Colombia, Ecuador, and Venezuela also planned to air the show. As of 2006, Televisa and CTW/Sesame Workshop produced ten seasons of *Plaza Sésamo* (with three more seasons scheduled for production) and the program is distributed to

17 Latin American countries and Puerto Rico, and now the United States as well.

For the second season of *Plaza Sésamo* in 1973 Televisa created 50 percent of the program content and the other 50 percent came from CTW footage. New Muppets joined some of the U.S. "regulars," and the characters were placed in a town square that was expected to be more familiar to Latin American audiences. Additionally, producers tailored a number of the educational aspects of the program for Latin American children. For example, while the U.S. program concentrated on teaching children letters, the Latin American version focused more on whole words (an approach that coincides more closely with how reading is taught in Latin America). *Plaza Sésamo* also stressed reasoning and problem solving and included segments that would build self-esteem for Latin American children. Hygiene and cleanliness were also emphasized (Meislin, C17). Finally, Rogelio Diaz-Guerrero et al. reported, "It was noticed that while Latin American subjects tend to be more attentive than the Anglo-Americans at the family level, one of the problems of Latin American societies is the lack of cooperation at the community level" (9). Therefore, some segments explicitly bolstered the idea of working with and being part of a community; being a good citizen.

The next season of *Plaza Sésamo* did not air until 1983, ten years after the second season.[8] The 130 half-hour episodes, created for $3.5 million, were distributed to 17 countries in Latin America and Puerto Rico (Meislin, C17). According to reports, this season the program focused less on reading and more on family and gender issues. Noting a distinct difference from the U.S. version, one executive for Televisa stated, "We want to show that 'Plaza Sésamo' is not a place where the sun always shines" (Meislin, C17). Televisa also brought in actors from across Latin America to offer audiences different accents and avoid association with a specific nation. Significantly, the program utilized "universal Spanish" rather than colloquialisms (Diaz-Guerrero et al., 10). And both Coca-Cola and UNICEF became primary sponsors for *Plaza Sésamo* throughout Latin America (Meislin, C17). This sponsorship continued into the fourth season, which started in the mid 1990s. Some of the Muppets were "touched up" for this season (color changes, for example) and new sets were built.

Muppets made specifically for *Plaza Sésamo* include Abelardo, Big Bird's giant parrot cousin, who is made up of bright green feathers on his body, a multi-colored tail, a pink and red head, and a yellow beak; Lola, a vivacious female Muppet who, like *Sesame Street*'s Elmo, speaks of herself in the third person; and Pancho, an Oscar the Grouch type of character who is blue and perhaps not as grouchy as Oscar. The program also incorporated live action segments produced in Peru, Argentina, Bolivia, and Colombia, and stressed the importance of children learning about the different cultures in Latin America. The program's producers further recognized the children of recent U.S. immigrants as a target audience for the program, a clear acknowledgment that *Plaza Sésamo* would now be seen in the United States.

In April 1995, coinciding with the start of the program's fourth season, Univision began testing *Plaza Sésamo* on its stations in Miami, Los Angeles, and Dallas, where the program was stripped Monday through Friday at 7:30 A.M. PBS stations in these same three markets also aired *Plaza Sésamo* on weekend mornings. In December 1995 Univision picked up *Plaza Sésamo* for the rest of its eleven stations and the program became available for all interested PBS stations. The General Manager for Univision's Los Angeles station expressed his excitement about airing the program, stating, "'Plaza Sésamo' is really the first quality children's programming in Spanish" (qtd. in Patton, B5). In 2000, Univision moved *Plaza Sésamo* to its new TeleFutura network, which targets the Spanish-speaking youth market. By 2004 *Plaza Sésamo* reportedly reached 84 percent of U.S. Hispanic households (Castleman, 57). Additionally, in at least one market *Plaza Sésamo* was broadcast right after a Spanish-language instructional program, illustrating its usefulness for teaching Spanish to English-speaking adults and children. Univision's role in bringing *Plaza Sésamo* to U.S. audiences must be considered along with those of CTW and Televisa. By examining these organizations, we can get a clearer sense of the industrial, cultural, and economic motivations that help to shape *Plaza Sésamo*'s impact on children's notions of citizenship.

CTW/Sesame Workshop is one of the most respected organizations in television. Praise is heaped on the not-for-profit creators of *Sesame Street* for producing educational and entertaining children's programming and for sustaining itself financially at a time of de-creased public funding. With the decline in federal funding, CTW has been responsible for larger portions of its budget. Consequently, while *Sesame Street*'s popularity overseas may have initially been an "accident," it soon became a financial necessity—as did the mer-chandising of toys, apparel, and other *Sesame Street* products both in the United States and abroad.

As early as 1982 a CTW spokesperson acknowledged that "reve-nues from overseas versions and product licensing provide financial support for the production of the American version" (Fraser, TG3). More recently, announcing *Plaza Sésamo*'s renewal for three more seasons, Sesame Workshop's vice president of global television dis-tribution said, "Our goal was to develop an integrated business plan with the support of key broadcast and production partners to extend the brand's message" (qtd. in Sutter, 12). This quotation obscures the brand's message, which is presumably still about educating children, in a cloud of business-speak. Increasingly the brand, along with its merchandising and licensing, seems to be more important than the brand's message. Nevertheless, CTW is necessary to *Plaza Sésamo* for its reputational capital as well as its production know-how. CTW, for example, contributes its significant library of material for use in *Plaza Sésamo* and its extensive research on educational television. Ad-ditionally, CTW brings the original *Sesame Street* brand, which connotes "quality" programming and includes a vast marketing ma-chine for the sale of products surrounding the program that in turn attracts viewers to the *Sesame Street* and *Plaza Sésamo* programs and videos.

If CTW brought educational credibility to *Plaza Sésamo*, Tele-visa brought Latino credibility. As Rhea Borja notes, "When the Mexican *Plaza Sésamo* first aired in 1973 it was seen as trying to force-feed American culture to Mexican children" (8). But, a content consultant for CTW explains that "people came to realize that this was produced in Mexico by Mexican producers and Mexican edu-cation specialists" (Borja, 8). Production of the program within Latin America and by a Latin American company gives *Plaza Sésamo* cultural legitimacy (whether deserved or not). Although Hendershot claims that versions of *Sesame Street*—regardless of its language and co-production process—are still seen as U.S. products overseas (1998, 186), in the United States, at least, *Plaza Sésamo* is considered a Latin American program. In this way, *Plaza Sésamo* functions like the imported British shows discussed in Chapter 2 by using its national affiliation to increase its value. Televisa's involvement with *Plaza Sésamo* undoubtedly contributes to this branding.

Within the Latin American community, Televisa had to work hard to make sure that *Plaza Sésamo* appealed to the Latin American export markets as well as the Mexican market. Televisa's overall emphasis on export became apparent in the 1980s, at the same time that, as America Rodriguez explains, the Hispanic market in the United States "had been created and recreated as a pan-ethnic national minority" (369). Signifying the growing interest in the "Hispanic" market, Coca-Cola became a sponsor for the 1983 season of *Plaza Sésamo*. Significantly, this increased emphasis on export occurred around the same time as the decline in the Mexican economy when Televisa found itself in need of export dollars in order to sustain itself. As John Sinclair notes, "The strategy which Televisa has followed . . . has been the reduction of imports and the increase of exports, an ironic inversion of what was thought to constitute media dependency or imperialism in the 1960s and 1970s: whereas the United States exported out of a position of strength in the world market, Televisa . . . does so out of a position of weakness" (1990).

Although not a producer of *Plaza Sésamo*, Univision is important as *Plaza Sésamo*'s primary outlet for reaching Latino children in the United States. While many of the PBS stations tend to ghettoize *Plaza Sésamo*, airing it with other Spanish-language programs often early in the mornings, Univision works actively to promote *Plaza Sésamo*. During *Plaza Sésamo*'s initial season in the United States, Univision provided CTW with a $75 million grant to create supporting materials that stations could distribute to audience members ("La Promesa Programs/New York") These pamphlets instructed parents on how to discuss elements of *Plaza Sésamo* with their children in a "participatory and interactive manner" ("La Promesa Programs/New York"). By creating these educational materials, Univision gained publicity for the program's broadcast in the United States and encouraged viewers to watch the program. Certainly the potential for high ratings supported Univision's decision to pick up *Plaza Sésamo*; however *Plaza Sésamo* also fit into Univision's business and marketing strategies in other ways.

First, Univision was, until recently, partly owned by Televisa and had the right of first refusal for all of Televisa's programs in the United States. This connection made *Plaza Sésamo* readily available to Univision and probably at a fair price. Additionally, as demonstrated by Dávila, among others, Univision has been consistently invested in creating the concept of the Hispanic market in the United States (62). One of Univision's main goals has been to connect audiences across nationalities and avoid the segmentation of audiences on the basis of country of origin. This concept of the general "Hispanic" audience certainly dovetails with *Plaza Sésamo*'s production strategies and allows Univision to continue to create for advertisers the concept of the generic Hispanic viewer—even at a very young age. In fact the move of the program to TeleFutura indicates Univision's attempt to segment the audience by age rather than nationality. Finally, *Plaza Sésamo*'s appeal for Univision very simply came from advertisers who expressed immediate interest in the program and hence in the Hispanic market. According to Augustin Martinez, the general manager for the Los Angeles Univision station when *Plaza Sésamo* began airing there, "There will be no commercial breaks within the entire show, but the flexibility to sell adjacencies was the kind of incentive we needed to pick up the show" (qtd. in Freeman, 1995, 6). Burger King, for example, planned to take a "significant position" in the four minutes before and after the program, perhaps as a counter to McDonald's controversial sponsorship of *Sesame Street* on PBS (Freeman, 1995, 6). *Plaza Sésamo* has proven successful on Univision. According to Carole Postal, CTW's regional vice president of sales, marketing and licensing for the Americas, in its first week as a nationwide broadcast, *Plaza Sésamo* was Univision's highest rated children's show (66).

The success of *Plaza Sésamo* in the United States undoubtedly excited the program's producers. The growing Latino market in the United States and the recognition of this audience by advertisers and television executives has been well documented. Although interest in the Latino market is not new, the 1990 census identified Hispanics as the fastest growing minority in the United States (Deitz, 32). In the mid 1990s, more than 49 percent of children ages two–11 living in Los Angeles County were identified as Hispanic (Postal, 66). Additionally, Hispanic Americans, research showed, were very loyal to brands and spent more money on their children than non-Hispanics (Castleman, 57). Certainly, by the early 1990s, the pan-ethnic Hispanic audience had been successfully constructed as a significant market segment within the United States. The possibility to prosper from this market would be clear to Televisa, which saw potential in the U.S. Spanish-speaking audience in the early 1960s when it initially founded the television network that would become Univision. And CTW soon recognized the growing Hispanic community in the United States as a source of additional revenue. In 1996, Postal wrote in *Playthings*:

> At CTW, we are taking the 'Plaza Sésamo' show and the licensed product we have developed from it to what is essentially undeveloped territory. Our early growth plan is to fill a market void with specifically targeted product based on 'Plaza Sésamo.' However, we believe there are strong crossover opportunities beyond the Latino market, once we have taken the time to let awareness build for the program and its new characters.... With the untapped and fast-growing Hispanic market effectively serviced, we look forward to a natural progression of crossover for these products to the Anglo and other markets, and to a healthy sharing of Spanish-English learning tools by all children. (66)

This "crossover" questionably began in 2004 when CTW started selling *Plaza Sésamo* apparel in the United States at stores such as Sears, JCPenney, and Mervyns, which are putting the clothing in their "designated Hispanic market stores" (Castleman, 57). At this time Heather Hanssen, the marketing director for Sesame Workshop, said, "For us, the *Plaza Sésamo* brand is a way to tap into the Hispanic consumer. We plan to put a big push into this product" (qtd. in Cipolla, 4).

This focus on the "Hispanic consumer" for *Plaza Sésamo* products suggests that this program may not be any different than other kids' programs in its position of children as consumers—not citizens. We must not ignore, however, that *Plaza Sésamo* does offer Latino children a glimpse of a world in which speaking Spanish is not "different" or, as recent U.S. laws suggest, "wrong." Additionally, with its focus on curriculum, *Plaza Sésamo*, like *Sesame Street*, at least attempts to teach children about the world in which they live and their places in it. *Plaza Sésamo* has clear potential to bolster the political and cultural citizenship of Spanish-speaking pre-school children. We must examine what *Plaza Sésamo* actually does with this potential. First, however, we must briefly consider what programming already exists for Latino children.

According to Barbara Franklin's analysis of Latino representations in U.S. children's television programs, "television portrayals of ethnicity, whether good or bad, fair or unfair, are most likely to affect those children who are already among the most vulnerable" (104). She presents Latino children as incredibly vulnerable in this way because they "face daily challenges to their self-esteem from a society in which they occupy a position of permanent disadvantage. If televised portrayals of Latino ethnicity are also negative, if they lack . . . recognition and respect, the Latino child is then doubly victimized" (Franklin, 104). Franklin's extensive study concludes that representation of Latino culture and characters are quite limited. Despite the growing number of characters that are represented on programs, they tend to present assimilationist images in which the characters are Latino but do not have any "cultural markers" (Franklin, 337). Or Latino qualities are treated as "signs" that appear on the surface but there is no history or deep cultural understanding supporting them (Franklin, 337). Latino culture, in programs like *Dora, The Explorer* becomes defined by empty signs such as accents, names, music, and food, that are never clarified or explained.

Certainly some children's programs have made efforts to depict difference in substantial ways. One early, regional program *Carrascolendas* was produced specifically for Mexican American children in Texas. The program, which aired in the early 1970s and sounds very similar to *Sesame Street* in its use of short vignettes, an educational curriculum, and puppets, was set in a mythical town in South Texas (Williams and Natalicio, 301). According to Frederick

Williams and Diana Natalicio, "*Carrascolendas* not only gives the Mexican-American child a program in which he and his ethnic group are represented, but these media in an educational sense are adapted directly to the needs and attitudes of that child" (308). That this program did not go on to its intended goal of national PBS distribution is perhaps not surprising considering its limited target audience; however, we must recognize the importance of offering a program designed to address the particular needs and interests of bilingual children in the United States.

The U.S. version of *Sesame Street* aims to "teach differences meanwhile emphasizing many similar experiences." (Mandel, 9). According to psychiatrist Chester Pierce, *Sesame Street* "moves children to become 'planetary citizens' living in harmony with others and developing 'a wider view of the world'" (qtd. in Mandel, 12). In 1990, for example, *Sesame Street* started a four-year race relations curriculum. Each year the show would focus on one group (African Americans, Native Americans, Latinos and Asian Americans) and show viewers "that people with different skin color, hair texture or eye shape can become good friends" (Lowe, 32). Because *Sesame Street* targets a large, national audience, differences are generally utilized to show commonalities among groups rather than to explore the meanings and effects of these differences. While viewers may be happy to see Latino characters included in *Sesame Street*, the program rarely speaks to and for them in the way that cultural citizenship suggests.[9]

According to Dávila, programs that target Latino audiences specifically tend to be imported from Latin America (14). While *Plaza Sésamo* may seem to fit into this category, its position as an international co-production complicates matters. CTW's involvement, and the strict standards imposed by this U.S. organization connect the program to dominant capitalist values and ideals about education and citizenship. At the same time, however, CTW's insistence that its co-productions address the needs of the local culture may actually impede *Plaza Sésamo*'s ability to resonate with young Latinos.

Political citizenship on *Plaza Sésamo*, as in most children's programs (as discussed above), is not dealt with in terms of direct political activities such as voting or government bodies. Even if desired, the need for *Plaza Sésamo* to address a pan-Hispanic audience would make any attempts at this impossible. After all, as many scholars have noted, the "Hispanic" population is incredibly diverse. The attempt to reach a general Hispanic audience does not account for differences in race, class, language, gender, when they arrived in the United States, and their geographic location within the United States (Obler, 1). Instead, *Plaza Sésamo*, like *Rolie Polie Olie*, teaches children generalities about getting along within a community and responsibility to others. Whereas on *Sesame Street* these issues come up frequently in segments that involve the Muppets learning from adults, *Plaza Sésamo* limits these conversations and lessons. The small number of Muppets and live characters come together often as they watch television together, dance and sing, and ride the bus. Interestingly, on *Plaza Sésamo*, characters appear to spend more time in big rather than small groups, perhaps illustrating the focus on community (rather than an insular concern for family) that early versions of the program hoped to emphasize. Additionally, with its attempts to teach problem solving, *Plaza Sésamo* frequently has characters asking for and getting help from others. In one segment, for example, Abelardo sees a note fall from the sky. He can't read so he asks Carmen to help him. Carmen tells Abelardo that the message says "Throw Hay." Carmen does not understand the note, but instead of walking away, she solicits Pablo to help; Pablo then asks Pancho. Pancho understands the message and throws hay on the floor in time for a Muppet wearing a parachute to fall from the sky and land in the hay. This team work, and the fact that none of the characters moved on after performing their function, illustrates the importance of belonging to a community and one's responsibility to help others within this community.

Beyond the acknowledgement of Latino children as a significant consumer group within society, economic citizenship can also be seen in *Plaza Sésamo*'s seeming recognition of the process of work. As on *Sesame Street*, money does not change hands in *Plaza Sésamo*; however *Plaza Sésamo*'s video segments frequently stray out of the plaza and into the real world of the marketplace. While money is still not shown, the representation of real places where people buy things at least concedes the existence of the world of consumerism where people work and shop. One particularly interesting segment featured

Figure 3.2 Children gather to learn a lesson in *Plaza Sésamo*. *(Photo courtesy of Photofest.)*

a young boy explaining how he builds a model car. Images of the boy are intercut with shots of workers in a Latin American GM factory putting together a real car. Although undoubtedly unintentional, the boy's narration emphasizes the importance of doing a good job in a way that eerily foreshadows his future as a plant worker for a U.S. company that has shipped its work overseas for cheap labor. Through this type of skit, and in its inclusion of a "blue collar" worker as a live character (a type of character that does not exist in *Sesame Street*), *Plaza Sésamo* foregrounds the respectability of doing manual labor and the importance of working hard. The program to some extent, while focusing on educating Latin American children, also prepares them for a working class life. This message may seem strange to U.S. Latino children who are bombarded with messages about upward mobility and the disgrace of being working class.

The acceptance of working class status, however, is part of the cultural citizenship afforded Latino children through *Plaza Sésamo*. Clearly, the inclusiveness of *Plaza Sésamo* for U.S. children—the depiction of Spanish-speaking characters, the respect afforded to

Latino adults, children, and Muppets—grants them some amount of cultural citizenship. *Plaza Sésamo*, much more than *Sesame Street*, includes many children in singing and dancing numbers (at least one in each episode and it is usually some kind of traditional game that is played through song and dance). Seeing so many Spanish-speaking children (at the beach, in a park, on a bus) must empower Latino children to some extent. Two concerns, however, are clearly at odds with the notion of cultural empowerment on the part of children. The first, involves the use of "neutral" Spanish on the program. Rose K. Goldsen and Azriel Bibliowicz recognized in 1976 that "there is no such thing as an acultural language. Language doesn't deliver culture. Language is culture" (124). By erasing the cultural differences of language for all Latin American and U.S. Latino children, *Plaza Sésamo* limits access to cultural citizenship to those, primarily of the upper classes, who speak and understand proper Spanish. For Latino children, this form of language may actually make them feel that they are "wrong" in their use of language rather than make them feel better about speaking Spanish (Dávila, 167). The second concern about the program's potential to grant cultural citizenship is that, because this is a program produced for and starring Latin Americans, children in the United States will still not see their experiences and their voices represented (Dávila, 162). Additionally, because the program needs to reach large international audiences of Latin Americans it, like other Hispanic programs described by Dávila, "completely eliminates and marginalizes cultural differences in the name of 'universal similarity,' among and across Latina subgroups" (163). In this way, while cultural citizenship is afforded to Latinos, they are recreated as a new generalized culture of Latinos or Hispanics. Rodriguez refers to this process as the "denationalization and then renationalization of members of a social construct called Hispanic USA" (371). By delocalizing the program, to make it accessible for international export, *Plaza Sésamo* weakens the meanings of cultural citizenship for Spanish-speaking audiences by eliminating the connections between nation and culture. What is left is a washed out cultural citizenship that relies primarily on (official) language to create a pan-ethnic Hispanic culture, and in the process "relegates U.S. Hispanics to the level of consumers rather than producers of representations of Latinadad" (Dávila 163).

We can see then that although *Plaza Sésamo* makes attempts to create a sense of citizenship for its young viewers, the program's international considerations limit its potential. In the appeal to international audiences, *Plaza Sésamo*, like *Rolie Polie Olie*, must make compromises. A program like *Plaza Sésamo*, which has limited international appeal and a strong curricular agenda, appears to have a greater chance of promoting citizenship. The program's need, however, to speak to Latin American audiences first, limits its ability to empower Latino children whose lives and cultures are very different. Like *Plaza Sésamo*, *Rolie Polie Olie* presents a limited depiction of difference. In this case, the program's need to conform both to international requirements and to the Disney ideology results in a show that promotes family structure even at the expense of individuality. In both cases, however, we see that the primary goal of the co-producers is to create a strong market for ancillary products. In this way, we may begin to believe that consumer citizenship really is both inevitable and necessary. International co-production, as a harbinger of globalization, clearly exemplifies a production model that promotes this representation of citizenship for children.

4 / Global Truths

Documentaries for the World

The ability of television to educate its viewers as citizens and shape their ideas about citizenship perhaps most obviously plays out in documentaries. As David Hogarth explains, global television has the potential to "document places and issues of collective importance for citizen-viewers around the world" (2). With their collaborative production and distribution techniques, international co-productions provide unique opportunities for documentaries. We must explore, then, what the international co-production, as a particular form of global television, does with its potential to depict the world for international audiences.

Although a widely researched topic, film and television documentaries are generally studied in seemingly homogenous ways. Books about filmic documentary tend to start with Robert Flaherty or John Grierson and explore the documentary's ability to enlighten viewers about the world. More recent studies of such documentaries that include mention of television documentary, particularly since the 1980s, tend to dismiss these programs whose "artistic quality was limited and whose veracity was sometimes questionable" (Ellis and McLane, 294). Similarly, research on television documentary, a smaller and more recent field of study, tends to make large generalizations about the format, focusing on these programs as products of the global conglomerates that often fund their production. While, acknowledging the significance of the international market in television's documentary production, these researchers generally avoid intense explorations of the relationship between contemporary documentary production and the kind of culture that is created in the process. Focusing on international co-production, this chapter will explore the theoretical underpinnings of such television documentaries and the resulting thematic, ideological, and cultural statements that these programs create. Ultimately, internationally co-produced documentaries, in their attempts to appeal to international audiences for branded niche channels, offer particular representations of their subjects that must be supported with a specific kind of evidence in order to shape citizens that sustain commercial capitalism.

The history of the relationship between U.S. television documentaries and the international market will first be examined, followed by a consideration of the epistemological questions surrounding such documentaries. The chapter will conclude with two case studies: *The Nazis: A Warning from History*, a co-production of A&E and the BBC that aired on The History Channel in 1998, and *Jesus: The Complete Story*, a co-production of The Discovery Channel and the BBC from 2000.

Documentaries in the New Television Environment

Although documentary programming was initially the province of educational television, the 1960s saw such programming increase on the United States' three major networks. As Michael Curtin explains, at this time, multiple pressures came to bear on the networks. Investigation by the Federal Communications Commission (FCC) for industrial practices, political pressure by the federal government, and a leveling off of the U.S. programming market instigated the production of documentaries with a particular social and political agenda. The high cultural value of documentaries, particularly those that tackled social and political issues, allowed the networks to illustrate that television was more than a vast wasteland (Curtin, 82). The high prestige of documentaries also helped to sell network programs in Europe, which provided a significant portion of the networks' syndication market (Curtin, 72). Social and political documentaries elevated U.S. programming above mere representations of sex and violence, justifying the European broadcasters' import of U.S. television shows (Curtin, 82). And finally, these documentaries allowed the networks to fulfill the government's request that they distribute programming overseas with pro-American messages (Curtin, 88). At this time, Curtin explains, television was seen as a "crucial medium that would help illiterate populations see beyond the boundaries of tribe, custom, and tradition" (80). Television was considered a tool for modernizing "underdeveloped" nations. Furthermore, global television was expected to unify the Free World around pro-American ideologies. Documentaries like *Brazil: The Rude Awakening* (CBS, 1961) and *Angola: Journey to War* (NBC, 1961) were seen as a powerful means of communication to potential partners in the Cold War. These 1960s documentaries, then, were strongly shaped by their functions in the international market and their national origins. Their examinations of political and social issues was marked by their intention to promote U.S. ideals and modern development to viewers overseas.

The networks' interest in documentary production, however, was short lived. By the 1970s, with the pressures off of them, the networks returned to a focus on entertainment. Documentary programming was picked up by the newly formed Public Broadcasting Service (PBS), which frequently acquired these programs from overseas or coproduced the shows with international partners. PBS' dominance of U.S. documentary programming remained in place until the late 1980s, severely limiting the number of documentaries seen on U.S. television. Quoted in *Variety*, one documentary producer described the U.S. market as "particularly tough" ("Docu Firm Stretching Out with Fiction Coproductions," 117). This condition continued until the late 1980s and early '90s when the spread of cable both opened up space for niche channels and generated an interest in low-cost programs that could fill airtime (Haley, 46).

Documentaries had many benefits in the new television environment. These programs could be sold easily overseas, where many

European broadcasters still applied their public service standards; they were relatively inexpensive to produce and acquire; and, with the proper choice of topic, they could easily be re-run without losing their currency (Hogarth, 31). Documentaries could also be used to program specialty channels (Fursich, 141–142). Niche cable networks as diverse as MTV, E!, and A&E used inexpensive documentaries to round out their schedules. Oftentimes, these documentaries were the only original programming offered on these networks, which, at least initially, scheduled many off-network programs. These documentaries had a double onus of not just providing information, but doing so in a way that matched the specialty networks' brands and appealed to their target audiences. Early on, shows such as MTV's *The Real World* illustrated that a program about "real life" could also be considered entertaining.

Furthermore, the documentary format cultivated its own niche audience by appealing to regular viewers of PBS documentaries. The success of documentary channels such as The Discovery Channel and The Learning Channel, as well as the popularity of documentary offerings on other specialty channels (such as *Biography* on A&E), led to an increase in the number of documentary channels. In 1995 A&E started The History Channel and Discovery started The Military Channel.

The 24-hour documentary channels strove to create programming that brought in audiences, advertisers, and ultimately money. Unlike the occasional documentary scheduled on PBS, these documentaries were responsible for generating ratings. They needed to inform and entertain (not necessarily in that order). First and foremost, they had to be documentaries that people wanted to see. Topics such as science, nature, travel, and health, all presented in a non-controversial fashion, dominated and continue to dominate the documentary channels (Fursich, 145). Historical documentaries, for reasons similar to those discussed in Chapter 1 in relation to historical fiction, also proved successful in the international arena. Relying heavily on computer generated images and reenactments, these documentaries attempt to serve the viewers' "desire to feel rather than know" (Hogarth, 114). As Cynthia Chris explains, such documentaries "emphasize sensationalism, promote the entertainment industry . . . , or offer content of dubious historic or scientific value" (11). Richard Kilborn and John Izod describe a common critique of these documentaries as "mostly a bland form of programming which will not stir up controversy" (179). Jack Ellis and Betsy McLane write that what they find "insidious for the documentary tradition is that the merchandise in these cases often became far more important to the presenting channel than anything the documentarian might have to say on the subject" (295). Hogarth concurs with the declining importance of the subject matter, writing that these channels are "selecting topics as much for their digital spin-off potential as for their intrinsic truth or significance" (114).

As will be discussed below, with their success many of the documentary channels quickly entered a stage of expansion. Several of the documentary channels spread overseas, targeting audiences in Europe, Asia, Latin America, and occasionally Africa. Programming, therefore, was evaluated not just for its potential in the United States but also for its international playability. The extension of documentary cable channels encouraged the production of programming that could be screened on cable networks all over the world.

In an attempt to appeal to international audiences and advertisers, according to Elfriede Fursich, global "non-fiction entertainment" programs tend to be (at least overtly) non-critical and non-political (132). These programs, she writes, must be "international enough to generate wide sales but also 'neutral' enough (not reflecting or upsetting specific national interests, tastes or themes) to appeal to a global audience" (Fursich 137–138). Science, nature, travel, and health are subjects that easily generate this kind of universal appeal, as long as they are "non-offensive, non-political, non-investigative or culturally constrained" (Fursich, 145). As with the historical narratives discussed in the first chapter, the goal of global documentaries, then, was to focus on a subject that was appealing enough to generate viewer interest, but not too culturally specific to tie the program to any one nation. This situation was enhanced by the growing trend of co-production, which often allowed the various producing partners to re-edit, or reversion, the program for their national markets. The ability to localize the documentaries by removing offending material, shifting the theme of the program to match national interests, and changing the narrator to someone local all contributed to the "glocalization" of the international documentary. For example, the U.S. broadcast of the 1987 international co-production *Reach for the Skies* (CBS International, BBC, and Turner Broadcasting) on Turner Broadcasting Station removed references and segments related to air vehicles created outside of the United States (Seigel, 33). This ability to localize, which in some sense removes the power of global documentaries to share culture around the world, must still begin with a single topic and approach that is acceptable to all of the co-production partners.

The difficulties involved in creating a documentary co-production are undoubtedly outweighed by the benefits to producers. Not only do co-producing partners help with financing, but also, as with other co-production ventures, they allow for a cultural exchange that makes the program easier to sell into additional markets and offer additional resources. As explained by an executive from New York's public station WNET at a panel on documentary co-production, "foreign partners can offer things other than funding—such as experience, equipment, facilities, and production personnel" (qtd. in Seigel, 32). Additionally, co-production partners can increase the "pool of potential subjects" for documentaries by easing access to research, images, interviewees, and photographs (Solomon, 1998).[1] The importance of international co-production for documentary is apparent in the estimate that by the mid 1990s almost 25 percent of international co-productions for television were documentaries; by 2001 industry research estimated that documentaries comprised the "world's single most common type of coproduction" (Hogarth, 31). U.S. co-production partners, especially the major cable networks, were considered particularly important as they could increase interest in the project among other possible investors and distributors. One documentary producer recommended attaching a U.S. partner like Discovery first, thus making it easier to get other co-production partners (Seigel, 33). U.S. documentary cable outlets participated heavily in co-productions. In 1996, National Geographic estimated that one-third of all of its productions were co-productions (Samuels, 15).

Two the most popular forms of recent co-produced documentaries are the historical documentary and the science documentary.

The former very quickly became the staple of The History Channel, which has in jest also been called the "War Channel" or the "Hitler Channel." Historical documentaries are often lower budget programs that attempt to unravel some sensationalistic element of the past using historical footage, interviews, and reenactments. Science documentaries, frequently associated with The Discovery Channel, are generally larger budget, technologically sophisticated documentaries. They make use of experts and digital imaging to explain some element of science or nature. Sometimes these programs attempt to unravel mysteries of the past or well known myths by re-creating the world in which these events occurred (such as Discovery's highly popular *Walking with Dinosaurs*).

Internationally co-produced documentaries bring together many of the concerns mentioned in the previous chapters. Like the historical fiction programs discussed in Chapter 1, documentaries face problems about the representation of space, place, nationalism, globalism, and localism. Documentaries, particularly historical documentaries, must represent nations without celebrating or maligning any particular country; they must encourage the understanding of different places that may no longer even exist. The importance of branding for cable channels, discussed in Chapter 2, is seen in the documentary channels' efforts to establish themselves as trustworthy, knowledgeable, and relevant. As with mystery programs and prestige dramas, documentary channels often rely on British productions (particularly those from the BBC) to instill an air of quality. And certainly, as with the children's programs in the previous chapter, documentary channels must carefully carve out their representations of citizenship as they attempt to balance their focus on consumerism and enlightenment.

One thing that might tie all of these issues together for documentary programming more so than an analysis of the knowledge/content put forth in these internationally co-produced documentaries is a consideration of the types of knowledge that they value. This chapter will argue, therefore, that the international co-production process and the globalization of the major documentary producers result in documentaries that promote certain frameworks of knowledge. The characteristics of the documentaries produced through the process of international co-production—such as the tendency to focus on science, history, and nature in a non-critical and non-controversial manner—are used to encourage particular ways of knowing that foreground objectivity, rationality, and progress with the ultimate result of bolstering consumer capitalism. By looking at the ways of knowing, the basis for the truth claims within the documentaries, we can see that these documentaries are, in many ways, not much different than the television documentaries of the 1960s as they promote Western notions of the modern, the real, and the true. They must do so, however, without making claims about particular nations and while promoting the values important to global consumerism.

The Epistemology of Co-Produced Documentaries

To understand how co-produced television documentaries present and represent the world first requires an examination of documentaries in general and their aesthetic, industrial, and social operations. We must further consider the relationship between documentary and the nation in terms of the genre's function to provide knowledge about communities and the world in which they operate.

As many theorists have argued, simply defining "documentary" is a difficult task. Bill Nichols explains that the definition of documentary is always "relational and comparative" (2001, 20). In general, however, Nichols argues that documentaries are films that attempt to represent the world (3). Dirk Eitzen defines documentary as a film about which we can ask: "Might it be lying?" (89). In other words, documentaries are presumed to be true. To support this truth, documentaries mobilize various forms of evidence and rhetorical devices. In the past, many of these elements of documentary were based on nationally accepted truths and common sense. Many early and well known documentaries, in fact, were primarily designed to support national goals. From John Grierson's Empire Marketing Board in the United Kingdom to the United States' Resettlement Administration to the 1960s television networks, documentaries have been used to create (as well as criticize) national communities. Documentaries, like other forms of history, help to determine what is remembered and what is forgotten within the national memory.

The move to documentary production by conglomerates with global aspirations and their utilization of the international co-production process has complicated this matter, making the use of national forms of knowledge difficult—and in many cases undesirable. Instead, knowledge is disconnected from its national associations and presented in a manner that allows it to universalize its "national biases" (Shumway, 358). Discursively, many documentaries, including most of the television documentaries produced for cable channels, attempt to demonstrate their "objectivity." Nichols explains, however, that even objective documentaries, which claim simply to present evidence for viewers to evaluate, are hiding an ideological or institutional bias. Nichols writes: "What objectivity itself cannot tell us is the purpose it is meant to serve since this would undercut its own effectiveness. . . . And yet what we need to know above all else about this complex and highly persuasive form of discourse is the purpose to which it is put" (1991, 198). To support their objective findings, global television documentary producers rely on scientific research, historical "facts," eyewitnesses, technology, and academic experts. These seemingly unbiased and indisputable forms of evidence are used to "shape historical events into a meaningful narrative framework" (Ashuri, 424). In addition to giving us information about the world, global documentaries shape the way we think of knowledge and truth. As Vinay Lal explains, "In our era of globalism, then, when the same icons of popular culture are to be found throughout the world, trade disputes come under the jurisdiction of the WTO, and financial markets are inextricably linked, nothing is more global than modern knowledge and its categories" (109).

The support of objective science can be seen as part of a larger attempt to encourage the "ordering of all modern societies according to a particular narrow principle of reason" (Tomlinson, 145). Examining the nature of cultural imperialism, John Tomlinson determines that what is really at stake with the expansion of global culture is the spread of what Cornelius Castoriadis terms the social imaginary significations of Western society. Castoriadis writes:

the construction of its own world by each and every society is, in essence, the creation of a world of meaning, its social imaginary significations, which organize the (presocial, 'biologically given') natural world, instaurate a social world proper to each society (with its articulations, rules, purposes, etc.), establish the ways in which socialized and humanized individuals are to be fabricated, and institute the motives, values and hierarchies of social (human) life. (41)

Applied to internationally co-produced documentaries, we can see that the attempts to objectively present science and history for global audiences, in the end, promote the social imaginary significations of Western, modern thought, which ultimately, Tomlinson explains, shapes how people conceptualize what is possible and what is good and right (167). What is important, then, is not necessarily the content of the documentaries, but the underlying strategies that are used to make truth claims about the world in which we live. Arguing against the dismissal of contemporary science documentaries as postmodern appeals to spectacle and hyperrealism, Jos van Dijck writes, "Perhaps more interesting than identifying and lamenting the postmodern genre of science documentary is to examine how the multimedia mix of words, sounds and images transforms our *claims* to knowledge" (21).

We must, therefore, consider the ways that internationally co-produced documentaries ask viewers to understand and evaluate science and history, and how these methods result in particular representations that support dominant assumptions of reason, modernity, progress, and development that cultivate economic citizenship. To do so we will now examine two co-produced documentaries and how they promote particular social imaginary significations of Western thought. First, we will consider the World War II documentary *The Nazis: A Warning from History* and its grounding in humanist thought as a means of understanding the Holocaust. Then we will turn to *Jesus: The Complete Story* to consider the role of experts, science, and technology in replacing religious myths. These case studies will illustrate the powerful impact resulting from the attempt to create documentaries that appeal to global audiences who must all be engaged as consumer citizens in a branded environment.

History's War: Internationally Co-Produced Documentaries of the Holocaust

"People want to understand history. And history is about people and the decisions they either made or didn't make, and how and why they made them."

MICHAEL MOHAMAD, THE HISTORY CHANNEL'S
SENIOR VICE PRESIDENT OF MARKETING (12)

"The secular world is the world of history as made by human beings. Human agency is subject to investigation and analysis, which it is the mission of understanding to apprehend, criticize, influence and judge."

(SAID, 878)

Despite concerns expressed both by right wing conservatives and postmodern critics that people are increasingly forgetting the past and ignoring history, since the 1990s television (as well as film) has illustrated a growing interest in history. For various industrial reasons, including those discussed above in relation to documentary in general, producers and programmers recognized the appeal of historical documentaries. Many of these cable networks attracted older viewers who were gripped by their past and their place within it, an interest amplified in the 1990s by the upcoming end of the millennium (Solomon, 6). Furthermore, historical documentaries were popular overseas as well as in the United States, thus representing a program type with increased revenue potential.

The growing number of historical documentaries reflected (and promoted) larger questions of historical representation within the mass media that have long been a point of contention. Alejandro Baer frames the debate in terms of the rhetoric of apocalypse versus the rhetoric of optimism. Those who see historical representation of the mass media as apocalyptical are epitomized by the Frankfurt School, which argues that the sensationalistic, melodramatic tendencies of the media opposes the reasoned enlightenment required for historical understanding. Optimists, on the other hand, argue that the combination of televisual techniques with historical subjects makes history more accessible for audiences and allows viewers to understand history on a more emotional and "human" level (Baer, 492–493). In terms of the debate on representation and history, the Holocaust is frequently put forth as one of the more complicated moments for mass mediated representation.

Despite the many difficulties in the depiction of the Holocaust and World War II, The History Channel (created by A&E in 1995) quickly earned the nickname of the "War Channel" or the "Hitler Channel" by airing a steady stream of documentaries about World War II. The source of these documentaries varied. Some were older films (from PBS, the BBC, or A&E) that The History Channel acquired cheaply, some were acquired from independent producers, and some were produced or co-produced by The History Channel itself. Common assumptions about U.S. television would suggest that the Holocaust—at least documentaries about the Holocaust—would not be the most appropriate subject for commercial television. After all, documentaries about mass murder and terror hardly promote consumerism. We must examine, then, The History Channel's decision to focus on this time period. We must also consider the evidence used in these documentaries and what story they tell viewers not only about World War II and the Holocaust but also about national communities and citizenship.

There are several industrial factors that support the production and programming of World War II documentaries. In addition to the backlog of documentaries that exist about this event, such documentaries are frequently inexpensive to produce and garner public interest. Documentaries specifically about the Holocaust can easily draw on the horrors of this historical period to propose questions that engage audiences who cannot quite fathom how this happened. Many documentaries about the Holocaust are co-produced, sometimes with various European partners but primarily with the BBC, which takes a surprisingly strong interest in the topic. These programs have international appeal and they benefit from international involvement as this makes resources (such as images, data, and interviews) more easily available. While the financial appeal of such documentaries can be easily explained, the cultural and social reasoning behind them, particularly on a commercial cable network, is perhaps a bit more confusing. The History Channel, however, has made this work—primarily because of the networks' history, brand, and position in the marketplace.

The History Channel premiered in January of 1995 as a subsidiary of A&E Television Networks and quickly became one of the fastest growing cable networks. A&E had been successful with its historical documentaries, and additional research illustrated that an audience existed in the specialized cable audience for a 24-hour network of documentaries. This research proved correct. In 1996 The History Channel reached approximately 19.2 million homes (Zoglin, 101); by 1998 the channel was seen in 47 million U.S. homes and in 50 countries (Worrell, 76). Initially, to keep costs down, The History Channel did not produce its own programs (Taves, 8). Programming came from the existing A&E library as well as licensed narrative films with historical themes from the United States and overseas (Taves, 9). Although Brian Taves argues that the use of non-U.S. documentaries allowed The History Channel to air alternative (non-nationalistic) views of history (9), over time the network decreased its number of acquired programs and increased its original productions. In 1998 the network estimated that it aired 40 percent original programming with the goal of increasing that number to 75 percent in the next year (Worrell, 76). Throughout the 1990s, The History Channel targeted a primary demographic of older, educated, and well-off men. In 1998, Dan Davids, the executive vice president and general manager of The History Channel, described The History Channel viewers as "mostly well-educated, 65% male, 35–54 year olds" (qtd. in Worrell, 76). To appeal to this target audience, The History Channel played a good number of films about war and military actions many of which were nationalistic in their descriptions of military victories and defeats.

Regardless of some criticisms of the excessive reliance on World War II documentaries, The History Channel created a successful and strong brand image with slogans like "all of history, all in one place" and "where the past comes alive." The History Channel, seeking the "cultural mantle of PBS" (Taves, 14), attempted to brand the network as "an avenue to actually experience history" (Mohamad qtd. in Kim,

6). The History Channel, then, cultivated a quality brand image that could appeal to people by making history accessible and interesting. A&E very quickly chose The History Channel to lead A&E's expansion into the international market. According to Nickolas Davatzes, the president and CEO of A&E Television Networks, The History Channel was chosen to be A&E's "international flagship" because of its universal appeal (McConville, 60). By the end of 1995, its first year in operation, The History Channel introduced a three-hour program block into the United Kingdom through BSkyB, with plans to expand into a full channel (McConville, 60). In 1996 The History Channel partnered with a regional television company to enter Latin America with a program block ("History Channel Launching in Latin America," 16). And in 1997 a deal was made with a local company to launch operations in the Nordic and Baltic regions (Katz, 39). In fact, by 1997 The History Channel had deals with the United Kingdom, France, Italy, Scandinavia, the Middle East, Israel, and Latin America (Galetto, 44). Then in 1998 a company in Spain signed on to create indigenous language versions of the channel for Spain and Portugal (Donohue, 16). And in 1999, additional agreements were imminent for Japan, South East Asia and India, and China, with the network also working on deals for Pakistan and Turkey (Forrester, 42). In each of these regions, The History Channel partnered with local companies and created a programming mix of A&E-owned shows and local programs. According to Mike Galetto, A&E/The History Channel executives indicated that "production of programs for specific markets as well as shows that can be used globally is sure to increase" (44). This mix of programming highlighted the balance that The History Channel needed to create between the nationalistic pull of history and the international push required by the global brand.

The determination to produce programs that could appeal to the global audience of The History Channel shaped their form and content. According to John Cuddihy, the vice president and managing director of the International Division of A&E Television Networks, the company did not want to spread the "American point of view of history around the world;" instead, Cuddihy explained, "We're consciously making programming with a global appeal" (qtd. in Galetto, 44).

This drive for global appeal resulted in programs with many of the same qualities as the historical shows discussed in Chapter 1: a strong focus on international or local communities and a downplaying of nationalism; a reliance on international sets and "actors;" a focus on well known events; and a tendency to assign blame only to acceptable "bad guys." The programming on The History Channel, then, was designed to appeal to a global audience without being U.S.-centric. At the same time, however, the kinds of programs created for this global market could not avoid promoting the social imaginary significations embedded within U.S. (and Western) society as these were, after all, commercial endeavors.

World War II offered a compelling topic that could be explored in ways that could produce universal appeal. Commenting on the deal with the company in Spain, one A&E executive said, "We have a lot of war material. We won't put anything on to offend the people there, but the appetite for World War II programming [in Spain and Portugal] is insatiable" (qtd. in Donohue, 16). This insight into the approach to the international market is telling, illustrating that The History Channel saw World War II as an internationally appealing topic that could be produced without offending audiences in any particular nation. Controversy could be avoided specifically by focusing on the people who suffered or the people who caused the suffering.

According to A&E executive Davids, A&E and The History Channel developed separate identities because "A&E focuses on people and History focuses on events" (qtd. in Flinn, 6). As indicated by the quotation at the beginning of this section, however, the way that these events tended to be explained turned on the decisions made by individuals. In this way, The History Channel's documentaries reflect Edward Said's description of humanism when he writes, "Humanism is centered upon the agency of human individuality and subjective intuition, rather than on received ideas and approved authority" (878). Said probably was not a fan of The History Channel and its globalized, Western-centered view of history; however, that The History Channel relied on notions of the rationality, autonomy, and an unchanging core of humanity seems clear. By focusing on individual "humans," particularly in analyses of the Holocaust, The History Channel presented a somewhat horrific moment of history without controversy and without condemning the multiple nations that did very little to stop the Nazis. In a sense, the Holocaust documentaries on The History Channel represent an extreme version of the forms of representations discussed in Chapter 1. The nation (Germany) is clearly depicted as evil; the international community (the Allies) is seen as the saviors of the smaller local groups (the Jews, Roma, homosexuals) who are innocent victims of the Nazi atrocities. Furthermore, the ideas about citizenship discussed in Chapter 3 also play out within these documentaries, as they tend to depict the Holocaust as caused not simply by the stripping of the victims' political citizenship but perhaps more importantly by their eradication as economic citizens who could own property and cultural citizens who could be depicted positively within and contribute significantly to German culture.

Many critics of documentaries on the Holocaust express concerns about the potential of humanizing the Nazis. In an argument for documentaries that mobilize modernist aesthetics, Hayden White writes that creating a traditional documentary about the Holocaust risks " 'humanization' of the perpetrators" (31). This humanization of the Nazis is exactly what is necessary, however, for global documentaries. Writing about British television coverage of the Holocaust in 1995, Judith Petersen explains that the BBC, as well as the commercial television stations in England, dealt only minimally (if at all) with the British government's complicity, or at least lack of action (258). To avoid creating controversy, the documentaries tend to stay away from examination of the actions of various world governments and instead "blame" the particular pathology of a group of people (while still acknowledging that these people were shaped by their societies) and question how "human beings" could do such horrible things. One producer working on a BBC co-production on the Holocaust explained, "It always comes back to concentrating on the focus on the human being inside the backdrop of whatever's going on" (qtd. in Solomon, 6). The essentialist appeal to notions of humanity, reason, and autonomy allow the programs to find a common denominator among international viewers while not suggesting that they themselves may have done something similar in such situations. These documentaries, then, operate in two major ways. First they focus on individuals through their topics (for example, *Hitler's Henchmen*), evidence (interviews, diaries), and structure (focusing on how particular people affected the course of the war). Second, these documentaries ascribe many of these actions to "human nature" run amok within a society that supported and rewarded cruelty. In some ways, showing how the Nazi perpetrators acted "rationally" according to their own understanding of the world illustrates that reason did not fail, but was misused by particular psychotic individuals. Reason and rationality are thus reaffirmed as primary social imaginary significations.

Perhaps no program went further to analyze the perpetrators of the Holocaust than *The Nazis: A Warning From History*. This five-hour miniseries produced by the BBC and A&E in 1997 aired on The History Channel in February of 1998. Two episodes were broadcast on Sunday February 8, 1998 (9:00 P.M. EST) and then one-hour episodes on Monday–Thursday (9:00 P.M. EST). The episodes, in order, were: "Helped into Power," about the forces that allowed Nazism to take hold in Germany; "Chaos and Consent," about the chaotic mode of government created by Hitler and how this fueled his followers; "The Wrong War," about Germany's expansion throughout Europe; "The Wild East," about Germany's invasion of Poland; "The Road to Treblinka," about the events and forces that fed into the creation of the concentration camps; and "Fighting to the End," about the war with the Soviet Union and Germany's defeat.

As yet another Holocaust program on The History Channel, the miniseries received little media attention in the United States. One review, however, was very positive, praising the documentary for its coverage of new information, its large numbers of interviews, and for answering complex questions "patiently, clearly and without fear of running counter to common wisdom" (Bianculli, 112). The program was also overwhelmingly popular in the United Kingdom, getting the highest ratings ever for a documentary (Bianculli, 112). A review of the DVD release of the documentary in 2005, also very positive, concludes, "This 'warning from history' suggests that this was no isolated anomaly but something in human nature that can be let loose at any time" (LaSalle and Hildebrand, 32). Speaking about the program, its writer/producer Laurence Rees explains that the documentary was ultimately trying to understand how people could do this (Rees, 147). He concludes, "It seems to me, in a broader sense, that what we're talking about here is something that is a profound part of the human condition—the search for scapegoats, the desire to have a quiet life, the desire for personal gain, the tendency to victimize particular groups and so on" (152).

The documentary framed the actions of the Nazis as part of the "human condition" through the matter-of-fact way that many of the interviewees spoke about their past. That the individual is at the center of the series is clearly suggested in the opening of the program. Each episode begins with a tight shot of a black-and-white photograph of a young boy's face. Frequent viewers of documentaries about the Holocaust might expect that this young boy was a victim of the Nazis. As the image widens, however, we see the boy, surrounded by soldiers in Nazi uniforms, performing the Nazi salute. This introduction clearly tells us both that this program will focus on the Nazis (rather than the Nazis' victims) and that it will do so by examining individuals and their actions within the Nazi regime.

The series goes on to use some of the mainstay forms of evidence of historical documentaries: "facts" told to us by a (British) narrator; Nazi propaganda films; newsreel footage; letters and documents uncovered in archives; and audio from Hitler's speeches. A *Warning from History* is distinguished, however, by its extensive use of particular interviews. As in other Holocaust documentaries, a few of these interviews are with victims of Nazi atrocities. Most of the interviews, though, are with the perpetrators of these atrocities and those who were part of the Nazi system. Interview subjects include members and leaders of Hitler Youth organizations, German soldiers, past members of the Nazi party, German citizens who witnessed particular events, a woman who informed to the Gestapo on her neighbor, and a housekeeper for one of the Nazi leaders in Poland. Several of those interviewed had actually met Hitler. Within their interviews, these people are asked to discuss what they did during the war, how they felt at the time about what was happening, and why they did what they did. The interviewers walk a fine line between letting the subjects speak for themselves and asking them direct (and often difficult) questions; in other words, focusing on the individual without humanizing the

Figure 4.1 A young "Brown Shirt" with Hitler in *The Nazis: A Warning from History.* *(Photo courtesy of Photofest.)*

Nazis. For example, in "Chaos and Consent," the interviewer questions one woman who had sent a letter to the Gestapo implicating a neighbor as a Jewish sympathizer when she claims not to remember ever writing such a letter. As the interviewer shows her the letter, the woman claims, "The address is correct, my signature is correct. But where it comes from I don't know." She goes on, "I mean, I didn't kill anybody, didn't murder anyone." She explains that she had not even joined the Hitler youth group for girls because her father did not want her going into town at night. The documentary clarifies that the woman who had been accused did die in a camp, thus allowing the viewer to question the claim that this informant had not killed anyone. The connection is therefore made between ordinary German individuals and their complicity in the atrocities of World War II.

While some of the interviewees do not express remorse (regardless of what they may actually feel), others do illustrate an understanding of their role during the war. The episode "Fighting to the End" tells of one Nazi officer who prosecuted a German soldier who had been heard badmouthing Nazi strategy toward the end of the war. Following a perfunctory trial the soldier was hanged in his own village while his wife watched. The Nazi officer tells the interviewer, "It is terrible for a woman like that to witness her own husband, to whom she has been married for forty years or more, being hanged in front of their door by a couple of madmen." The interviewer asks "And you were one of those madmen?" He replies, "You could say that, yes." Following the war, this officer spent six years in prison for his involvement with this execution. These two examples illustrate the kinds of people who were interviewed for this documentary (from Nazi officers to everyday citizens) and the way that the documentary connects the events of World War II with the actions of people who made decisions about their own behavior. By focusing on these individuals and hearing them talk about their feelings at the time, and seeing their reactions today, viewers are asked to understand these atrocities as something done by individuals who, for the most part, made choices that their victims did not have the luxury of making. In the end, these actions are tied to the chaos of extreme nationalism and stopped by the power of the caring international community.

The documentary also attempts to create a context for the behavior of the Nazis, although not an expansive political and economic context. The series overtly rejects the notion that German citizens were somehow brainwashed into following Hitler. A *Warning from History* illustrates that the actions of the Nazis and those who supported the government stemmed *rationally* from the sadistic and psychologically twisted ideologies created by the Nazis. Interview after interview explains the reasons for particular actions. These included the economic relief offered by the Nazis (under the Nazis, Germany was "a better and safer time than today"); the self-esteem imparted by involvement in the movement ("we were somebody"); fear of being turned in by other Germans (you could resist "yes, of course, if you risked your own life, or at least your job"); and false propaganda created by the Nazis ("it was the general feeling that Jews had gone too far. Too many lawyers or theatre directors.") Using interviews, eyewitness accounts, and archival footage, *The Nazis: A Warning from History*, establishes the perverted rationality behind the Holocaust and grounds that perversion in individual people (from army officers to everyday citizens) who lacked the morality to wield the power they were given. In "Chaos and Consent," the narrator explains that Hitler's "personality determined the way in which Germany was governed." At no time does the documentary question the importance of individual people, their reason, or their autonomy. Rather, the horrors of the Holocaust occurred because human beings at their core need proper governance (though not dictated by extreme nationalism) to keep particular individuals from perverting reason to their own psychotic ends. The modern social imaginary significations of reason and humanism are reaffirmed in this documentary through the suggestion that one of the most horrible events in the recent past occurred not because there was a breakdown in how society operates and prioritizes, but because the "normal" social mode of operations were distorted and twisted by a few insane, overly nationalistic people.

While *The Nazis: A Warning From History* clearly uses eyewitness testimony and interviews, another strain of global documentaries relies on science and facts to present an "objective" representation of the world. Petersen highlights *Victory*, which she describes as a "major international co-production," as the most "objective" of British television's World War II documentaries (267). Including no eyewitness testimony or interviews, *Victory* (clearly intended for an international audience) relies primarily on archival footage, photographs, and press clippings to make its points (Petersen, 267). Petersen writes, "*Victory*'s almost obsessive privileging of the hard evidence of contemporary historical discourse over the soft evidence of memoirs and testimonies seems to reveal a determination to create a semblance of historical and objective truth" (268). This reliance on the primacy of science is another modernist, Western social imaginary signification that we see promoted in non-fiction entertainment, as will be discussed in the next case study.

The Complete Story: Analyzing Myth through Science

"I'm not a religious person, but this series is not about belief, it's about fact."

JEREMY BOWEN (QTD. IN WELLS).

Jeremy Bowen, the narrator for the British documentary *Son of God*, created controversy in the United Kingdom in 2001 when he repeatedly, and publicly, proclaimed that he was not a believer. Rather, the former Middle East reporter for the BBC claimed that he was drawn to *Son of God* for its historical and scientific information (Webb). Some Christians in the United Kingdom expressed concerns about the involvement of a non-religious man with this documentary on Christ, particularly since the publicity materials surrounding the documentary explained that the series would question several stories of the Gospel. When the documentary aired in the United States on The Discovery Channel as *Jesus: The Complete Story*, Bowen's narration was replaced with that of American actor Tom Hodgkins. This change appears to have eliminated the majority of controversy surrounding the documentary, despite the best efforts of the BBC and Discovery Communications (which co-produced the documentary along with funding from France 3) to create debate about the documentary's findings.

Both the BBC and Discovery focused their promotional campaigns on the science and technology that went into the program, with the focus of the publicity being a computer generated image of what Christ might have actually looked like. Stories on both the BBC and Discovery web sites highlighted this "scientific breakthrough" and reported on the potential controversy that a "true" rendering of the Christ of history (as opposed to the Christ of faith) might cause (Lorenzi, Webb, "BBC Unveils Hi-Tech Jesus," "Why Do We Think Christ Was White?"). The "problem" the producers expected with the rendering was that it did not match the white, blue-eyed, and noble image of Christ that is popular in most of the Western world. Instead, the Discovery web site explains that archaeological, forensic, and historical scholars created a "swarthy, coarse, vacant-eyed, short haired man" as a historically "accurate" model for Christ (Lorenzi). The controversy surrounding the rendering of Christ, however, never seemed to come. Although some press outlets in the United States ran stories about the documentary's physical depiction of Christ, many did not even review the program (and some that did simply ran edited versions of the Associated Press' short news item about the documentary).[2]

The lack of protest to the representation of Christ is at the same time both surprising and predictable. Only four years earlier, a black man cast as Christ in a New Jersey passion play received death threats ("Black Jesus in Union City," 12). So, would not a depiction of Christ as a Middle Eastern peasant generate at least a mild reaction? At the same time, however, Discovery, as a global media conglomerate would not be expected to connect itself with controversial material. This controversy, however, much like the fear of "humanizing" the Nazis in *The Nazis: A Warning From History*, was controlled by the documentary's reliance on foundational modernist ideas; in this case the truth of science as illustrated through experts and technology, which is quite possibly the foundation upon which rests all programming on The Discovery Channel.

Discovery Communications Inc. is one of the most prominent producers of global non-fiction entertainment. With operations in over 170 countries, the company currently owns (or co-owns) over 90 networks, including The Discovery Channel (which has numerous versions including Discovery Espanol, Discovery International, Discovery Asia, and Discovery Middle East), TLC, Animal Planet, and BBC America ("International Networks"). The shareholders of Discovery Communication include three of the most powerful media companies in the United States (Liberty Media, Cox Communications, and Advance/Newhouse Communications) along with Discovery's founder, John S. Hendricks (dsc.discovery.com). Discovery's international popularity is quite strong, as evidenced by the fact that, in the late 1990s Discovery became one of the few cable channels to show a profit on its international operations. As Fursich explains, Discovery is a company that relies on international programs. The channel does not "glocalize" its programming but produces programs for the global audience. Fursich writes:

By emphasizing the localizing or 'glocalizing' strategies of transnational media conglomerations over the last few years, international communication scholars tended to overlook the fact that there are still companies such as Discovery that intentionally rely on global content and programming as their core product. Beyond inexpensive voice-over changes in different languages, Discovery programs are from the outset produced to work across borders, Discovery's content is global; only its promotions tend to be local. (148)

Discovery's product is generally bought from independent producers or co-produced by Discovery, frequently with companies from other countries (Fursich, 142). Discovery's 1998 agreement with the BBC represents its most high-profile international agreement. According to the deal, Discovery and the BBC would co-produce programs and create new cable channels together (such as BBC America). Discovery also gained the right of first refusal for both co-financing and U.S. airings of all new BBC documentaries (Mifflin, 1998, 2D).[3]

The deal between BBC and Discovery was considered an important opportunity for both organizations, although some critics bristled at the spread of Discovery's documentary techniques to the BBC. One British critic likened Discovery to lead in the drinking water. Discovery, he said, would drive British documentaries into "a state of imbecility" while making them "taste better" (Sutcliffe, 14). Along with a critique of Discovery's reliance on sensationalism and dramatization of somewhat frivolous subjects, another consistent criticism of Discovery is its tendency to create documentaries within a "safe, quality environment" (Berger, 16). As the *Washington Post* television critic Tom Shales said, "They [Discovery's documentaries] tend to be apolitical, and they shy away from anything that may breed controversy" (qtd. in Berger, 16).

That Discovery agreed to co-produce, with the BBC, a documentary about the "true" story of Christ, a topic that could potentially generate a great deal of controversy, is perhaps surprising, then. The subject, however, is also a wonderfully universal one that many people around the world, regardless of their religions, would find

Figure 4.2 Liron Levo reenacts the crucifixion in *Jesus: The Complete Story* *(Photo courtesy of Photofest.)*

interesting. Christianity, furthermore, is a growing religion, especially in Latin America, Asia, and Africa (Jenkins). This documentary therefore had good potential to attract audiences throughout the world. Furthermore, Van Dijck argues that although documentaries that rely heavily on digital technologies and recreations are often critiqued as postmodern for their focus on spectacle over content (6), the technology deployed in these documentaries actually reaffirms modern notions by "anchoring the documentaries' truth-claims in accepted realist conventions" (van Djick, 15).

Jesus: The Complete Story premiered in the United States on Easter Sunday (April 15) 2001.[4] The three-hour documentary, which was broken up into three parts, cost £1.5 million—approximately $2.8 million (Wells). According to reports, *Jesus: The Complete Story* intended to focus on "facts and theories that both back up and challenge common beliefs about Jesus" (Zad, Y04) and it was an "effort at a strictly scientific investigation into the Messiah of Christendom" ("Documentary Hypothesizes," 7). This program, which focuses on the Christ of history, utilized scholarship, science, and technology both to question and support the stories of the Gospels. As one *Washington Times* reviewer observed, while some of the theories may "ruffle the feathers of some Christians who are more fundamentalist, the special is certainly thorough. The three parts feature 21 experts from the fields of archeology, theology, astrology, and even criminology" (Warner, D1). For example, historians question whether Jesus was born in a stable (since people in Palestine kept their animals in caves not stables), whether Mary and Joseph were alone when Jesus was born (childbirth was a very dangerous experience and Mary and Joseph probably had relatives in Bethlehem who would have helped), and whether Jesus worked with Judas to arrange his turn-over to the Romans (based on an updated translation of the New Testament). At the same time, scholars support the ideas that Jesus existed as a historical figure (an early historian included a reference to Jesus), that Christ's hands sweated blood in the Garden of Gethsemane (doctors have uncovered a rare medical condition that causes people to sweat blood when under extreme stress), and that a bright star was seen in the sky when Jesus was born (astronomers believe that, at this time, Jupiter was passing through the constellation of Aries making it appear like a very bright star).

High-end technology was also used to bring audiences closer to the historical Christ. Computer graphics rendered stunning images of what Palestine may have looked like while Jesus was alive by superimposing the ancient possibility over pictures of current ruins.[5] The highlight of technological innovation came in the last ten minutes of the program. Historians, archeologists, and computer specialists created a three-dimensional computer image of a first century Jew—a recreation that was promoted by BBC and Discovery as a recreation of what Christ might have looked like. According to promotional materials, to create "an image of Christ far removed from centuries of convention," the producers relied on a 2000-year-old Jewish skull along with ancient religious documents, computer software, and new forensic techniques (Lorenzi).

Most reviews of the documentary noted that the image of Christ created by the program was "a far cry from the pale, thin, long-faced, long-haired man of many depictions" (Zad, Y04). The *Washington Times* observed that the face created by the documentary is "wider, rounder and rougher" than typical depictions, and "the new image portrays Jesus as Middle Eastern with curly dark hair, dark eyes and a broad nose" (Warner, D1). Furthermore, the first century Jew rendered by the computer looks older than Jesus is typically depicted. According to historians, the hot environment and persistent sunshine generally caused wrinkles and early aging in men by their mid 30s. Furthermore, Christ more likely had short hair and a short beard (the documentary quotes a section from the Bible that states that long hair was considered "disgraceful"). And, scientists said, Christ's skin color would certainly be dark. Rather than relying on simple ethnic likelihood, one historian notes that Jesus would have to have had a dark skin tone in order to hide among the Egyptians, as the Gospels say he did. Additionally, he relies on Biblical references to Christ's genealogy (as a descendant of David), which included Afro-Asiatic ancestors who would cause him to have a darker skin tone.

Despite the numerous ways that the documentary altered the idealized Western image of Christ, the program generated little controversy. Perhaps the focus on the Christ of history and the historical fact that Christ was actually from the Middle East allowed people to accept the scientific "truths" presented by the program. As Ann Rodgers-Melnick notes, "Elements that publicists used to hype the film won't amaze anyone who attended Sunday School in the 20th century. Outside of a few fringe groups no one in America thinks Jesus was likely to have had blue eyes or blond hair" (36).[6]

The continuous mobilization of science and technology in *Jesus: The Complete Story* undoubtedly diminished the controversy surrounding the program. The documentary repeatedly referred to "remarkable discoveries in science and history," "new evidence," and "breakthroughs in science and archeology." Scientists were shown working in laboratories, historians were surrounded by books, and archeologists were wandering around ruins. These discourses of science and the fetishization of technology allowed the program to present its information as "neutral." Of course, as Michel Foucault has illustrated, this is a false objectivity that hides true motivations of power and control (84-85). Since the science is used both to support the Gospels and debunk them, we must ask why a global corporation might be interested in bolstering and tearing down one of the largest organized religions in the world. This can be related to the modernist project that seeks to replace tradition, custom, and myth with rationality and science.

One of the most interesting projects of these objective documentaries is to scrutinize traditional myths. Arash Abizadeh explains that national myths are not lies, but stories that are frequently used to inspire people within a national community (293). The attempt to hold up national myths "to rational scrutiny according to standards of truth is itself a modernist conceit" (Abizadeh, 293). It seems, in fact, that global documentaries are attempting to apply rational, secular humanist, and modern "knowledge" to traditional stories and myths whose "truth" was never necessarily significant. Derek Paget argues that "through the mass media and the information agencies, facts and information have begun to supply religion's place as a provider of certainties" (Paget, 18). At the core of this attempt is the desire to replace many of the ideals of religion with the social imaginary significations of global consumer capitalism.

Certainly there are elements of Christianity that strongly support global capitalism and the benefits that it might bring to the world. However, there are also Christian groups that question the role of global capitalism in breaking down nationalism, in focusing on wealth rather than good deeds, and in spreading the ideals of consumerism around the world. A writer in the in *National Catholic Reporter* explained that there are a number of Catholic organizations that are lobbying for "a reversal of the trends that are concentrating economic power in a few super corporations" (Ruether, 16). The rules of global capitalism, Rosemary Ruether writes, "are creating unemployment, hunger, poverty and devastation of the earth through much of the world. They need to be replaced by a process that breaks up such large corporations and favors locally owned farms and businesses that are responsible to the communities in which they are based" (16). If there are Christian organizations that are powerfully questioning the benefits of global capitalism (particularly in the markets of Asia, Africa, and Latin America where Catholicism is growing and global corporations are spreading), then perhaps there is motivation for global media corporations to attempt to question the faith. At the same time, however, this questioning cannot be overt.

Focusing on the science and technology of faith has the potential to move the center of historical understanding toward the mass mediated truth of the "neutral" sciences.

Although the topics have changed since the 1960s, television documentaries are still active in their promotion of Western ideals. Rather than being overtly nationalistic and political as they were in the '60s, today's television documentaries quietly support the ideas of consumer capitalism. The ways of knowing represented in these co-produced documentaries for the specialty cable networks promote the primacy of humanism, objectivity, rationality, and progress that bolster consumer culture. These representations also tell people what is important and what to believe. Certainly these are powerful social imaginary signifiers to be spreading throughout the world. We must also recognize, however, their impact on U.S. audiences. The promotion of objective experts who know the truth, of keeping emotions and faith out of our decision making, and of believing that technology will continue to make the world a better more enlightened place are strong messages that reinforce particular ideas about what the world is, what it should be, and what is possible.

Conclusion

Transculturation or the Expansion of Modern Capitalism

G*lobal Television Co-Producing Culture* is expressly concerned with the culture created by the industrial process of international co-productions in television. John Tomlinson suggests that we think of culture as "the resources through which people generate narratives of individual and social meaning and purpose" (173). In this case, we need to examine internationally co-produced television programs not only as artistic products but also as conveyors of ideology and identity that help to shape how people live. Television programs are clearly examples of the former. While some may argue about the quality of television shows, that they are a form of expression can no longer be denied. As for the latter, with so many people spending so much time watching television, we must accept that television has become a force that helps people—in the United States and around the world—understand the world and their places within it. International co-production, this book has argued, creates a particular kind of global culture. The industrial consequences of international co-production contribute to the resulting culture.

As demonstrated throughout the proceeding chapters, international co-productions have clear and significant benefits and drawbacks for industry participants. Access to resources such as locations, cast members, information, and documents allows for the creation of programs that have greater potential for international distribution. *Highlander: The Series, The Odyssey, Pride and Prejudice* and *Jesus: The Complete Story* all relied on multiple locations as well as international casts. Documentaries such as *Jesus: The Complete Story* and *The Nazis: A Warning from History* also required information from international sources. And children's programs such as *Rolie Polie Olie* and *Plaza Sésamo* benefited from technological and cultural international talent. Additionally, tax incentives and cost sharing allow international co-production partners to create programs with higher production values that would not be otherwise possible to fund. Miniseries, documentaries, and weekly action series can be very costly to produce. If they could have been produced at all, the programs discussed throughout this book would have been significantly different—in terms of production values, talent, and locations—without the co-production partners. Finally, co-production partners can bring to the television shows information and ideas about what will work in various markets. All of the programs discussed throughout this book benefited, at the very least in terms of distribution, from being produced by multiple international partners.

Of course, certain drawbacks also exist for international co-production. As illustrated perhaps most clearly by *Highlander: The Series*, there can be bureaucratic problems in trying to organize too many international partners. A loss of control can also lead to the reshaping of the programming. As discussed in Chapter 2, questions have been raised about the BBC's selection of television programs, which, critics have argued, is influenced by the aim to please its U.S. partners. Additionally, as the children's programs most clearly demonstrated, the need to meet regulatory requirements in multiple countries can be limiting in terms of storylines, characters, and conflict resolution.

The drawbacks to international co-productions, however, are probably most clearly seen in the cultural realm. Concerns rightfully exist about the creation of Europudding, which, in its attempt to bend to all international funding regulations and cultural norms, ends up pleasing no one. The desire to attract international audiences certainly affects all internationally co-produced programs. This drive for "universal" appeal, particularly for shows aiming for access to the U.S. market, necessitates particular aesthetics and content strictures such as high production values, Hollywood-style editing and camerawork, and the use of the English language. Additionally, in terms of content, the reliance on action-adventure, history, travel, "universal" themes (such as love, friendship, and family), spaceless narratives, and "objective" documentaries all contribute to the creation of programs that are understandable and relatable to large, diverse audiences. Interestingly, however, we must also note that most of the programs discussed in this book are not mainstream shows; they are not the prime time programs that consistently attract large audiences. Rather, the shows that are most often internationally co-produced are documentaries and children's shows, high budget miniseries, and independent or cable dramas. To some extent, though embraced by many different factions within the television industry, international co-production is still the mark of an alternative production. The majors, though involved in international co-production, have not embraced the process in the search for international audiences. Formatting, rather than international co-production, has emerged as the more prominent means of globalizing primetime, broadcast television.

Nevertheless, in the 1990s, international co-productions still demonstrated great potential to become a gateway to global culture. The examples within this book have illustrated that television in the United States in the 1990s was perhaps more "global" than it may have initially appeared. By airing co-productions, U.S. television—broadcast and cable, independent and network—offered U.S. audiences a taste of programming designed for international audiences. Furthermore, international co-productions created particular cultural constructs about the increasingly global world and highlighted certain means by which individuals could understand and navigate this world. In other words, while creating internationally appealing programs that shaped their brand images, television networks exposed audiences in the United States (and around the world) to television programs that shaped their understanding of how the world operates, how the world should operate, and what is possible.

The television programs, genres, and networks explored throughout this book demonstrate some patterns in terms of the way they ask viewers to see the world and their place within it. For instance, glob-alization is, for the most part, depicted as something that is beneficial. *Highlander: The Series, The Odyssey,* and even, to some extent, *Jesus: The Complete Story, Pride and Prejudice,* and *Plaza Sésamo* illustrate that travel provides benefits and knowledge. Nationalism, on the other hand, is viewed more negatively. In their attempt to break national borders, international co-productions frequently depict national ties as harmful. *Highlander: The Series* and *The Odyssey* are the most blatant in their attack on nationalism, but the negative effects of national ties can also be seen in *Pride and Prejudice, Cracker,* and even *The Nazis: A Warning from History,* which is in some sense a warning against per-verted nationalism. Rather than proposing national allegiances, in-ternational co-productions tend to focus on the local, most specifically the family. The children's programs *Rolie Polie Olie* and *Plaza Sésamo,* along with many of the fictional narratives discussed throughout *Global Television,* indicate the benefits of strong family connections and the ultimate responsibility to family. Citizenship and identity are tied to family rather than larger national communities.

In addition to expressing ideas about how the world operates, the international co-productions addressed in this book also demon-strate ideas about how the world *should* operate. Notions of consumer citizenship—privileged over political citizenship—teach children that to be part of a society means having buying power. Additionally, modern capitalist ideas about knowledge that privilege science, rea-son, technology, and experts are promoted not only in the doc-umentaries discussed in Chapter 4 but also in *Highlander: The Series,* where McLeod becomes the expert in all that he learns through global travel; *Cracker,* in which Fitz is depicted as the flawed but expert psychiatrist; *Pride and Prejudice,* which is ultimately about modern reason and its relationship with love; and *Rolie Polie Olie,* which is a celebration of technology through both its means of production and its content. These, like all television programs, tell audiences what is good, helpful, and reliable in the world and what we, as individuals, should believe in and strive for. In the end, international co-produc-tions have a particular message about all of these topics.

Certainly, this book does not intend to argue that television pro-ducers are sitting around a room trying to figure out how to reinforce hegemonic ideas about global capitalism to international audiences. Rather, television producers are trying to figure out how to create television shows that sell in international markets. As this analysis has illustrated, the process of creating global television and global brands lends itself to certain ideologies. Focusing on the benefits of particular nations or national events would not necessarily create shows that would have "universal" appeal. A program that highlights the importance of family, however, is more likely to resonate with audiences in multiple countries. In another example, creating documentaries based on subjective and personal ideas from a particular person may not seem appealing to international gatekeepers; however, a program that claims objectivity through the use of science and technology may have a better chance of being accepted. The ideologies found within international co-productions, then, are outgrowths of the increasingly global media environment.

I would like to return to the quotation that opened *Global Television: Co-Producing Culture*. John Frow writes: "To speak of the globalization of culture is to speak in the first instance of the globalization of *capitalism*, and hence of a globalization of the commodity form which is expressed in a fully internationalized, interdependent and interlocking market" (9). *Global Television: Co-Producing Culture* has illustrated that, although globalization is about the expansion of capitalism, it is also about the spread of ideas about the world, forms of knowledge, and identities. What ultimately becomes clear is that international co-productions have the potential, perhaps more so than other forms of international media production, to expose viewers to "global" culture. International actors, locations, techniques, and so forth are all required in the industrial and financial deals that make such productions beneficial. In the end, however, these ideas may not lead to an idealized transculturation but to a supportive environment for late modern capitalism.

Notes

Introduction: McTelevision in the Global Village

1. A less pessimistic theory of the blending of local and global culture can be seen in the concept of transculturation, which suggests the potential for a merging of two cultures to create a new and inclusive culture.

2. Another form of international co-production is "twinning." In this process each partner makes a distinct program of similar format and budget. Although the programs tend to retain their national feel, the programs are counted as "national" in both countries and receive equal treatment (in terms of incentives and distribution). This process is rarely used and will not be discussed in great detail.

3. Although this study attempts to integrate the history of co-productions between the United States and Europe, Asia, and Latin America, a very limited amount of research has been done on Asian and Latin American co-productions. This is certainly an area that is open for further research. Additionally, I have been unable to find research on co-productions with African nations (and only one or two mentions of actual co-productions between U.S. and African companies), which raises further questions about the idea that in our "global" media environment all nations are considered equally important markets.

4. In 1947, the British government placed restrictions on films imported into Britain. The government imposed a 75 percent customs duty on the earnings of U.S. films in Britain, thus beginning what became known as the Anglo-U.S. film war (Macnab, 73; "U.S. Exports," 103). In protest, the U.S. film industry quickly announced a boycott of the British market (Kulik, 295). The

boycott was ended in 1948 with the two-year Anglo-U.S. Film Pact. This pact limited the amount of money the U.S. companies could take out of Britain to $17 million a year. Additional funds could be taken out of Britain in proportion to the amount of money that British films earned in U.S. theatres. ("Provisions of Anglo-U.S. Film Pact," 9). Although some Latin American countries attempted to implement similar restrictions, according to John King, the U.S. government was able to strong arm the governments into dropping them (41).

5. Although David Hubka does state that the ability to gain the rights to a particular animated character can be a major motivation for animated international co-productions (Hubka, 2002, 243).

Chapter 1: History without Nation— Global Fiction

1. As is well documented, Canada, for example, is often seen as a "gateway" to the American market (Acheson and Maule, 407).

2. This argument is itself critiqued for its assumption that the use of the English language by non-native speakers will simulate U.S. English and automatically envelope participants into commercial culture. Cultural studies scholars have shown us that culture is more complicated than this, and, throughout his work, Mikhail Bakhtin particularly has illustrated that language use is complex and multifaceted. Although non-native English speakers do adapt the language for their own, potentially non-hegemonic, purposes, there are still many valid concerns about the use of the English language within European productions.

3. Over time, English has gained a certain amount of prestige in Europe (particularly for young people) and has developed into what has been termed a hypercentral language that allows people of different national languages to communicate in the fields of technology, science, business, and politics (de Swaan,52).

4. For example the French government offered a crash course in French culture to senior diplomats from ten countries about to join the European Union in 2004, this included lessons in the French language as well as French art, food, and wine (Willsher, 31).

5. As is well known, the French government has very actively protected and promoted the French language. In 1992 French was named the country's official language. Laws were passed that created quotas for the amount of French music on the radio (40 percent) and the number of hours of French programs on television (40 percent). Most controversially, in 1994 the government passed the Toubon Law, which required that French be used in six different domains: education, commerce, the media, public service, the conference industry, and the workplace. Some of these requirements were found unconstitutional but much has remained in place.

6. See, for example, Robert Burgoyne's *Film Nation*, the essays in Vivian Sobchack's *The Persistence of History* and Robert Rosenstone's *Visions of the Past*.

7. Recently some television series are taking on qualities of the miniseries format. For example, programs such as *Third Watch* and *Heroes* utilized story arcs to connect several episodes within a season. Also, other programs, such as *NYPD Blue*, had such short seasons that their length might be equivalent to some miniseries. However, in these cases, although the arc and the season might end, the program and the characters continued either the next week or the next season (until cancellation). With the miniseries, once the episodes are finished, the characters and the story are not expected to continue. (Although there are occasional miniseries sequels they cannot be anticipated by the viewers at the time of the original.) Furthermore, some series that air overseas as weekly series (such as *Cracker* and *Prime Suspect*) have been televised in the United States as special event miniseries. In these cases, viewers do know that the characters will return but they may not know when or for how long.

8. Reasons offered for the decline of these miniseries include a decreasing viewership for miniseries (and broadcast television in general), the lack of residual value for miniseries, and the expense of these programs (Forkan, 4).

9. The low ratings for *War and Remembrance* in 1988-89 are also cited in the trade press as one reason miniseries decreased in number in the 1990s (Brodie, 1).

10. The $32 million number is probably closer to the true budget since Halmi's son, the CEO of Hallmark Entertainment, explained that his father tended to exaggerate production budgets to the press (Bellafonte, 83).

11. According to reports Halmi, who was born in Hungary, was an anti-Nazi freedom fighter who was eventually captured in Poland. He was sentenced to death but freed by the Soviets. He then became a spy for the Office of Strategic Services and again captured (by the Soviets) and sentenced to death. Halmi then escaped to the United States. Lisa Gubernick and Fleming Meeks question this story, though: "How do we know this is true? We don't. We're taking Halmi's word for it, not necessarily a good idea when dealing with a charming fellow who describes himself as 'a typical Hungarian b.s. artist'" (64).

12. The television version of the miniseries does not include all of Odysseus' adventures related in Homer's *The Odyssey*, but it is more what Ann Hodges referred to as "The Selected Adventures from *The Odyssey*" (3).

13. While many of these programs are also internationally co-produced (with the producer of the original program maintaining some amount of production control over all of the "copies"), this is a different scenario than were are considering here since each version of the program is created for a local audience and is not intended for global distribution.

14. In 1999 Gaumont let go of its holdings in Gaumont Television. It will be interesting to examine what this sale means for Gaumont's international strategy as it deals with its growth and development as a transnational conglomerate.

15. Gaumont produced Fellini's *City of Women* (1980) and *And the Ship Sails On* (1984); Bergman's *Fanny and Alexander* (1982); Wajda's *Danton* (1982) and *Love in Germany* (1983); Losey's *Don Giavonni* (1979); and Syberberg's *Parsifal* (1982). Gaumont also distributed Zeffirelli's *La Traviata* (1982).

16. *Fly By Night* was co-produced by Gaumont and the Canadian production company Alliance. *Counterstrike* was co-produced by at least nine companies at different times, including Gaumont, Alliance, USA Television, and TF1.

17. Charret bought the Gaumont Television holdings from Gaumont in 1999, forming GTV.

18. Immortals only learn they are different than mortals once they have been "killed" and wake up again, at which point they stop aging and cannot be permanently hurt unless beheaded.

19. *Highlander*'s method of creating an image of a world separated rightfully into unique religious and ethnic groups suggests neo-conservative tendencies on the part of the program, which potentially bolsters fear and prejudice while seemingly promoting warmth and harmony.

20. The exception, perhaps, may be the positive depiction of the French resistance to Nazi control. Even here, however, the resistance fighters are seen as fighting to save lives not to free their nation.

21. Burns, a psychiatrist and a friend of MacLeod's, was an occasional recurring character on the show. Avid *Highlander* fans would know, even before this episode explains it, that MacLeod had killed Burns during a time when MacLeod was overcome by the evil of all of the Immortals he had killed and had himself, in a special two-part episodes, become evil.

22. Furthermore, Darius is killed in the second season when Werner Stocker, the actor who played him died.

Chapter 2: Clear, Strong Brands—British Television as a Marketing Tool

1. One A&E executive explained that video sales depend heavily on branding: "Our logo becomes a kind of Good Housekeeping Seal of Approval" (Sherber, 59). The brand associations with A&E's logo, therefore, must drive audiences to purchase videos and of course watch A&E.

2. A&E did more co-productions with the BBC than any other U.S. TV outlet (Rich Brown, 24).

3. The first episode reached 3.72 million homes, the second 3.66 million homes, and the third 3.76 million homes ("A&E Reaps Record Ratings").

4. Concerns about the show's violence were most prevalent. One series, "To Be a Somebody," was even suggested as a model for a real-life killing that was committed shortly after the show aired (Baily, T8; "Killer 'Copied TV,'" 3).

5. The 2006 episode of *Cracker*, which received mediocre reviews, aired in the United States on BBC America.

6. The U.S. television program *Brooklyn South* (CBS, 1997-1998) attempted to create connecting story arcs between a small number of episodes. The success of this strategy cannot be determined as the program was cancelled after only one season.

7. This decision was probably influenced by the BBC's 1997 announcement that it would, with The Discovery Channel, create BBC America.

Chapter 3: The Three C's—Children, Citizenship and Co-Production

1. A 1992 estimate states that 40 percent of the U.S. population did not have access to cable (Committee on Communications, 343).

2. The limits were no more than 12 minutes per hour during the week and 10.5 minutes per hour on the weekend.

3. Co-producers included Hanna-Barbera, NBC, SEPP International, and Wang Co.

4. Disney removed the Zoog Disney name from its tween lineup as part of a 2002 rebranding to make Disney Channel more hip.

5. Alternatively, later (post 9/11) seasons of *Bear in the Big Blue House*, also on Disney Channel, showed the program's characters venturing out of the big blue house and into the community of Woodland Valley where they helped rebuild the destroyed library and performed other various community services in culturally specific ways that may have increased the program's cultural discount in the international market.

6. CTW changed its name to Sesame Workshop in 2000. This paper will continue to use CTW since this was the name in use during the period under discussion.

7. Heather Hendershot explains that while the co-productions may attempt to cater to different national audiences, they retain culturally imperialistic tendencies through the imposition of a particular style of co-production that became the standard for creating "quality" educational television (1998, 170–171).

8. One reason for such a long time gap between seasons involves the expense incurred by performing all of the research and testing required by CTW in order to create the curriculum for the program. These costs, along with the standards of production quality set by CTW and its requirement that no ads run during any version of *Sesame Street* (even if aired on a commercial station), continue to make sustaining the program difficult for many producers (Hendershot, 1998, 164–175).

9. The character of Rosita certainly offers an interesting representation of a Latina. According to Barbara Franklin, however, her strong connection with

Latina culture has resulted in her being sidelined on the show and used primarily to do small business, such as introduce the "Spanish word of the day" (267).

Chapter 4: Global Truths—Documentaries for the World

1. As Jamie Holland explains, at this time more government files and footage, particularly in Eastern Europe, were becoming declassified, increasing interest in gaining access to new information (7).

2. See "Is This the Face of Jesus?" in *The Atlanta Journal-Constitution*; "Jesus Doc Features New Image" in *The Toronto Star*; and "TV Documentary Challenges Conventional View of Jesus" in *The Seattle Times*.

3. This move was devastating for PBS, which had until then been the main outlet for BBC programs in the United States. Although PBS could still work with the BBC on documentaries, it could only be on projects that Discovery passed on first.

4. The documentary aired on the BBC earlier, starting on April 1, 2001, over a period of three nights.

5. This historical information also added an element of tourism to the program, thus allowing people around the world to "see" the land of Jesus' birth, both as it was at the time and today.

6. Also significant is the fact that this program aired before September 11, 2001, when representing Christ as Middle Eastern was not tied up with the same meaning, or nationalism and ethnic fear, as it might be today. Now this Middle Eastern image, particularly with its short beard and everyday expression, might be more controversial. The rendering of a first century Jew, which the documentary held up as a possible model for Christ, looks more like a mug shot than the noble images of Christ with which we are most familiar. Perhaps it is telling that Mel Gibson cast a white, blue-eyed man in his 2004 *The Passion of the Christ*. While speaking Aramaic may be acceptable, perhaps the Western world is no longer prepared to think of Christ (particularly the Christ of faith) as Middle Eastern.

Works Cited

"A&E Reaps Record Ratings from 'Pride and Prejudice.'" The Associated Press, 18 January 1996. LexisNexis, University of Arizona. Accessed 22 May 2007.

Abizadeh, Arash. "Historical Truth, National Myths and Liberal Democracy: On the Coherence of Liberal Nationalism." *Journal of Political Philosophy* 12 (2004): 291–313.

Acheson, Keith and Christopher J. Maule. "International Regimes for Trade, Investment, and Labour Mobility in the Cultural Industries." *Canadian Journal of Communication* 19 (1994): 401–21.

Adilman, Sid. "The Little Company that Could: Nelvana Celebrating its 20 Years of Success in Animation." *The Toronto Star*, 25 September 1991, B1.

Amdur, Meredith. "Shrinking Budgets Make for Smaller World." *Broadcasting*, 20 April 1992, 37.

"Anglo-American 'Cracker.'" *Broadcasting and Cable*, 15 February 1999, 70.

Artz, Lee. "Monarchs, Monsters, and Multiculturalism: Disney's Menu for Global Hierarchy." In *Rethinking Disney: Private Control, Public Dimensions*, ed Mike Budd and Max H. Kirsch, 75–98. Middletown, CT: Wesleyan University Press, 2005.

Ashuri, Tamar. "The Nation Remembers: National Identity and Shared Memory in Television Documentaries." *Nations and Nationalism* 11 (2005): 423–42.

Attallah, Paul. "Canadian Television Exports: Into the Mainstream." In *New Patterns in Global Television: Peripheral Vision*, ed John Sinclair,

Elizabeth Jacka, and Stuart Cunningham, 161–91. New York: Oxford University Press, 1996.

Baer, Alejandro. "Consuming History and Memory Through Mass Media Products." *European Journal of Cultural Studies* 4 (November 2001): 491–501.

Baily, Paul. "Cracking Up Under the Strain." *The Guardian*, 18 October 1994, T8.

Banet-Weiser, Sarah. " 'We Pledge Allegiance to Kids': Nickelodeon and Citizenship." *Nickelodeon Nation*, ed Heather Hendershot, 209–40. New York: New York University Press, 2004.

Barber, Benjamin. *Jihad vs. McWorld*. New York: Ballantine Books, 1995.

Bawden, Jim. "New Code on Violence Has Little Effect." *Toronto Star*, 5 January 1994, E5.

Bazalgette, Cary and David Buckingham. *In Front of the Children: Screen Entertainment and Young Audiences*. London: British Film Institute, 1995.

BBC News Online, 27 March 2001. http://news.bbc.co.uk/1/hi/entertainment/tv_and_radio/1243339.stm. Accessed 20 March 2005.

Bellafonte, Ginia. "Forget Cliffs Notes." *Time*, 12 May 1997, 83.

Berger, Warren. "The Brains Behind Smart TV." *Los Angeles Times*, 25 June 1995, 16.

Bergfelder, Tim. "National, Transnational or Supranational Cinema? Rethinking European Film Studies." *Media, Culture and Society* 27 (2005): 315–31.

———. "The Nation Vanishes: European Co-Production and Popular Genre Formula in the 1950s and 1960s." In *Cinema and Nation*, ed Mette Hjort and Scott MacKenzie, 139–52. London: Routledge, 2000.

Bernstein, Paula. "A&E has Hammerlock on Highbrow." *Variety*, 7 February 2000, 27.

Betz, Mark. "The Name above the (Sub)Title." *Camera Obscura* 16 (2001): 1–45.

Bianculli, David. "Irrefutable 'History' Nails Nazis." *Daily News* (New York), 6 February 1998, 112.

Bickley, Claire. "$40 Million Odyssey." *The Toronto Sun*, 18 May 1997, TV3.

Bita, Natasha. "One Tongue Wraps Itself Around the Languages of Europe." *The Australian*, 8 November 2004, T06.

"Black Jesus in Union City, NJ, 'The Passion Play' Stirs Community Racism." *Jet*, 24 March 1997, 12.

Borja, Rhea. "Venerable U.S. Children's Show Reaches Around Globe." *Education Week*, 2 October 2002, 8.

Brennan, Patricia. "Jane Austen's Story of First Impressions." *The Washington Post*, 14 January 1996, Y07.

Briller, Bert. "The Globalization of American TV." *Television Quarterly* 24 (1990): 72.

Brodie, John. "Minis Measure Up with Majors Again." *Variety*, 1 March 1993, 1, 77.

Brown, Barry. "Geographies of Technology: Some Comments on Place, Space and Technology." http://www.dcs.gla.ac.uk/~barry/papers/place%20and% 20space.pdf. Accessed 21 May 2007.

Brown, Rich. "Programming Investment Provides Boost for A&E." *Broadcasting and Cable*, 1 March 1993, 24.

Buckingham, David. *After the Death of Childhood: Growing Up in the Age of Electronic Media*. Cambridge: Polity Press, 2000.

Budd, Mike. "Introduction: Private Disney, Public Disney." In *Rethinking Disney: Private Control, Public Dimensions*, ed Mike Budd and Max H. Kirsch, 1–36. Middletown, CT: Wesleyan University Press, 2005.

Burgi, Michael. "Cable's Promised Land." *Mediaweek*, 27 March 1995, 26.

———. "Cable's Menu Expands with Original Fare." *Mediaweek*, 11 April 1994a, 24.

———. "Arts and Entertainment Revamps Format." *Adweek*, 7 February 1994b, 12.

———. "A&E: Ten Years After." *Mediaweek*, 7 February 1994c, 9.

Burgoyne, Robert. *Film Nation: Hollywood Looks at U.S. History*. Minneapolis: University of Minnesota Press, 1997.

Caldwell, John. *Televisuality: Style, Crisis, and Authority in American Television*. New Brunswick, NJ: Rutgers University Press, 1995.

Canclini, Néstor Garcia. *Consumer and Citizens: Globalization and Multicultural Conflicts*. Minneapolis, MN: University of Minnesota Press, 2001.

Cantanzariti, Therese. "You've Got a Friend." In *Media Focus: Co-Productions*, ed Nigel Palmer, 10–11. London: SJ Berwin, 2001.

Carvell, Tim and Joe McGowan. "Showdown in Toontown." *Fortune*, 28 October 1996, 100–08.

Castleman, Lana. "Licensors Heat up Hispanic Merch Programs to Feed Retailer Demand." *Kidscreen*, 1 March 2004, 57.

Castoriadis, Cornelius. *Philosophy, Politics, Autonomy: Essays in Political Philosophy*. New York: Oxford University Press, 1991.

Chan-Olmsted, Sylvia and Yungwook-Kim. "Perceptions of Branding among Television Station Managers: An Exploratory Analysis." *Journal of Broadcasting and Electronic Media* 45 (2001): 75–91.

Chapman, James. *License to Thrill: A Cultural History of the James Bond Films*. New York: Columbia University Press, 2000.

Charret, Christian, interview by Serge Siritsky. "Highlander Clearances." *Television Business International*, 1 March 1996, 50.

Chris, Cynthia. "All Documentary, All the Time? Discovery Communications, Inc. and Trends in Cable Television." *Television and New Media* 3 (February 2002): 7–28.

Cipolla, Lorin. "Translating Sales." *Promo Magazine*, 1 April 2004, 4.

Clark, Jennifer. "CBS, Berlusconi Partner on Coprod'n." *Daily Variety*, 26 June 1992, 22.

Clark, Victoria. "Export Boom as British Television Captures a World Audience." *The Guardian*, 7 October 1996, 7.

Clarke, Steve. "ITV Gets 'Cracker'-ing." *Daily Variety*, 27 August 1997a, 10.

———. "'Fitz' Hits with Int'l Sales." *Daily Variety*, 16 June 1997b, 15.

Cohen, M. L. "Gaumont SA." In *International Directory of Company Histories*, ed Laura E. Whitely, 172–175. Detroit: St. James Press, 1999.

Committee on Communications, American Academy of Pediatrics. "The Commercialization of Children's Television." *Pediatrics* 89 (February 1992): 343–44.

Crary, David. "Government Pledges Production Funds to Counter U.S. Television." Associated Press, 10 September 1996. LexisNexis, University of Arizona. Accessed 27 June 2006.

Creeber, Glen. "Old Sleuth or New Man? Investigations into Rape, Murder and Masculinity in *Cracker*." *Continuum: Journal of Media and Cultural Studies* 16 (2002):169–83.

Crystal, David. *English as a Global Language*. Cambridge: Cambridge University Press, 1997.

Culf, Andrew. "Granada in Foreign Deal." *The Guardian*, 13 November 1996, 6.

Curtin, Michael. *Redeeming the Wasteland: Television Documentary and Cold War Politics*. New Brunswick, NJ: Rutgers University Press, 1995.

Daly, John. "A Global Vision." *Maclean's*, 14 October 1991, 38–39.

Dann, Michael. "The 'Street' That Runs Around the World." *The New York Times*, 6 August 1972, D13.

Davatzes, Nickolas, interview by Steve McClelland. "Making History at A&E." *Broadcasting and Cable*, 10 March 1997, 55.

Davies, Alistair. "From Imperial to Post-Imperial Britain." In *British Culture of the Postwar: An Introduction to Literature and Society 1945–1999*, ed Alan Sinfield, 125–38. London: Routledge, 2000.

Davies, Hannah, David Buckingham, and Peter Kelley. "In the Worst Possible Taste: Children, Television and Cultural Value." *European Journal of Cultural Studies* 3 (2000): 5–25.

Dávila, Arlene. *Latino, Inc: The Marketing and Making of a People*. Berkeley: University of California Press, 2001.

Dean, Sherrie. "Jane Austen One of Hollywood's Hottest Properties." *Showbiz Today* Transcript No. 1002–3. LexisNexis, University of Arizona. Accessed 22 May 2007.

Deitz, Roger. "Carl J. Kravetz: Hispanic Marketing Executive." *The Hispanic Outlook in Higher Education*, 29 August 2005, 32.

Dempsey, John. "Brooke Bailey Johnson." *Daily Variety*, 16 March 1999, A3.

———. "Cablers Strike Up the Brand." *Variety*, 22 June 1998, 1.

——. "Cable Starting Mini Renaissance?" *Variety*, 15 April 1996, 45.

Diaz-Guerrero, Rogelio, Raul Bianchi Aguila, and Rosario Ahumadade Diaz. *Investigación Formativa de Plaza Sésamo: Una Introducción a las Técnicas de Preparación de Programas Educativos Televisados*. Mexico: Editorial Trilhas, 1975.

Dobie, Madeline. "Gender and the Heritage Foundation." In *Jane Austen and Co.: Remaking the Past in Contemporary Culture*, ed Suzanne R. Pucci and James Thompson, 247–60. Albany, NY: SUNY Press, 2003.

"Docu Firm Stretching Out with Fiction Coproductions." *Variety*, 28 September 1983, 117, 124.

"Documentary Hypothesizes Dark-Skinned Jesus." *National Catholic Reporter*, 6 April 2001, 7.

Dole, Carol M. "Austen, Class, and the American Market." *Jane Austen in Hollywood*, ed Linda Troost and Sayre Greenfield, 58–78. Lexington, KY: University Press of Kentucky, 1998.

Donohue, Steve. "A&E on the Road: Spain, Portugal to Spur Latin Channels." *Electronic Media*, 9 November 1998, 16.

Dorland, Michael. "Quest for Equality: Canada and Coproductions, a Retrospective (1963–1983)." *Cinema Canada*, October 1983, 14–18.

Doyle, Marc. *The Future of Television: A Global Overview of Programming, Advertising, Technology, and Growth*, ed National Association of Television Program Executives. Lincolnwood, IL: NTC Business Books, 1992.

Drohan, Madelaine and Alan Freeman. "English Rules." *Globe and Mail* (Canada), 12 July 1997, D1.

Eaton, Leo. "Co-Production in International Television: Making the Marriage Work." Paper presented at the East-West Center 2nd Meeting, Honolulu, 1992.

Ebeling, Ashlea. "Toon In." *Forbes*, 6 September 1999, 166.

Eitzen, Dirk. "When is a Documentary? Documentary as a Mode of Representation." *Cinema Journal* 35 (Fall 1995): 81–97.

Elley, Derek. "Co-Productions: Who Needs Them?" *International Film Guide*, 1993, 18–20.

Ellis, Jack and Betsy A. McLane. *A New History of Documentary Film*. New York: Continuum Press, 2005.

"European Television Production Not Unified." *European Media Business and Finance*, 23 October 1995. Factiva. Accessed 25 February 2008.

Fabrikant, Geraldine. "For TV Movie Producers, What Plays in Peoria Does Not Pay Abroad." *The New York Times*, 10 November 1997, D1.

Falicov, Tamara. "U.S.-Argentine Co-Productions, 1982–1990: Roger Corman, Aries Productions, 'Schlockbuster' Movies, and the International Market." *Film and History* 34 (2004): 31–38.

Farhi, Paul and Megan Rosenfeld. "American Pop Penetrates World Wide Nations." *The Washington Post*, 25 October 1998: A1.

Farquhar, Peter. "Managing Brand Equity." *Marketing Research*, September 1989, 24–33.

Featherstone, Mike. "Localism, Globalism, and Cultural Identity." In *Global/Local: Cultural Production and the Transnational Imaginary*, ed Rob Wilson and Wimal Dissanayake, 46–77. Durham, NC: Duke University Press, 1996.

Feretti, Fred. "'Forstye Saga' will unfold on Channel 13." *The New York Times*, 4 October 1969, 70.

Fisher, William. "Let them Eat Europudding." *Sight & Sound* 59 (1990): 224–27.

Flinn, John. "It's All History Now." *Adweek*, 29 April 1996, 6.

Fore, Steve. "Golden Harvest Films and the Kong Kong Movie Industry in the Realm of Globalization." *Velvet Light Trap* (1994): 40–58.

Forkan, James P. "Mini-Serious: Networks Making Mega-Cuts as Costs of Production Climb." *Advertising Age*, 18 May 1987, 4.

Forrester, Chris. "History, Nickelodeon Are Advancing in Asia." *Multichannel News*, 8 November 1999, 42.

Foucault, Michel. *Power/Knowledge: Selected Interviews and Other Writings 1972-1977*, ed Colin Gordon. New York: Pantheon Books, 1980.

Franklin, Barbara. "An Honest Self? Searching for Latinos in U.S. Children's Television." Diss. Tulane University, 1999.

Fraser, C. Gerald. "Sesame Street Worldwide." *The New York Times*, 21 November 1982, TG3.

Freeman, Michael. "Now, Big Bird en Espanol." *MediaWeek*, 3 April 1995, 6.

———. "MGM, Reteitalia Get Together." *Broadcasting*, February 10, 1992, 33.

Friedman, Wayne. "Disney Adds Ads to Kids' Cable Net." *Advertising Age*, 25 February 2002, 1–2.

Frow, John. "Cultural Markets and the Shape of Culture." In *Continental Shift: Globalisation and Culture*, ed Elizabeth Jacka, 7–24. Sydney, Australia: Local Consumption Publications, 1992.

Frutkin, A. J. "Art Takes a Hit." *MediaWeek*, 4 April 2005, SR56–58.

Fry, Andy. "Brit Producers Play Format Game." *Variety*, 19 January 1998, 74.

Fursich, Elfriede. "Between Credibility and Commodification: Nonfiction Entertainment as a Global Media Genre." *International Journal of Cultural Studies* 6 (2003): 131–53.

Galetto, Mike. "History Channel, No Ugly American." *Electronic Media*, 20 October 1997, 44.

Gallo, Phil. "Cracker." *Variety*, 15 September 1997, 40.

Garcon, Francois. *Gaumont: A Century of French Cinema*. New York: Harry N. Abrams, 1994.

Gershon, Richard A. *The Transnational Media Corporation: Global Messages and Free Market Competition*. Mahwah, NJ: L. Erlbaum, 1997.

Ginsburg, Marla. "Lessons to Learn from the Highlander Coproduction." *Electronic Media*, 25 January 1993, 130.

Glaister, Dan. "Cracker Lite Proves Thin on Danger." *The Guardian*, 25 August 1997, 7.

Glenn, Adam and Meredith Amdur. "New World TV Order Evident at Mip." *Broadcasting*, 29 April 1991, 23.

Godard, Francois. "Canadian TV Searching for Identity." *Broadcasting and Cable*, 13 January 1997, 98.

Goldsen, Rose K. and Azriel Bibliowicz. "*Plaza Sésamo*: 'Neutral' Language or 'Cultural Assault'?" *Journal of Communication* 26 (1976): 124–25.

Gould, Jack. "Galsworthy's Social Trilogy, 'Forstye Saga' Here From Britain." *The New York Times*, 6 October 1969, 94.

Grahnke, Lon. "Mad Gods and Monsters: Odyssey Is Still a Wild Trip." *Chicago Sun-Times*, 16 May 1997, 49.

Grimes, William. "An Austen Tale of Sex and Money in Which Girls Kick Up Their Heels." *The New York Times*, 14 January 1996, 3.

Gritten, David. "This One's Rated BC." *Los Angeles Times*, 16 February 1997, 3.

Grossberger, Lewis. "Media Person: Odyssey and Oddities." *MediaWeek*, 26 May 1997, 30.

Guback, Thomas H. *The International Film Industry: Western Europe and America since 1945*. Bloomington: Indiana University Press, 1969.

Gubernick, Lisa and Fleming Meeks. "Trust Your Instincts." *Forbes*, 7 June 1993, 64.

Guider, Elizabeth. "Strange Bedfellows Make Good Biz Sense in TV Co-prods." *Variety*, 9 May 2000, 1–3.

Haley, Kathy. "The Documentary Climbs to New Heights." *Broadcasting and Cable*, 3 November 1997, 46.

Harrington, C. Lee and Denise Bielby. "Global Television Distribution: Implications of TV 'Traveling' for Viewers, Fans and Texts." *American Behavioral Scientist* 48 (2005) 902–20.

Harrison, Kathryn. "Coupez a la Car Chase." *Forbes*, 3 May 1991, 60.

Hart, Kenneth. "Duel to the Death?" *Communications International*, May 1994, 7–11.

Heath, Carla. "Children's Television in Ghana: A Discourse About Modernity." *African Affairs* 96 (1997): 261–75.

Hendershot, Heather. "Introduction: Nickelodeon and the Business of Fun." In *Nickelodeon Nation* ed Heather Hendershot, 1–14. New York: New York University Press, 2004.

———. *Saturday Morning Censors: Television Regulation Before the V-Chip*. Durham, NC: Duke University Press, 1998.

Herman, Edward S. and Robert McChesney. *The Global Media: The New Missionaries of Corporate Capitalism*. Washington, DC: Cassell, 1997.

Hill, John. *British Cinema in the 1980s: Issues and Themes*. Oxford: Clarendon Press, 1999.

Hipsky, Martin. "Anglophil(m)ia." *Journal of Popular Film and Television* 22 (1994): 98–107.

Hirsh, Michael. "Funding Co-Productions: A Complicated but Tasty Recipe." *Animation World Magazine*, 10 January 1998. http://mag.awn.com/index. php?ltype=search&sval=michael+hirsh&article_no=612. Accessed 9 October 2003.

"History Channel Launching in Latin America." *Electronic Media*, 19 August 1996, 16.

Hobsbawm, E. J. *Nations and Nationalism Since 1780*. Cambridge: Cambridge University Press, 1992.

Hodges, Ann. "Homer's Epic Tale Becomes Miniseries." *The Houston Chronicle*, 18 May 1997, 3.

Hoffman, Katjah. "Survey—Creative Business." *Financial Times*, 22 May 2001, 18.

Hogarth, David. *Realer than Reel: Global Directions in Documentary*. Austin: University of Texas Press, 2006.

Holland, Jamie. "Tales of Ordinary Heroes: Why is the Second World War Dominating Films and Books as Never Before?" *Daily Telegraph* (London), 20 December 2000, 7.

Hoskins, Colin and Stuart McFadyen. "Canadian Participation in International Co-Productions and Co-Ventures in Television Programming." *Canadian Journal of Communication* 18 (1993): 219–36.

Hoskins, Colin, Stuart McFadyen, and Adam Finn. *Global Television and Film: An Introduction to the Economics of the Business*. Oxford: Clarendon Press, 1997.

Hubka, David. "Globalization of Cultural Production: The Transformation of Children's Animated Television, 1980 to 1995." In *Global Culture: Media, Arts, Policy, and Globalization*, ed Diana Crane, Nobuko Kawashima, and Ken'ichi Kawasaki, 233–55. London: Routledge, 2002.

———. "Globalization of Cultural Production: Children's Animated Television, 1978 to 1995." Diss. Carleton University, 1998.

Ingrassia, Joanne. "Canadian Producers Endorse Kids TV." *Electronic Media*, 15 May 1995, 20.

"International Networks." Discovery Communications Inc. http://corporate. discovery.com/brands/networks_abroad.html. Accessed 25 May 2007.

"Is This the Face of Jesus?" *The Atlanta Journal-Constitution*, 29 March 2001, 1D.

Jackel, Anne. "European Co-Production Strategies: The Case of France and Britain." In *Film Policy: International, National and Regional Perspectives*, ed Albert Moran, 85–97. London: Routledge, 1996.

Jarvik, Laurence. *Masterpiece Theatre and the Politics of Quality*. Lanham, MD: Scarecrow Press, 1999.

Jenkins, Philip. "A New Christendom." *The Chronicle of Higher Education*, 29 March 2002. http://chronicle.com/free/v48/i29/29b00701.htm. Accessed 20 March 2005.

Jensen, Elizabeth. "Turner Will Offer Preschoolers a Show with Ads as 'Bookends.'" *The Wall Street Journal*, 31 May 1996, B3.

Jensen, Robin M. "Jesus Up Close." *Christian Century*, 20 September 2003, 26–30.

"Jesus Doc Features New Image." *The Toronto Star*, 28 March 2001. LexisNexis, University of Arizona. Accessed 28 February 2008.

Johnson, Brooke Bailey. Interview by Debra Johnson. "A&E is Home Sweet Home to British Drama." *Broadcasting and Cable*, 13 January 1997, 92.

Johnston, Carla B. *International Television Co-Production: From Access to Success*. Boston: Focal Press, 1992.

Katz, Mike. "A&E and MTG Pair for History." *Broadcasting and Cable*, 25 August 1997, 39.

Kavanagh, Michael. "Is Costume Drama Going Out of Style?" *Electronic Media*, 19 January 1998, 86–87.

Keller, Kevin Lane. "Conceptualizing, Measuring, and Managing Customer-Based Brand Equity." *Journal of Marketing* 57 (1993): 1–22.

Kelly, Brendan. "Nelvana Jumping into 3D." *Daily Variety*, 22 October 1997, 8.

Kilborne, Richard and John Izod. *An Introduction to Television Documentary: Confronting Reality*. Manchester, UK: Manchester University Press, 1997.

"Killer 'Copied TV'." *The Guardian* (London), 20 October 1994, 3.

Kim, Hank. "These Ads Are History." *Adweek*, 4 August 1997, 6.

King, John. *Magical Reels: A History of Cinema in Latin America*. London: Verso Press, 1990.

Kirby, Andrew. "A Sense of Place." *Critical Studies in Mass Communication* 6 (1989): 322–26.

Kulik, Karol. *Alexander Korda: The Man Who Could Work Miracles*. London: W. H. Allen, 1975.

"La Promesa Programs/New York." National Latino Children's Institute. http://nlci.org/States/NewYork.htm#PlazaSésamo. Accessed 24 May 2007.

Lal, Vinay. *Empires of Knowledge: Culture and Plurality in the Global Economy*. London: Pluto Press, 2002.

Langway, Lynn. "The Selling of the Smurfs." *Newsweek*, 5 April 1982, 56.

LaSalle, Mick and Lee Hildebrand. "The Nazis: A Warning from History." *The San Francisco Chronicle*, 10 July 2005, 32.

Lev, Peter. *The Euro-American Cinema*. Austin: University of Texas Press, 1993.

Levinsky, Andy. "Unintended Consequences." *Humanist* 59 (1999): 5–8.

Lieberman, David. "The Disney Channel Names President." *USA Today*, 22 February 1996, 2B.

Lief, Louise. "France's Gaumont Takes Aim at the American Market." *The New York Times*, 25 December 1983, 13.

Liner, Elaine. "Grecian Formula," review of *The Odyssey*. *Boston Herald*, 18 May 1997, 6.

Lorenzi, Rossella. "Jesus Remade in New Documentary." *Discovery News*, http://doc.discovery.com/news/briefs/20030414/jesus_print.html. Accessed 19 March 2004.

Lowe, Vanessa. "PBS Show Tries Race Relations." *Black Enterprise* 22 (1992): 32.

Macnab, Geoffrey. *J. Arthur Rank and the British Film Industry*. London: Routledge, 1993.

Mahan, Elizabeth. "Culture Industries and Cultural Identity: Will NAFTA Make a Difference?" *Studies in Latin American Popular Culture* 14 (1995): 17–36. From Ebsco Host Academic Search Premiere, University of Arizona. Accessed 21 May 2007.

Mandel, Jennifer. "The Production of a Beloved Community: Sesame Street's Answer to America's Inequalities." *Journal of American Culture* 29 (2006): 3–13.

Mason, M. S. "NBC's Sumptuous Odyssey Is Must-Read TV," review of *The Odyssey*. *Christian Science Monitor*, 16 May 1997, 12.

Matthews, Kate. "Free Trade: Spotlight on the Children's Television Production Industry." *Australian Screen Education* 33 (2004): 32–37.

Mattleart, Armand. *Advertising International*. London: Routledge, 1989.

McAllister, Matthew P. and Matt Giglio. "The Commodity Flow of U.S. Children's Television." *Critical Studies in Media Communication* 22 (2005): 26–44.

McConville, Jim. "History Channel to Launch in London." *Broadcasting and Cable*, 9 October 1995, 60.

McKay, John. "CBC Promising Healthy Shows for Children." *Calgary Herald*, 20 September 1998, F7.

Meislin, Richard J. "... In Mexico, Latin Values Stressed." *The New York Times*, 29 September 1983, C17.

"MGM-BBC 26-Seg Galsworthy Saga." *Variety*, 30 March 1966, 1.

Mifflin, Lawrie. "BBC and Discovery to Develop Programming Together." *The New York Times*, 20 March 1998, 2D.

———. "Broadcasters and Producers Make Time for Children." *The New York Times*, 2 December 1996c, D1.

———. "TV Notes, That's Not All, Folks." *The New York Times*, 2 October 1996b, C18.

———. "Trying to Be Enticingly Eggheaded." *The New York Times*, 9 June 1996a, section 12, 55.

Miller, Jeffrey S. *Something Completely Different: British Television and American Culture*. Minneapolis: University of Minnesota Press, 2000.

Miller, Stuart. "Channels Get Hip to O'seas Savvy." *Variety*, 22 September 1997, M3.

Miller, Toby. "Cultural Citizenship." *Television and New Media* 2 (2001a): 183–86.

———. "Introducing . . . Cultural Citizenship." *Social Text* 19 (2001b): 1–5.

Miller, Toby, Nitin Govil, John McMurria, and Richard Maxwell. *Global Hollywood*. London: British Film Institute, 2001.

Mohamad, Michael, interview by Janoff Baroy. "Taking the Mystery Out of Marketing History." *Brandweek*, 18 April 2005, 12.

Montgomerie, Margaret. "Miniseries." *The Encyclopedia of Television*. Chicago: Museum of Broadcast Communications, 1997. http://www.museum.tv/archives/etv/M/htmlM/miniseries/miniseries.htm. Accessed 20 February 2003.

Morris, Meaghan. "Transnational Imagination in Action Cinema: Hong Kong and the Making of a Global Popular Culture." *Inter-Asia Cultural Studies* 5 (2004): 181–99.

Mullen, Megan. *The Rise of Cable Programming in the United States: Revolution or Evolution?* Austin: University of Texas Press, 2003.

"Necessary for Cable Growth." *Communication Daily*, 4 December 1987, 6.

Negrine, Ralph M. and Stylianos Papathanassopoulos. *The Internationalisation of Television*. London: Pinter, 1990.

Nichols, Bill. *Introduction to Documentary*. Bloomington: Indiana University Press, 2001.

———. *Representing Reality: Issues and Concepts in Documentary*. Bloomington: Indiana University Press, 1991.

Northam, Jean A. "Rehearsals in Citizenship: BBC Stop-Motion Animation Programmes for Young Children." *Journal for Cultural Research* 9 (July 2005): 245–63.

Nossiter, T. J. "British Television: A Mixed Economy." In *Broadcasting Finance in Transition: A Comparative Handbook*, ed Jay Blumler and T.J. Nossiter, 95–143. Oxford: Oxford University Press, 1991.

Obler, Suzanne. *Ethnic Label, Latino Lives: Identity and the Politics of (Re) Presentation in the United Sates*. Minneapolis: University of Minnesota Press, 1995.

O'Connor, John J. "For British Detective, Crime Pays." *The New York Times*, 29 March 1994, C18.

Olswang, Simon. "Introductory Paper." Paper presented at the Second Munich Symposium on Film and Media Law: European Coproduction in Film and Television, Munich, 1988.

O'Neil, Brian. "Yankee Invasion of Mexico, or Mexican Invasion of Hollywood? Hollywood's Renewed Spanish-Language Production of 1938–1939." *Studies in Latin American Popular Culture* 17 (1988): 79–104. Ebsco Host Academic Search Premiere, University of Arizona. Accessed 16 May 2007.

O'Regan, Tom. "The International, the Regional and the Local: Hollywood's New and Declining Audiences." In *Continental Shift: Globalisation and Culture*, ed Elizabeth Jacka, 74–98. Sydney, Australia: Local Consumption Publications, 1992.

O'Shaughnessy, John and Nicholas Jackson O'Shaughnessy. "Treating the Nation as a Brand: Some Neglected Issues." *Journal of Macromarketing* 20 (June 2000): 56–64.

O'Sullivan, John. "The Real British Disease." *The New Criterion*, September 2005, 16–23.

Paget, Derek. *True Stories? Documentary Drama on Radio, Screen and Stage.* Manchester, UK: Manchester University Press, 1990.

Palmer, Edward L., Milton Chen, and Gerald S. Lesser. "Sesame Street: Patterns of International Adaptation." *Journal of Communication* 26 (1976): 109–123.

Palmer, Nigel. "Double the Trouble?" In *Media Focus: Co-Productions*, ed Nigel Palmer, 4–5. London: SJ Berwin, 2001.

Paoli, Pascale. "MIP-TV Special Report: France Taking Co-Production Lead." *Kidscreen*, 1 April 1996, 64–67.

Parsons, Patrick and Robert Frieden. *Cable and Satellite Television Industries.* Needham Heights, MA: Allyn and Bacon, 1998.

Patrick, Aaron O. "In Tots' TV Shows, A Booming Market, Toys Get Top Billing." *The Wall Street Journal*, 27 January 2006, A1.

Patton, Susannah. "'Sesame Street' Broadens Into a Plaza As It Extends Reach to Other Cultures." *The Wall Street Journal*, 10 April 1995, B5.

Pecora, Norma. "Nickelodeon Grows Up: The Economic Evolution of a Network." In *Nickelodeon Nation*, ed Heather Hendershot, 14–44. New York: New York University Press, 2004.

Pendakur, Manjunath. *Canadian Dreams and American Control: The Political Economy of the Canadian Film Industry.* Detroit: Wayne State University Press, 1990.

Petersen, Judith. "How British Television Inserted the Holocaust into Britain's War Memory in 1995." *Historical Journal of Film, Radio and Television* 21 (2001): 255–72.

Peterson, Richard and N. Anand. "The Production of Culture Perspective." *Annual Review of Sociology* 30 (2004): 311–34.

Popper, Margaret. Christian Charret interview. *European Media Business and Finance*, 9 October 1995, 1.

Porter, Vincent. "European Co-Productions: Aesthetic and Cultural Implications." *Journal of Area Studies* 12 (1985): 6–10.

Postal, Carole. "Breaking Down Barriers." *Playthings*, June 1996, 66.

Powell, Chris and Peter York. "Beyond Ann Hathaway's Cottage." *New Statesman*, 6 May 2002, 28.

Preston, Elizabeth Hall and Cindy White. "Commodifying Kids: Branded Identities and the Selling of Adspace on Kid's Networks." *Communication Quarterly* 52 (2004): 115–28.

"Production Deals." *European Media Business and Finance*, 17 November 1997. LexisNexis, University of Arizona. Accessed 22 May 2007.

"Provisions of Anglo-U.S. Film Pact." *Variety*, 17 March 1948, 9.

Quill, Greg. "Tough New Broadcast Code Zaps TV Violence." *The Toronto Star*, 29 October, 1993, A1.

Rees, Laurence. "The Nazis: A Warning from History." In *Holocaust and the Moving Image: Representation in Film and Television Since 1933*, ed Toby Haggith and Joanna Newman, 146–53. London: Wallflower Pres, 2005.

Regan, Tom. "Kids' TV Opens to Northern Exposure." *Christian Science Monitor*, 25 August 1999, 6.

Robertson, Virginia. "Disney Channel Tunes in With a New Logo." *Kidscreen*, 1 September 1997, 16.

Rodgers-Melnick, Ann. "Messiah Complexity." *Pittsburgh Post-Gazette*, 13 April 2001, 36.

Rodriguez, America. "Creating An Audience and Remapping a Nation: A Brief History of U.S. Spanish Language Broadcasting." *Quarterly Review of Film and Video* 16 (1999): 357–74.

Rohter, Larry. "Learn English, Says Chile, Thinking Upwardly Global." *The New York Times*, 29 December 2004, A4.

Rosenstone, Robert. *Visions of the Past: The Challenge of Film to Our Idea of History*. Cambridge: Harvard University Press, 1995.

Ross, Chuck. "Cable TV: Marketer of the Year: A&E." *Advertising Age*, 8 December 1997, S1.

Rothstein, Edward. "Jane Austen Meets Mr. Right." *The New York Times*, 10 December 1995, section 4, 1.

Ruether, Rosemary. "Global Capitalism a New Challenge to Theologians." *National Catholic Reporter*, 7 February 2003, 16.

Said, Edward. "Orientalism Once More." *Development and Change* 35 (2004): 869–79.

Samuels, Rich. "International Co-Productions." *International Documentary*, December 1995/January 1996, 14–15.

Saunders, Dusty. "Indecisive 'Odyssey' Sails Off Course," review of *The Odyssey*. *Denver Rocky Mountain News*,18 May 1997, 16D.

Schlesinger, Philip. "From Cultural Defence to Political Culture: Media, Politics and Collective Identity in the European Union." *Media, Culture and Society* 19 (3, 1997): 369–91.

Schmuckler, Eric. "Brats' Open Kids Season." *MediaWeek*, 12 January 1998, 5.

Schneider, Michael. "Nelvana Will Look After CBS Kids." *Electronic Media*, 12 January 1998, 120–21.

Scott, Tony. "A&E Mystery Movie Cracker." *Daily Variety*, 17 January 1995. LexisNexis, University of Arizona. Accessed 22 May 2007.

Seigel, Robert L. "It's a Small World Market After All II: International Documentary Co-Production." *The Independent*, March 1993, 32–33.

Sharkey, Betsy. "Going Wide, Wider, Widest." *Mediaweek*, 16 March 1998, 9.

———. "Television's Man of Letters." *Mediaweek*, 26 February 1996, 25.

Sherber, Anne. "Cable Shows Corner the Vid Market." *Billboard*, 12 April 1997, 59.

Sherwood, Rick. "Historic Agreement." *The Hollywood Reporter* Highlander Special Issue, 3 December 1996, S30.

Shochat, Lisa. "*Our Neighborhood:* Using Entertaining Children's Television to Promote Interethnic Understanding in Macedonia." *Conflict Resolution Quarterly* 21 (2003): 79–93.

Shumway, David R. "Nationalist Knowledges: The Humanities and Nationality." *Poetics Today* 19 (Fall 1998): 357–73.

Sierz, Aleks. *In-Yer-Face Theatre: British Drama Today*. London: Faber Press, 2001.

Sinclair, John. "Mexico, Brazil and the Latin World." In *New Patterns in Global Television: Peripheral Vision*, ed John Sinclair, Elizabeth Jacka, and Stuart Cunningham, 33–66. Oxford: Oxford University Press, 1996.

———. "Spanish-Language Television in the United States: Televisa Surrenders its Domain." *Studies in Latin American Popular Culture* 9 (1990): 39–64. Ebsco Host Academic Search Premiere, University of Arizona. Accessed 13 November 2003.

Sinclair, John, Elizabeth Jacka, and Stuart Cunningham. "Peripheral Vision." In *New Patterns in Global Television: Peripheral Vision*, ed John Sinclair, Elizabeth Jacka, and Stuart Cunningham, 1–32. Oxford: Oxford University Press, 1996.

Snyder, Beth. "Fisher-Price Embarks on Saturday Morning TV." *Advertising Age*, 8 February 1999, 3.

Sobchack, Vivian. "Introduction: History Happens." In *The Persistence of History: Cinema, Television, and the Modern Event*, ed Vivian Sobchack, 1–14. New York: Routledge, 1996.

Solomon, Harvey. "History Lessons." *The Boston Herald*, 21 June 1998, 6.

Sonntag, Selma K. *The Local Politics of Global English: Case Studies in Linguistic Globalization*. Lanham, MD: Lexington Books, 2003.

Sparks, Colin. "Is There a Global Public Sphere?" In *Electronic Empires: Global Media and Local Resistance*, ed Daya Kishan Thussu, 108–24. London: Arnold, 1998.

Spring, Greg. "Canada's Nelvana, CBS a Match Made By Kids Rules." *Electronic Media*, 2 March 1998, 3.

Stanley, T. L. "Spread the Risk, Share the Riches?" *Brandweek*, 2 June 1997, 22.

Sterngold, James. "Reinventing the Box: How Cable Captures the Mini-Series and the High Ground." *The New York Times*, 20 September 1998, 86.

Stevenson, Nick. "Cultural Citizenship in the 'Cultural' Society: A Cosmopolitan Approach." *Citizenship Studies* 7 (2003): 331–48.

Stewart-Allen, Allyson. "Heritage Branding Help in the Global Markets." *Marketing News*, 5 August 2002, 7.

Stock, Paul. "Dial 'M' for Metonym: Universal Exports, M's Office Space and Empire." *National Identities* 2 (2000): 35–47.

Street, Sarah. *British Feature Films in the United States*. New York: Continuum Press, 2002.

Strover, Sharon. "Recent Trends in Coproductions: The Demise of the National." In *Democracy and Communication in the New Europe: Change and Continuity in East and West*, ed Farrel John Corcoran and Paschal Preston, 97–123. Cresskill, NJ: Hampton Press, 1995.

Sullivan, Andrew. "Trash Pickup." *The New Republic*, 4 November 2002, 19.

Sutcliffe, Thomas. "Now for a Programme Right up your Strata." *The Independent on Sunday* (London), 17 June 2001, 14.

Sutter, Mary. "Sesame Pacts with Discovery, Televisa." *Daily Variety*, 23 April 2004, 12.

Swaan, Abram de. *Words of the World: The Global Language System*. Oxford: Oxford University Press, 2001.

Taubin, Amy. "Murder, She/He Wrote." *Village Voice*, 3 May 1994, 45.

Taves, Brian. "The History Channel and the Challenge of Historical Programming." *Film and History* 30 (2000): 7–16.

Taylor, Paul. "Responding to the Shock of the New: Trade, Technology and the Changing Production Axis in Film, Television and New Media." Diss. University of Washington, 1998.

Taylor, Toper. "Keeping the US in Balance with the Rest of the World." *Kidscreen*, 1 December 1998, 33.

Thompson, Kristin. *Exporting Entertainment: America in the World Film Market 1907–34*. London: BFI Publishing, 1985.

Thompson, Robert J. *Television's Second Golden Age: From Hill Street Blues to ER*. New York: Continuum Press, 1996.

Tinic, Serra. "Going Global: International Coproductions and the Disappearing Domestic Audience in Canada." In *Planet TV: A Global Television Reader*, ed Lisa Parks and Shanti Kumar, 169-185. New York: New York University Press, 2003.

Tomlinson, John. *Cultural Imperialism: A Critical Introduction*. London: Pinter Publishers, 1991.

"Too Much of a Good Thing." *Economist*, 18 December 2004, 97.

"TV Documentary Challenges Conventional View of Jesus." *The Seattle Times*, 28 March 2001, A4.

Urban, Ken. "Towards a Theory of Cruel Britannia: Coolness, Cruelty, and the 'Nineties'." *New Theatre Quarterly* 20 (2004): 354–72.

"U.S. Exports: End of Boom." *Business Week*, 16 August 1947, 103.

Van Dijck, Jos. "Picturizing Science: The Science Documentary as Multimedia Spectacle." *International Journal of Cultural Studies* 9 (2006): 5–24.

Walley, Wayne. "Disney Channel No Fantasy." *Advertising Age*, 1 December 1986, S10.

Walmsley, Ann. "A Bearish Move with Bullish Results." *Maclean's*, 27 May 1985, 54.

Warner, Bethany. "Discovery Puts Context Into the Life of 'Jesus.'" *The Washington Times*, 14 April 2001, D1.

Wasko, Janet. *Understanding Disney*. Malden, MA: Blackwell, 2001.

Webb, Alex. "Looking for the Historical Jesus." 26 March 2001. *BBC Online*. http://news.bbc.co.uk/1/hi/entertainment/tv_and_radio/1243954.stm. Accessed March 20, 2005.

Wells, Matt. "Is This the Real Face of Jesus Christ?" *The Guardian*, 27 March 2001. http://www.guardian.co.uk/print/0,3858,4160069-103690,00.html. Accessed 19 March 2004.

Westcott, Tim. "Indie Producers Look to Boost Biz Abroad." *Variety*, 14 December 1998, 79.

White, Cindy and Elizabeth Hall Preston. "The Spaces of Children's Programming." *Critical Studies in Media Communication* 22 (2005): 239–55.

White, Hayden. "The Modernist Event." In *The Persistence of History: Cinema, Television and the Modern Event*, ed Vivian Sobchack, 17–38. New York: Routledge, 1996.

"Why Do We Think Christ Was White?" *BBC News Online*, 27 March 2001. http://news.bbc.co.uk/1/hi/uk/1244037.stm. Accessed 20 March 2005.

Wilinsky, Barbara. *Sure Seaters: The Emergence of Art House Cinema*. Minneapolis, MN: University of Minnesota Press, 2001.

Williams, Frederick and Diana S. Natalicio. "Evaluating *Carrascolendas*: A Television Series for Mexican-American Children." *Journal of Broadcasting* 16 (1972): 299–309.

Williams, Michael. "English Lingo Sounds Good to Gaumont." *Variety*, 26 October 1998, 34.

Willsher, Kim. "Paris Offers EU Newcomers Crash Course in French." *Sunday Telegraph* (London), 7 March 2004, 31.

Worrell, Kris. "The Past is Present on History." *Broadcasting and Cable*, 4 May 1998, 72, 76.

Worsdale, Andrew. "Cinematic Notions on Sale." *Electronic Mail and Guardian*, 13 November 1997. http://www.chico.mweb.co.za/mg/art/reviews/97nov/13nov-filmmarket.html. Accessed 16 May 2007.

Zad, Martie. "The Jesus Story: A Scientific View." *The Washington Post*, 15 April 2001, Y04.

Zahed, Ramin. "Mr. Joyce Goes to Hollywood." *Daily Variety*, 30 September 1997, 20.

Zbar, Jeffrey D. "Wishing Upon a Star Only the Beginning." *Advertising Age*, 10 April 2000, S12.

Ziegler, Regina. "Introductory Paper." Paper presented at the Second Munich Symposium on Film and Media Law: European Coproduction in Film and Television, Munich, 1988.

Zoglin, Richard. "A Show From Our Sponsors: A Cable Network Cancels a Series of Corporate-Made 'Histories' As TV's Lines of Demarcation Get Hazier." *Time*, 17 June 1996, 101.

Index

Barbara J. Selznick is an Associate Professor in the School of Media Arts, The University of Arizona, and author of *Sure Seaters: The Emergence of Art House Cinema*.